110141

9 - 0 - Area code & number

Constant Ring 82072

9 - 0 - A

8207.

B
MCDANIEL   Jackson, Carlton.
           Hattie

$18.95

DATE		

110141

Hattie

THE LIFE OF HATTIE McDANIEL

Hattie

THE LIFE OF HATTIE McDANIEL

CARLTON JACKSON

MADISON BOOKS
LANHAM • NEW YORK • LONDON

British Cataloging in Publication Information Available

Library of Congress Cataloging-in-Publication Data

Jackson, Carlton.
Hattie : the life of Hattie McDaniel / by Carlton Jackson.
p.   cm.
Bibliography: p.
Includes index.
1. McDaniel, Hattie, 1895–1952.   2. Motion picture actors and actresses—
United States—Biography.   I. Title.
PN2287.M165J3   1989
791.43'028'0924—dc19   89–30903 CIP
[B]

ISBN 0–8191–7295–2 (alk. paper)

The paper used in this publication meets the minimum requirements of American
National Standard for Information Sciences—Permanence of Paper for Printed Library
Materials, ANSI Z39.48–1984.   ∞

*To my beautiful daughters, Beverly and Hilary;
and my fine sons, Daniel and Matthew*

Contents

A section of photographs follows page 104.

Acknowledgements

M any people helped me to write this book, and I wish to thank
them. As always, nothing could have been done without good
libraries and efficient librarians. Tim Spragens, Paul Bailey, and
Prentiss Moore, were very helpful to me at the Ransom Humanities
Library at the University of Texas in Austin. Ned Comstock and his
colleagues also provided good services at the University of Southern
California.

Maxine Fleckner and her staff of the Wisconsin Center for
Film and Theater Research, at the University of Wisconsin, and the
staffs at the Library of Congress and NAACP in Washington, D.C.,
went out of their way to help me, and I am appreciative. At the
University of Kentucky Library in Lexington, Rob Aken supplied
me with some helpful information.

In Denver, Joan Reese provided me with some much needed
research, as did Brian E. O'Connell in New York. I thank them
both for their help.

Others whose cooperation was essential to the successful completion of this biography include Carlton Moss, Joel Fluellen, Jester
Hairston, Wonderful Smith, Elzi Emmanuel, James and Eva Goodwin, Ernest Anderson, Ken Nelson, Frances Williams, Frances

Melton, Michael St. John, Ethel Jordan, Olivia de Havilland, Butterfly McQueen, and Jack Mertes.

No author would get very far without good editors behind him. I have been extremely fortunate in having some of the best. Professor Thomas Cripps of Morgan State University in Baltimore, Maryland, edited the entire manuscript, and improved it considerably. Also, my friend and colleague at Western Kentucky, Professor Joe Millichap, read it and gave critical and much appreciated advice. Linda Busetti, at Madison Books, did a superb job of editing and proofreading. I wish especially to thank the associate publisher at Madison Books, Charles Lean, for his constant encouragement and help.

I wrote much of this book while on an extended visit to Dhaka, Bangladesh. I thank my friends there: Mary Furgal, David Grimland, Joe Foote, and others who encouraged me and helped develop the manuscript in various ways.

Here at Western Kentucky University, I was aided by grants from the Faculty Research Committee. To each member of that committee: thank you. My student assistant, Jim Johnson, was indispensable as he performed dozens of useful tasks in the research phase of this book; and librarian Susan Tucker, was most cooperative and helpful. To all these people, I give my sincere thanks.

And finally, to my family, Pat, Beverly, Daniel, Matthew Hilary, Steve and Grace; and to Colleen, Megan, Kate, Travis, Patrick, and Austin: thanks.

Carlton Jackson
Western Kentucky University

Introduction

Hattie McDaniel was the black woman who played Mammy in *Gone With the Wind*. As the movie approaches its fiftieth anniversary in 1989, Hattie's fame as Mammy shows every sign of becoming increasingly strong.

Her role as Mammy has remained the most remembered of her motion picture performances. As the years have passed since the movie was made in 1939, her part in it has evolved in the minds of movie fans almost to the point of being equated with the roles of Rhett Butler and Scarlett O'Hara. The scene on the stairway where Mammy tells Melanie Wilkes that "Mr. Rhett" won't let his daughter, Bonnie, be buried, has lingered as one of the great moments in movie history. More than any other, it was that scene that won her the Academy Award for Best Supporting Actress in 1939. She was the first black ever to win an Oscar.

Hattie's Mammy image is somewhat unfortunate because it tends to obscure many of the other things she did. She played in over 300 movies and received screen credit in more than eighty of them. She played a maid or cook in the majority of these roles, which made Hattie a target for the National Association for the

Advancement of Colored People. As a consequence, she spent much of her time in the mid and late 1940s defending herself.

Her role as Mammy, too, has caused many people to overlook Hattie's contribution to radio. She started out when radio was in its infancy in the 1920s, and ended in the early 1950s, just as radio was beginning to give way to television.

For half a decade Hattie played Beulah on the radio, and in that role, I shall argue, she diminished some of the "stereotypical" image of black subservience with which the NAACP had charged her. She refused to use dialect in "Beulah," a program that became the most popular offering in radio history. It was heard each night by around 20 million people.

Her role as Beulah probably did more to enhance black careers than Hattie and the people around her realized, and it would be fair to say that Hattie became an "unwitting" reformer. That is, as I shall maintain, she did not start out—as the NAACP did—deliberately to change the system; she changed it by example rather than by words. Perhaps that feat was her greatest accomplishment.

In this book I try to present a balanced picture of Hattie McDaniel's triumphs as well as her defeats; and to show that she was strong-willed enough to overcome most of her adversities. Those people who saw her as the jolly, bubbling, and happy-go-lucky maid in one movie after another, did not realize the often traumatic experiences she was undergoing in real life. Likewise, the radio audience for "Beulah" didn't realize how unhappy Hattie really was when she performed in some of her shows.

By adapting her many talents to the technological achievements of the day, Hattie McDaniel made a significant contribution to her race, and to the film, radio, and television arts.

CHAPTER ONE

"That Talented McDaniel Family"

The event at Denver East High School that night in 1910 was not exactly Carnegie Hall fare, but it did bring out a sizeable portion of the city's population. They came to hear a highly publicized program sponsored by the Women's Christian Temperance Union.

The participants were to recite poems showing the deleterious effects of alcoholism. One by one they appeared and told the prim and proper WCTU ladies about once happy homes destroyed by demon rum. Then they regaled their audience with idyllic images of health and good fortune that could be achieved through abstinence. All in all, the recitations brought vigorous nods of agreement from the partisan audience.

One contestant, the only black entry, chose demented violence as a theme of alcoholism. She wanted to show how quickly strong drink can take over and control a life.

This competitor was a jovial young lady, popular with her fellow students in high school. Her dark face was pleasantly plump, and she had a huge smile that accentuated brilliantly white teeth. Her name was Hattie McDaniel.

Hattie, who had already begun a singing and dancing career

in Denver, and had been cited by her teachers for her talents, chose a brutally unhappy piece to present to the assembled ladies. Called "Convict Joe," it was written in 1888 by Alexander G. Murdoch, and it described the inexorable road to ruin caused by too much familiarity with the bottle. It began:

> Did I know Convict Joe? *Yes I knew him,*
> *And I ne'er knew an honester lad,*
> *Til he took head and heart to the bottle,*
> *And went with a rush to the bad.*
> Ah, *Joe's was a pitiful case, Sirs,*
> *And show, you'll allow it I think*
> *That granting* his *part in the business*
> *Joe was less in the blame than the drink.*[1]

The stanza brought a general buzz of approval from the audience. Hattie sensed their enthusiasm, and as the poem continued, she became increasingly emotional.

Joe, a shipwright, had once been happily married. One night, though, he went on a "rare spree," and was abusive to his wife and children once he did get home. Dismissing his family, Joe sat in the living room fighting off the alcohol inspired demons, creatures, and monsters, who kept tormenting him. Hearing him call out, his wife rushed to comfort him, and then the worst happened:

> *"Wife, Wife!" in his horror he shouted,*
> *And towards his presence she flew;*
> *"Joe dearest! My husband!" No Woman!*
> *Black, horrible monster! Not you!*
> *His brain hot with fury, he clutched at a*
> *Hatchet!—One terrible blow*
> *Next moment, Death's presence stood by him*
> *With a forefinger pointing at woe!*

The sheer brutality of the image shocked the audience, and some began to cry, but it definitely got their attention. This very kind of incident—all too accurate as seen from real life newspaper accounts—was exactly what the WCTU wanted to use to get their anti-alcohol message across to the public.

After Joe killed his wife, he "flung himself down alongside her, and slept til the dawning of day." He dreamed peacefully, but awoke to horror.

> Was it only a nightmare? *Ah, no Sirs:*
> *Rough hands on Joe's shoulders were laid*
> *And voices, all harsh, took his hearing,*
> *As he started, and stared, half-afraid.*
> *God! What could it mean—the crowd round him—*
> *Thus to wake in the hands of the law?*
> *Ah, that form stretched all stirless before him!*
> *Surrounded by horror and awe.*

At the subsequent trial, Joe wanted to be put to death by hanging, so that the sadness over his heinous deed would be ended. The judge, though, imprisoned him for life, so that Joe would be in constant torment.

> *Why lengthen a heart-moving story?*
> *The law took its just-handed course;*
> *Joe, escaping the terrible gallows,*
> *was doomed to eternal remorse,*
> *A lifetime of penal exactments,*
> *Felon chains, with their soul-searing chime*
> *But, if tears are accepted in Heaven,*
> *Joe has wept out all trace of his crime.*[2]

As she finished this searing presentation, Hattie herself was in tears, barely able to finish the last sentence. The audience's applause soon grew into a standing ovation, and all the while Hattie stood on the stage, with tears streaming down her face.

There was no question that night about the winner of the WCTU's Gold Medal for the best performance. The uncontested victor was Hattie McDaniel. More important for Hattie was that she realized how the sound of applause affected her. It gave her an indescribable feeling, she later said, of joy, love, and even sadness.

Hattie McDaniel's background was natural for an entertainer, because her family was richly endowed with musical abilities. Her father, Henry McDaniel, was born into slavery as a fieldhand on a Virginia plantation near Richmond. Her grandmother was the plantation's cook and Mammy. In later years, Hattie remarked that she took after her paternal grandmother, and perhaps that was why she came up with so many Mammy roles in the movies. She also ascribed her love of cooking and good food to her grandmother (whom she never met).[3]

During the war, Henry was a soldier in the Union Army seeing non-combat service in various campaigns in Virginia. For some time after the conflict ended, large groups of black people roamed the open roads of the South, living off the land as best they could, vulnerable to climate, illnesses, and mean spirited white people. In one of these groups was twenty-five-year-old Henry McDaniel.

Henry drifted into North Carolina, working at odd jobs, such as chopping wood for his supper, planting tobacco, and gathering hay. When the opportunities arose, he sang and danced for the enjoyment of his white employers. Black minstrel groups were popular during the last quarter of the nineteenth century, and Henry frequently played a banjo and guitar, and sang with these performers.

Henry existed hand to mouth for ten years after the Civil War ended, roaming throughout Virginia and the Carolinas. A decade of wandering was not really unusual for that day and time. Thousands of Henry's fellow freedmen remained nomadic much longer than ten years.

By 1875 Henry's meanderings brought him to Nashville, Tennessee. By the age of thirty-five he had become a part-time Baptist preacher. His experiences of slavery, emancipation, breaking ties with his family, and then grubbing for existence, turned Henry into an introspective, meditative man. He began to express the philosophy that he could best help his fellow freedmen through singing, oratory, and preaching.

In Nashville Henry traveled from one black church to another, preaching and singing. It was inevitable that he come into contact with other singing groups. One was an all female chorus that made regular tours of Nashville and surrounding towns and counties, singing gospel music. Performing in one of these groups was a young lady named Susan Holbert, who had gained fame in Nashville as a religious singer. She was nine years younger than Henry, and he fell in love with her. Soon after they met, Susan and Henry were married.[4]

A year or so after their marriage in 1875, Henry and Susan decided to leave Nashville, perhaps prompted by the end of congressional reconstruction in 1877, under President Rutherford B. Hayes. Without the direct protection of the federal government, Negroes in the South were targets for vengeful legislation regarding civil rights. (It is true that Tennessee pulled out of the Civil War before the other Southern States, and was therefore not "congressionally reconstructed." Nevertheless, there was enough resentment toward newly freed black people to make them uncomfortable.)

Moving again was no great task for Henry, for he had done it so often. Susan, however, hated to leave Nashville. Henry reckoned that life for black people was easier in the West than in the reconstructed South. In fact, the entire West became a boom area as tens of thousands of rootless war veterans, from both north and south, picked up their lives for new starts. Many of these travelers to the West were blacks, going out to become cowboys, ranch hands, range riders, and bronco busters. Henry and Susan were thus not alone in making their westward trek. They joined thousands of blacks doing the same thing.

Henry and Susan left Nashville, and traveled west by train to Memphis, and on into Arkansas. From there, they went by whatever conveyance (foot, wagon, river) they could find, following the Arkansas River through Oklahoma territory, finally winding up in Wichita, Kansas.

Wichita in the late 1870s and on into the 80s, was one of those boom towns caused by constant migrations to the West. The site of the city, not only on a river, but also on a railroad, enhanced its importance as a center of cattle shipping and an agriculturally productive hinterland.

Henry stopped in Wichita, prepared by his versatility to survive in its booming western economy. Hundreds of new structures—houses, stores, churches, schools, train stations—had to be built, and by now Henry had become adept in the building trades. He was a multi-talented person, necessary to survive the harshness of the post civil war period, and was now a banjo and guitar player, singer, dancer, minstrel player, Baptist preacher, carpenter, teamster, and construction worker. Many times both Henry and Susan conducted services at various churches in the Wichita area. Henry preached and Susan sang. They lived at 925 N. Wichita Street,[5] where their fame spread very quickly throughout the black community.

Before going to Wichita, and during their stay there, Henry and Susan started what ultimately became a large family of thirteen children.[6] Over half of them died either at birth or shortly thereafter.[7] The youngest, born on June 10, 1895, was a bouncing baby girl, whom they named Hattie.[8]

But life for the young Hattie did not settle down until her father's wandering urge carried the family to turn-of-the century Colorado, first in Fort Collins and then in Denver.

In Fort Collins Henry worked as a teamster. The family lived in the 300 block of Cherry Street.[9] Two blocks away on North Meldrum lived Hattie's dearest friend, Ruth Collamer, a white girl. Ruth and Hattie were inseparable, as they walked with each other every morning, hand in hand, to the Franklin School, where they were classmates.[10]

At school, Hattie and Ruth played jacks on the flagstone sidewalks, and a game called, "Pom pom pullaway." Hattie taught Ruth how to bounce a rubber ball while repeating in rhythm, "one, two, buckle your shoe." Each afternoon after school Ruth's father drove his cattle to pasture, always passing by the McDaniel's residence on the way. Hattie frequently came out of her house and walked with the herd for a way, she and Ruth picking flowers (violets and "johnny jump ups" in the Spring), and, hand in hand, "hippety-hopping" through the fields.[11]

The picture of Hattie that Ruth always held was "of a sweet little colored girl about eight years old in a dainty ruffled bonnet, and a round face with one of the biggest smiles a girl could acquire. She had beautiful white teeth, which she showed very distinctly every time she smiled, and that was very often when we were together."[12]

In 1901, Hattie was again uprooted when the family moved to another boomtown, Denver, a short distance away. Henry saw working and living conditions as better for himself and family in Denver than in Fort Collins. Henry quickly got a job as a laborer on numerous construction projects, and his oldest son, Otis, became a porter in a barber shop, earning his share of the family upkeep by sweeping, and keeping the place clean. Over the next several years the McDaniels lived in at least ten different places in Denver from the time they arrived in 1901 to Henry's death in 1922.[13] Gradually, as they grew up, his family scattered throughout the city, his sons (including Otis, James, and Samuel) going into barber shop and hotel portering, and construction work, and his daughters (including Ruby, Adele, Orlena, Etta, and Hattie), generally became clerks. Hattie, for example, worked for some time as a clerk for the Charles Lind Bakery on Lincoln Street.[14] "Clerking" meant not only keeping books, but the place clean as well. Hattie probably got the job because of her friendly nature and her ability to "cipher." It was not, however, commonplace for blacks to become clerks in business establishments. All of the McDaniels had some talent in music and entertainment, and the children at least, who had not been directly involved with slavery, had outgoing personalities that caused them to seek employment beyond the usual maid and wash jobs. In addition, Denver was such a boom town with so many business establishments to be run that "color" was frequently put aside when managers looked for employees. Also in the western parts of the country around the turn of the century, Populist Party politics created a system in which blacks had at least a semblance of "place." Perhaps that political factor was one reason why Henry McDaniel, though frequently moving around in the city of Denver itself, stayed permanently after 1901 in the state of Colorado.

Even with all the changed ways of life Henry and Susan had left behind, the McDaniels—especially the men—could usually get only menial jobs in Denver. Their situation in the Colorado capital, however, was probably better than if they had stayed in the South. "White supremacy" took root in southern states and state legislatures put into effect a large number of "Jim Crow" segregation laws. On the other hand, much of the West at this time was so economically active, with enough work and adequate housing to go around, that there were generally too many activities for people's racial biases to become obsessive, as they had done in the South.

Nevertheless, there was some bigotry, even in Denver. In the Fall of 1916, a debate raged over a proposed ordinance to prohibit blacks from living on the same residential blocks as whites. The Denver Property Owners' Protective Association, was made up almost entirely of white real estate agents, and it supported the efforts to segregate Denver's housing.[15] (Ironically, during the late 1940s, Hattie battled exactly the same kind of housing discrimination in Los Angeles.)

Besides the housing problem, another cause for racial strife in Denver, as indeed around the country at the time, was the screening, in 1915, of D. W. Griffith's epic film, *The Birth of a Nation*. Based upon Thomas Dixon's *The Clansman,* the film glorified the Ku Klux Klan at the expense of black people, and for the first time depicted black villains on the screen. The newly formed (1909) National Association for the Advancement of Colored People fought against showing this film anywhere. The Denver chapter of the NAACP was formed in 1915, in no small part because of *The Birth of a Nation*. Thus, while Denver in the early twentieth century was quite liberal compared to other parts of the country, it did have its own racial problems.

These difficulties, though, remained unapparent to Henry and Susan's youngest child, Hattie. She was one of a few black students at Denver's Twenty-Fourth Street Elementary School, and her teachers and classmates loved her.

Her favorite teacher, Louise Poirson, often permitted Hattie to do what she liked best: to stand before the class reciting poetry or singing popular songs. Mrs. Poirson wrote to Hattie later on in

Hattie's career: "The reason I remember you so well is due to the fact that as a child you were so full of rhythm. You had an outstanding dramatic ability, an ability to project to your listeners your strong personality and your ever present sense of humor. I recall with pleasure the keen enjoyment of the pupils and myself whenever you sang or dramatized a story."[16] Hattie began singing at the Central Baptist Church in Denver almost as soon as she arrived, sang spirituals at school, and recited passages from the Bible for the pleasure of her classmates. Hattie herself said that she sang so much as a child that it sometimes got on the household nerves. "My mother would say, 'Hattie I'll pay you to hush,' and she'd give me a dime. But in just a few minutes I'd be singing and shouting again."[17]

From an early age, Hattie was a "take charge" person, a characteristic which remained her entire life. In grammar school she organized, improvised, and directed the activities of the other children, a foreshadowing of future successes and "firsts." Being first almost became a way of life for Hattie. Later, she would be known as the first black woman to sing on radio, the first black person to win an Oscar, even the first black to be buried in a previously all white cemetery.

Her best friend at Twenty-Fourth Street School was Willa May,[18] and after graduation Hattie and Willa went together to East Denver High School. The most "daring" thing the two friends did in high school was to have their initials tattooed in blue in the bend of their arms. Hattie could stare down at a big "HM" imbedded into her arm, while Willa gazed at "WM."[19]

Still the center of Hattie's life at East Denver was singing and dancing, and her theatrical abilities. She was always much in demand for school plays and musical performances, and excelled at a number of dances that were popular in that era. The most notable of these were the cakewalk, the juba, the fleetfoot softshoe buck, and the wing dance, and they were among hundreds that blacks brought from Africa, or created once they were in the United States. (See Appendix D for a description of these dances.)

In a way, the development of black music and dancing talents was one way of compensation for their conditions of servitude.[20]

Thus, when Hattie went through the rigors of "Convict Joe" that night at East Denver High, she exemplified many generations of black talent. Her natural abilities, coupled with Henry's and Susan's encouragement, turned Hattie, at an early age, into an important performer.

In fact, as early as 1908, when she was only thirteen, Hattie was billed as part of a minstrel show, J. M. Johnson's Mighty Modern Minstrels performed at East Turner Hall (later known as German Hall). The show featured "Happy Dick Thomas and the Merry Howards," and "just a few" of the "big, mighty company," included Etta, Hattie, Otis, and Samuel McDaniels (misspelled as even press agents would do for years to come). The show was as much a competition as a performance, because its program announced that the "challenging cakewalk, fleetfoot softshoe buck, and the wing," were "open to all comers,"[21] as they had been in plantation tradition.

A few months later, in March 1909, a minstrel group, the Red Devils, came to East Turner Hall, under the management of the Colored American Amusement Company, with Miss Hattie McDaniel, "Denver's favorite soubrette," at the bottom of the bill. Already, Hattie was acquiring a reputation of acting the coquettish maid.[22]

In 1910, Henry decided that he had had enough of hard labor and so he formed his own minstrel show, with his sons, Otis and Sam as regulars. For some time the two brothers had played with the All-Star Minstrels at both East Turner and the Empress. Otis and Sam were clog dancers; Sam played Pappy Rufe, and Otis played Aunt Miranda of the Lime Kiln Club, leaving "the house in a constant uproar of laughter and applause,"[23] according to one reviewer. The Henry McDaniel Minstrel Show was popular entertainment for people all over Colorado. With Henry at the top of the bill with his banjo and guitar the show toured Pueblo, Colorado Springs, Boulder, Fort Collins, and other cities. Although fifteen-year-old Hattie begged to travel and perform, her mother, Susan, forbade it, protecting her from the rigors of show business life, one-night stands, tiresome travel, and stays in segregated, inferior parts of towns they visited.

Generally, black performers preferred to travel by train rather than by car to engagements, because they were not as likely to be stopped by unfriendly policemen. Sometimes, however, a remote destination required several black groups to travel together by automobile, exposing them to dangers along the way. Susan also considered that since everyone in the show was black, hotel rooms were hard to come by, compelling a dependence on a black "bed and breakfast" circuit that flourished along the black entertainment routes.

For her part, Hattie seemed to be doing just fine as a student at East High. Nonetheless Hattie quit high school at the end of her sophomore year. While she waited for her "real" career to begin, Hattie continued to perform at local theaters such as the Empress, and at carnivals. Then, in 1910 she gave her famous rendition of "Convict Joe," and after that experience nothing could stop her from full time entertainment. She enlisted the help of her brother, Otis, in convincing Susan that the time had come. Reluctantly, Susan bowed to the inevitable, even though it meant giving up her cherished dream of seeing Hattie earn a high school diploma.

The next three years were among Hattie's busiest and happiest. She toured from Colorado to the West Coast, sometimes with a minstrel group called the Spikes Brothers Comedy Stars. Primarily, though, she traveled with her father and brothers, and frequently wrote the programs that her father's minstrel group performed. Also, she began to show a lively talent for writing songs, a talent that was fully developed during the 1920s.

But in 1916, tragedy struck. Her older brother, Otis, who had always been the star of "that talented McDaniel family," died of an undisclosed cause, at the unfulfilled age of thirty-five. His funeral was conducted at the Campbell Chapel of the African Methodist Episcopal Church, and he was buried in Riverside Cemetery.[24] For awhile it appeared that Henry's minstrel group would fall apart without Otis' guidance, and gaps increased between engagements. During these periods, Hattie worked in Denver cooking, clerking, and taking in washing. By the late 1910s, Henry had become inactive as the years and busy life began to catch up with him, forcing Hattie, Etta, and Sam, to turn to other outlets through which to display their talents.

At last around 1920 Hattie first came into contact with one of Denver's most noted black musicians, Professor George Morrison, and his "Melody Hounds," who gave her the "big break" that carried her to a greater exposure than she was accustomed to. She traveled with the Morrison Orchestra to Portland, Salt Lake City, El Paso, and even a short stint in Juarez, Mexico. Newspapers lauded Hattie's entertainment abilities. The *Portland Telegram* said that "the biggest show stopper of them all was Morrison's Orchestra and its Hattie McDaniel, billed as the female Bert Williams," (an internationally known black vaudeville performer). Hattie Mc-Daniel was "taken in riotous fashion," said *The Telegram*. The *Oregon Daily Journal* said that Morrison's work on the Pantages Circuit was "not exactly a jazz offering of the syncopated, slam-bang order," but a "refined and accomplished act which not only hits the musical high spots, but interjects a humorous surprise in Hattie McDaniel. . . . who did a hop, skip, and jump act on the stage while keeping up her vocal stunts. . . ." Another paper, the *Oregonian*, complimented Morrison's band for its "melodious play-ings" of its theme song, "By the Waters of Minnetonka," which took on "new and charming values." The paper described Hattie as a "large Negro woman who sings jazz songs." The *Evening News* of San Jose, California, called Morrison's band "as excellent a vaude-ville show as anyone would care to see," and Hattie a special feature whose dances blended "to the peppiest music ever heard in this man's town."[25]

In 1922 Hattie suffered two more losses. In his seventies, Henry had developed hearing and sight problems, which sharply curtailed his activities with the minstrel show. On December 5, 1922, he died, at the age of 82. He was buried in a special Grand Army of the Republic section of Denver's Riverside Cemetery. His death deeply affected Hattie: though she had always leaned most heavily on Susan for aid and understanding, she had adored Henry, and learned much of her musical craft from him.[26]

Hattie had married George Langford, from a prosperous black Denver family, a few months before her father's death. A short while later, Langford died—shot, according to one of Hattie's relatives—and Hattie became a widow. She did not marry again until the mid-thirties (a short-lived marriage to a man named Howard Hickman, not the same person who played John Wilkes in *Gone With the Wind*).

In the months following Henry's death, Hattie performed mostly in the Denver area, still singing with George Morrison's band. One great opportunity opened up to her on December 15, 1924. That was the date radio station KOA in Denver had its first broadcast.

Many sources indicate that Hattie was the first black person ever to sing on KOA. The Denver station broadcast its earliest black program on January 10, 1925, with the choir from the Shorter African Methodist Episcopal Church. Professor Morrison and his band started their KOA broadcasts on December 5, 1925, offering classical music and jazz, whose fans sent scores of congratulatory letters and telegrams.[27] Hattie, still affiliated with the Morrison Orchestra, thus may have been the first black soloist to sing on KOA. In any case, radio turned out to be Hattie's *tour de force*. Indeed, even though in the years ahead, she may have attained fame in the movies, radio probably remained her first love. In effect, she began her career with radio (KOA) and ended it in the same medium, as Beulah. Perhaps the notice given to her radio perform-ances led Hattie to a career—at least for awhile—as a performer on the western entertainment circuits, the most notable of which were the Pantages and Orpheum.

Alexander Pantages was a Greek who went from running a shoe shine parlor in Seattle to one of the world's greatest show producers. Entertainers on the Pantages Circuit were always ex-tremely popular, and they usually played to full houses.

The Orpheum Theatre Circuit was founded by Martin Beck originally from Czechoslovakia. In 1899 circumstances placed him in charge of the vaudeville entertainment at a saloon concert hall in San Francisco previously known as Gustave Walters' Orpheum, which became the first house "to dominate the big time west of Chicago."

Morrison contracted with the Pantages Circuit in 1924, and

on one of his tours, took Hattie and another Denverite, Jimmie Lunceford, with him. He said, "Hattie McDaniel and I got our act all worked up, practicing about seven or eight hours a day, every day, and got it down pat."[28] They opened, in 1924, in Minneapolis. "We were billed as George Morrison, the colored Paul Whiteman, and Hattie McDaniel, the female Bert Williams. . . ." They'd open each night with "Vesti la guibba" from Leoncavallo's *I Pagliacci* and proceed to "The Waters of Minnetonka." The tour in 1924 took Morrison and Hattie to Tacoma, Seattle, Portland, San Francisco, Los Angeles, Salt Lake City, Kansas City, and "a lot of little places."[29]

One other entertainer with whom Hattie was frequently compared was Sophie Tucker, and was often called the "black Sophie Tucker," because of the way she presented her songs. Hattie was the black "last of the red hot Mamas." That Hattie was black and Sophie white marked a world of difference between their two careers in the 1920s. Though reputedly, "talent" was the only important factor in choosing acts, no black actor or actress received top billing in the 1920s, and for that matter, well on into the 1930s.

While touring for Pantages and Orpheum, Hattie developed her song writing talent. On numerous occasions in the past she had written skits while she traveled with Henry and her brothers.

She wrote the words for "Sam Henry Blues," and the music by her friend, Richard Jones, of New Orleans fame, merged into the Jazz-Blues style of the 1920s.

> *Sam Henry was a gamblin' man,*
> *I loved him for myself*
> *I swore if I caught him cheatin'*
> *He won't cheat on nobody else.*
> *'Cause he'll be graveyard bound,*
> *Then he'll stop runnin' 'round.*[30]

The chorus exemplified the plight of a sweetheart who is in fact merely "one of many."

They say he's got me and six others too
But when he loves me, Lord what can I do
Now when I went down to that gamblin' shack
He'd just left with notorious Ida Black
I love my man, don't care what he do
Don't care if he got me and ten thousand, too!

Another McDaniel-Jones musical contribution was "Poor Wandering Boy Blues," like "Sam Henry Blues," written in 1927.

I'm just a wandering child
I'm just a wandering child
I've wandered 'round this world alone
No place to call my home
My mother told me so,
My mother told me when I was leaving
My home sweet home
She begged me not to go
Now when I get back home
Now when I get back home
When I get back to that old shack,
No more I'll roam.[31]

Hattie's other titles—to which she wrote both the lyrics and the music—included "Quittin' My Man Today," "Brown Skin Baby Doll," "I Wish I Had Somebody," "BooHoo Blues," "Wonderful Dream," "Lonely Heart," and "Poor Boy Blues." Still others, written in the late twenties, were "I Thought I'd Do It," "Just One Sorrowing Heart," "Destroyin' Blues," "Dentist Chair Blues," "That New Love Maker of Mine," and "Any Kind of Man Would Be Better Than You."

Some of these songs were recorded, with Hattie singing them, frequently accompanied by the Richard Jones Jazz Wizards. "Dentist" Jackson sang several duets with her when these songs were recorded by the Merritt Company in Kansas City, and on the Okeh and Paramount labels in Chicago. Most of Hattie's songs, however, remained as sheet music.

Though the Pantages and Orpheum circuits gave the greatest outlets for Hattie's talents, they were not always available to her. For one thing, she was generally not a headliner. Her performances were geared to the better known black stars, such as George Morrison, and even he did not always get engagements. For another, black entertainers were simply not treated as well as whites by the Pantages and Orpheum managements. These conditions made it logical for Hattie to work for other circuits, such as the black Elks Club and Shriners. These fraternal organizations sponsored "indoor circuses" around the country. As a part of their shows, the circuses frequently included minstrel performances, where Hattie McDaniel served her apprenticeship. She traveled with the Elks and Shriners to many American cities, and was even headlined in some of their shows.

By far, the organization that most frequently booked Hattie, and other black performers, was the Theatrical Owners Booking Association, or TOBA, as it was commonly called. TOBA was made up of black theatre owners, who, to keep their houses busy, shared booking responsibilities and arranged lodging and eating facilities for its guest performers.

Among all these outlets—Pantages, Orpheum, Elks, Shriners and TOBA—Hattie was kept fairly busy throughout most of the twenties, a "star" sometimes, particularly if she played for TOBA, but a "fill in" at other times, primarily for Pantages and Orpheum.

As the decade drew to a close, Hattie became involved with a TOBA sponsored road production of "Showboat," playing and singing "Queenie," as she did in the movie version. The group was performing in Chicago (where Hattie had played from time to time at the Royal Gardens, owned by black businessman, Virgil Williams) in October 1929, when the great stock market crash occurred. Her company announced its bankruptcy which, of course, left several black players, including Hattie, stranded.

By chance, Hattie heard that there might be some work up north, in Milwaukee, where Sam Pick's Club Madrid frequently hired new talent. But the black ladder to success started a few rungs down: she did get a job at the club—as the attendant in the ladies' washroom for $1.00 a night, plus tips.

The Club Madrid, located on Bluemound Road in Waukesha County, just across the county line from Milwaukee, attracted customers from Marquette University and State Normal School, with a whimsically unpunctuated sign, "Dancing Sandwiches." Done in middle western rococco with an exterior in Spanish motif, it was ringed by a stone wall complete with valet parking. Within its grounds were numerous sunken gardens, an interior featuring several lounges with velvet plush seats, a recessed band stand, and a huge raised stage. On the second floor were roulette wheels and gaming tables. Obviously, the casino attracted a wealthy clientele, enabling Sam Pick to hire better bands and singers for the enjoyment of the patrons on the first floor.[32] The consumption of bootleg liquor was protected by lookouts stationed at strategic locations throughout the road house, and its approaching thoroughfares.

As for Hattie, her first gig at the Madrid was no more than the classic black tale of servant—at first, anyway. Many people remember Hattie at the club.[33] She was widely referred to as the "lovely lady" in the washroom. She kept a "tip saucer" handy, and she considered a gratuity of a dime to be generous. Her work place was close to the stage, so washroom patrons were frequently amused to see her clapping her hands and dancing to the rhythms of the songs. Often she hummed the tunes, and sang them to herself, leading the ladies who used the washroom to suggest that Hattie become a regular performer. Unfortunately, the club's management did not agree. It seemed clear that Hattie's color kept her from singing at the predominantly white club, thereby wasting her vast experiences in vaudeville and in theatrical entertainment circuits.

Eventually, Hattie broke the color barrier and in melodrama style began to sing on stage. Various accounts attest to how Hattie happened to sing one night at Club Madrid. One story was that the ladies using the washroom brought so much pressure on Sam Pick that he finally yielded and let her perform, while another told of a slow night, with few of the club's clientele present. According to this version, the manager, trying to liven up the evening, exclaimed "I'd let the help sing if I thought it would do any good!"

The regular performers that night were Art Krueger's Columbian Band, and its soloist was Mark Steger, who remembered that Hattie "came to the band in a rather shy way and said, 'somebody wants me to sing.' "[34]

According to Steger, Hattie claimed that she "didn't know any tunes," (of course, quite untrue, since Hattie had been singing and writing songs for more than a decade), but thought, however, that she knew some of the words to "St. Louis Blues." Steger, who was "thoroughly surprised," for he "never knew Hattie, the washroom attendant, could sing," recalled:

> We figured out a decent key and away we went. She really had a good beat, and got a standing ovation from the few people in the club. . . . Soon people were coming out just to hear Hattie sing. That was the beginning for Hattie.[35]

Hattie's tip saucer that night had more than dimes in it. When she counted her "take," she had $90.36 in a day when $90 would buy a lot of food![36]

Night after night at Club Madrid Hattie belted out the "St. Louis Blues," and other songs, many of which she had written herself. Soon her fame spread throughout the Milwaukee area, and people traveled to Bluemound Road just to catch her nightly act. For Hattie, it was a "Cinderella" story. The more she sang before Club Madrid's well-to-do, success oriented, clientele, the more popular she became, and thus more receptive to the idea that she seek even greater things. One of her friends even suggested that she go to Hollywood, and try her hand at the movies.

CHAPTER TWO

"A Woman's Gifts Will Make Room For Her"

W hile Hattie toured the East with various vaudeville groups, her brother Sam and sisters Etta and Orlena sought their fortunes in California. The late twenties were boom years for Hollywood, and Sam and Etta got bit parts in movies, while Orlena ran a rooming house for Pullman porters. Like Hattie back East and all struggling performers, when they could get no entertainment work, they resorted to menial employment.

When Sam and Etta heard about Hattie's break at the Club Madrid, they begged her to join them in Hollywood. For Hattie this became an easy decision since Sam Pick's enterprises in Milwaukee suffered with the Depression, and Hattie's work and pay soon became irregular. She decided to go West and try the movies. There she could live with Etta and Sam until she got established.

Accounts of how Hattie traveled to Hollywood vary. According to one she and a group of friends from Milwaukee drove the distance in a ramshackle automobile; in another she rode a train to Los Angeles. Whatever the case, she arrived in California in 1931, with about $20 in the cheap, new purse she had bought as she passed through Denver. Also in her purse was a rabbit's foot, and a clipping from a Denver newspaper that Hattie, the "hometown girl," was on her way to movie stardom in Hollywood.[1]

Like every movie hopeful she faced the cold reality of sunny Hollywood, and her savings were soon depleted, as she went from one studio to another trying to get work. Many times producers told her that she probably did have a future in films; but just not with them. Accordingly, Hattie once again took on household jobs of sweeping, cooking, and ironing. Later in her life, she estimated that she washed three million dishes on her way to stardom.

Sam took Hattie to see Harry Levette, a veteran stringer who sold movie gossip to black press services, who had connections with the Tivoli (later Bill Robinson) Theatre in Los Angeles. Levette introduced Hattie to the Tivoli audience, and she sang with Sarah Butler's Old Time Southern Singers. Hattie's "sparkling smile and naturalness" at once made her a hit that night at the Tivoli.[2] Word got around the area about her unpaid performance, and she began to get more attention than in the past.

Yet another source of gigs in these struggling times was her brother, Sam, known as Deacon McDaniel, or The Doleful Deacon. He was performing for Los Angeles radio station KNX, on a program titled "The Optimistic Do-Nut Hour," sponsored by the Perfection Bakery Company. Hattie begged Sam to get her a spot on the show. Sam facetiously told his little sister, "Well, I don't know, Sis. This is big time, you know." In addition to Sam, "Optimistic Do-Nuts" featured such popular attractions as the Satchel McVey Orchestra and White Wash Weldon, a singer whose well known songs included "Asleep in the Deep," and "Ten Thousand Leagues Under the Sea."[3] Despite these popular regulars, Sam did get Hattie a place on the program, and she instantly became a hit with black West Coast listeners, writing her own songs and gags, and playing the cook in "Miss Ann's Kitchen."

For her first broadcast, Hattie came into the studio "dressed down like a debutante. . . ." She wore a formal evening gown, while the rest of the cast had on casual clothes. The cast took a look at her, and Tom Breneman, a KNX announcer, yelled, "Hattie's gone High Hat." From that day forward, she was known as Hi-Hat Hattie. She was, as one author put it, "a big, black, bossy, and beautiful maid who continually forgets her place." Some began to refer to her as Her Haughtiness.[4] Every Friday morning, another KNX announcer, Bert Betterworth, gleefully proclaimed the "Optimistic Do-Nut Hour," starring Hi-Hat Hattie McDaniel, but soon Hattie's effervescence took over and the show actually became known to some listeners as Hi-Hat Hattie and Her Boys.[5]

For each of her weekly performances, Hattie received $5.00. (Later, when she became a movie extra, she also got $5.00 for each appearance, causing her to quip that no-one in Hollywood could count above five).[6] Though she was "making it" popularly with Optimistic Do-Nuts, her salary was not enough to keep her solvent. Even in 1931, five dollars did not go very far. During the week, she worked as a maid in wealthy, Los Angeles households, and prayed that central casting would contact her for a movie part. She became so depressed under these circumstances that frequently letters from back home went unanswered. Fans in Denver were enthusiastic about her work in Hollywood, thinking she was going "like a ball afire." She was then in her mid-thirties, and her sojourn to Hollywood was in many ways a do or die situation. But she rarely spoke of her troubles at the time she had them. She'd always stop negative talk about her—or anyone else's—career, by saying, "Don't put that in the ether."[7] The admonition meant that if you didn't want something to happen, you didn't even speak of it—for words have power.

Hattie had to borrow car fare money to go for an interview at a downtown studio. A friend advised her not to let those movie people know that she was down and out. "Look breezy," and people will think you are,[8] was the good advice Hattie got; advice that in the years ahead she imparted to other young, struggling actors and actresses on their way up. When Hattie went into the studio (which, unfortunately, she did not name), for her interview, "she breezed past about twenty of her friends who were waiting, and landed the job."[9]

Hattie sang in choruses of Southern singers in several movies in 1931 and 1932. As merely one of dozens of such performers, she got no screen credit; she did, however, get $5.00 a movie for her services.

At last in 1932 she appeared in her first feature, Fox's *The Golden West*. A Romeo and Juliet like story, the film was set in the town of Preston, Kentucky, in 1845. Bad blood prevailed between the Summers and Lynch families. Betty Summers and Jerry Lynch loved each other, but could not marry because of their parents' obstinancy. Jerry moved West, and while he was away, Betty's father forced her to marry Calvin Brown. Jerry then married a girl named Helen, but was heartbroken because he had lost Betty. His sorrow ended when he was killed in an Indian raid.

Hattie, uncredited, portrayed one of the numerous house servants in the Summers household, and she tried, generally unsuccessfully, to ease Betty's pain caused by the intransigence of her family toward Jerry Lynch.[10] Her part here as a beloved black servant who also became a confidante of the young daughter of the family set a pattern for many of Hattie's future movies.

In 1933, Hattie got small, household maid parts in three movies. The first two were *The Story of Temple Drake* (Paramount—based on William Faulkner's *Sanctuary*) and *The Blonde Venus* (Paramount—directed by Josef von Sternberg). The third, *I'm No Angel*, (Paramount), starred Mae West, with the part of the maid, Beulah, played by Gertrude Howard. It was in this movie that Mae West spoke those "immortal" words, "Beulah, peel me a grape." In later years, journalists frequently misidentified the person to whom it was spoken as Hattie.

The next year, 1934, Hattie started out, unlisted in the movie's credits, with *Operator 13* (MGM). Set in the Civil War, it starred Gary Cooper and Marion Davies. Hattie played Annie, the cook for the U.S. Secret Service people who were spying on the Confederates. Etta and Sam were also in this movie, along with Louise Beavers and the Mills Brothers.

During one of the fight scenes in *Operator 13*, Hattie got tickled as she watched a man get punched in the stomach. She blurted out, "He hit him in the front and bulged him out in the back."[11] Though he never used the line, the director, Richard Boleslavsky, liked it, and it got Hattie some added attention. She always attributed this ad lib to the fact that soon after *Operator 13*, she got a leading part in a Will Rogers movie, *Judge Priest* (Fox).

The movie, adapted from an Irvin S. Cobb novel, starred Will in the title role, and was directed by the great John Ford. Hattie played Aunt Dilsey, the washerwoman for Kentucky Judge Priest.

Stepin Fetchit (Lincoln Perry, at the time riding the crest of Hollywood popularity, though it would be waning in two years' time), was also in the movie. Various critics suggested that Hattie "stole" some scenes from "Step," a fact that caused ill ease between the two in later years. A few days into the shooting, Will Rogers was heard to say, "It's a good thing this movie has got Hattie McDaniel in it."[12] This statement did not fare well with "Step," either, so while he did not exactly try to hold Hattie back in the movie, neither did he give her any particular encouragement. The truth was that "Step's" day was quickly passing; through the late 1920s he was a major star in silent movies, and was known for his roles of complete subservience to white people. Hattie, on the other hand, was on her way up; she and "Step" "passed" each other. While it is true that she played mostly obsequious parts, there was enough "sassiness" in her to make her style different from Stepin Fetchit's.

An important opportunity for Hattie in *Judge Priest* was that she demonstrated her singing abilities. She sang "Master Jesus Wrote me a Note, and Washed me White as Snow," and "Saving Daniel from the Lion's Den." Also, she participated in a moving rendition of "My Old Kentucky Home," and sang a duet with Will Rogers, "He Needs a Toddy Tonight."

Perhaps because of her singing Hattie reckoned that *Judge Priest* was her most important film to date. Widespread opinion was that this was the finest picture Rogers ever made, and Rogers himself credited Hattie, who became his close friend, with the picture's success.[13] Gaining the friendship of people like Will Rogers and John Ford certainly could not hurt Hattie's career. Hattie was listed in the credits of *Judge Priest,* but this did not mean that she would afterward routinely be credited. In fact, it was not until *Gone With the Wind* that she received regular billings.

As Hattie continued to obtain roles in the movies, her self-confidence grew, along with her salary. She was delighted to learn that Hollywood directors really could pay her more than $5.00 a movie; so much more in fact that she bought a house at 2177 West 31st Street in Los Angeles, and made her home there for the next several years.[14] Also, her face became familiar. One day she was on a streetcar in Los Angeles when a young admirer came up to her, and asked if she was Hattie McDaniel. He was Wonderful Smith, himself a black performer, and that chance encounter with Hattie began a friendship that lasted for the next twenty years,[15] during which time he gave Hattie some much needed driving lessons in her old Chevrolet.

Hattie in turn took Wonderful under her tutelage and taught him that success should make him humble, and helped develop Wonderful's considerable talent in singing and dancing. She became so much his confidante, advisor, and beloved friend that from time to time, newspapers hinted at romance between the two. It was Wonderful who escorted Hattie, many years later, to the crowning achievement of her film life—the night she won the Academy Award for playing Mammy in *Gone With the Wind*.

Smith somehow brought out Hattie's deep streak of folksiness. Once, when Duke Ellington and his band came to Los Angeles, Wonderful, a student of drama, played for him in a musical revue at the Mayan Theatre called "Jump for Joy." At the end of the engagement, Ellington offered Wonderful a seven-year contract, to travel with the band and, among other things, deliver a monologue, "Hello Mr. President." Wonderful went to Hattie for advice on whether or not to accept Ellington's offer, only to be put off for two days. Then Hattie told him that she had had a dream in which Duke Ellington, Hattie, and a number of other people were out 'possum hunting. They caught a 'possum, and put him in a large tow sack. As they carried the 'possum in the tow sack, Ellington held one end, while Hattie secured the other. While the old 'possum struggled to escape, the Duke put out one hand and pushed it on top of the 'possum's head. When Hattie saw that 'possum in the tow sack, it looked exactly like Wonderful Smith. Her advice: don't sign the contract. He didn't.[16]

Another black Californian of the early thirties who became Hattie's best friend, secretary, confidante, and "right arm" was a young journalist from Du Quoin, Illinois, Ruby Berkley Goodwin.

Ruby was in San Diego in 1934 working for a black service, the Calvin News Syndicate, when the editor wrote her a note: "We hear there is a colored boy in Hollywood who arranges music for Paul Whiteman. Get a story on him."[17] The "colored boy" turned out to be William Grant Still, who became one of a small circle of successful black composer-arrangers. While on the Still assignment, Ruby went to the Universal Studios, where *Showboat* was being shot, hoping to get an interview with Paul Robeson, the movie's black basso deckhand, Joe. On the *Showboat* set, Ruby saw a large, laughing, black woman surrounded by a crowd of black extras costumed as dancing girls and dockworkers. She wandered over, and recognized the woman as Hattie McDaniel, introduced herself, and instantly the two hit it off. The meeting led to some articles about Hattie,[18] and eventually friendship and a job for Goodwin four years later as a secretary. Hattie played Queenie in this version of *Showboat,* a part that had been filled by Gertrude Howard in 1927. Critics did not single out either Howard or Hattie for their respective performances, but they hailed the movie casts as a whole for their wonderful music which filled in rather long periods of melodrama. A *New York Times* critic, Frank Nugent, said the 1936 *Showboat* should make the "world grateful to Hollywood for restoring such grand entertainment." It really was "too good a piece to suffer neglect," Nugent claimed.[19]

McDaniel's friendship with Goodwin marked her movement in earnest into black Hollywood circles and away from her older "non-professional" relationships. In late 1938, Hattie received a book of Ruby's poems. She wrote back to Ruby, or "Goody," as she called her, that "I am enjoying the poems immensely. I love 'I Dream Alone Again,' rather fitting because I just received my divorce. Smile."

This reference to her divorce indicates that Hattie was married four times (instead of three usually mentioned in press books and film anthologies). Her second husband's name was Howard Hickman, but she never explained when she married him, or why she divorced him.[20]

By the mid-thirties, Hattie had become a respected, and recognized, but not particularly well-known actress. There were still many times when she did not receive screen credit for her film appearances. She worked on a picture by picture basis without any permanent contract with a major studio. The "star system" was so entrenched in the minds of movie goers that lesser luminaries had little chance of any recognition. Hattie rarely went on location with the movies in which she played, even when going on location became fashionable. The overwhelming part of her work was in the studio, or "stujo," as she tended to pronounce it. Sometimes she would not even leave town lest she get a precious call from the "stujo" to come in and do some work. Her usual workday in the "stujo" was 4 a.m. to 7:24 p.m.[21]

Her circle of film friends in the mid-thirties also expanded. In the black community, her closest friend was Ruby Goodwin. She was also close to Louise Beavers, Ethel Waters, Lillian Randolph, Frances Williams, Wonderful Smith, Carlton Moss, and Joel Fluellen. Included among the "big names" in Hollywood who knew her, and came to admire her work were Edward Arnold (a long-time friend, who got Hattie several movie parts), Joan Crawford, Olivia de Havilland, Bette Davis, Katharine Hepburn, Marlene Dietrich, Shirley Temple (who lovingly called her "Mama Mac"), Walter Pidgeon, Henry Fonda, Ronald Reagan, and "the king," Clark Gable. Still, Hattie must have sensed that she was just on the fringes of stardom. She kept waiting for her big break.

Hattie's first movie of 1935 was *The Little Colonel* (Fox), starring Shirley Temple, Bill Robinson, and Lionel Barrymore. Her performance as Mom Beck caused a stir among some members of the black community. It was, as film historian Edward Campbell in *The Celluloid South,* put it, as though the lessons of the Civil War had never been learned. "Colonel Lloyd (Barrymore) ruled over a magnificent estate tended by devoted servants. Blacks still gathered on the front lawn to sing "Carry Me Back to Old Virginia," and the Colonel still raised his glass to "the South and confusion to all its enemies."[22]

Some black critics complained that in *The Little Colonel,* Hattie expressed the thought, written into the script, that the economic security of slavery was preferable to the vagaries of freedom. They believed the movie unfairly stereotyped blacks, and gave the world the impression that they *wanted* to be slaves. This movie marked the beginning of a fight by some black activists against racial casting that heated up in the years ahead until it reached a boiling point in the late forties.

Actually, however, in the mid-thirties, Hattie's film image was not totally that of a servile, groveling menial. On the contrary, she became known to many movie audiences as an independently-minded, sometimes even sassy, operator of the household. A good example of this characterization was *Alice Adams* (RKO) in 1935, which starred Katharine Hepburn and Fred MacMurray. Directed by George Stevens, this adaptation of the Booth Tarkington novel concerned the social climbing antics of the Adams family. To impress a visitor (Fred MacMurray), Alice planned a sumptuous meal, prepared and served by a maid hired for the evening, but made to appear as a permanent employee. The maid was Malena Burns, played by Hattie McDaniel. Her "efforts" at advancing the Adams' fortune that evening were quite disastrous. First, Malena told Alice the weather was "too hot" to serve soup as an appetizer, and then she brought in some caviar sandwiches. Each time she appeared at the table, Malena loudly chewed gum and popped it, which added to Alice's consternation. Once while serving, Malena's head scarf fell onto the table, and then she tripped down the cellar steps.

Altogether, Hattie's performance in *Alice Adams* was a comic *tour de force*, a "Greek chorus" commenting on the Adamses. She was slow and bumbling like Stepin Fetchit, but beyond Stepin Fetchit, she was a cantankerous and, as one author put it, "talk back to whitey," maid.[23]

This image of Hattie did not fare well with Southern movie goers. *Alice Adams* was the first picture many of them had seen in which a black showed bossiness or impertinence to whites.

Ironically, by 1935, Hattie had two movie images. She was much too servile in *The Little Colonel,* for the liking of many blacks; she was much too independent in *Alice Adams* for numerous whites. Over the next several years she alternated in these characteristics.

In *Another Face* (RKO) she played Nellie, who was constantly told to "act more delicate," but she was quick to reply that she was a maid, and "I ain't no cook." In *Gentle Julia* (Fox) the story was the same: flippant Hattie acted the role of Kittie Silvers. When Julia wanted Kittie to wash the dog, Kittie responded, "No Ma'am, Miss Julia. I say I'm no dog washerwoman for nobody. . . . My job is cooking victuals for you and your pa. And I ain't playin' nurse to no dog." When Grandpa asked Kittie where the dog came from, she told him, "I don't know, sir, who done it, no more than the lilies of the valley, what toil, neither do they spin."[24]

In *Mad Miss Manton* (RKO), Hattie played Hilda and put another twist on her evolving persona as the fierce protectress of Barbara Stanwyck. Once when the doorbell rang persistently, Hattie shouted, "I heard it. I heard it. I ain't deaf. Sometimes I wish I wuz." Audiences had mixed reactions as Hattie threw a pitcher of water into Henry Fonda's face when he came with flowers in hand, calling on Barbara Stanwyck. Sure, Hattie was just "obeying orders," but in the America of the mid-thirties both North and South, it was something different, to say the least, to see a black person act this aggressively toward whites. One line in the movie was to some extent prophetic. A character remarked, "when the revolution comes, our help will turn against us." Hattie replied that she couldn't handle a gun. "I'se a pacifist."[25]

Star For A Night, a 1936 Fox production (originally called *The Holy Lie*) created a new dimension for Hattie: sex appeal. She played the usual maid, who one night while the family was out let her boyfriend in.

"Come on in, big boy!"

"Look out sister, here I goes, and what I does nobody knows."

"Nobody won't be back 'til 11:30. . . . Come on, big boy, in the kitchen and we'll make ourselves comfortable while I fixes us a drink."

"Where you leads I got to follow, and I won't stop for the red lights."

"You're telling me. Take a chair, big boy. Sure nuff. What a night!"[26]

Hattie largely reverted to racial stereotypes as they were written for her roles in most of her other movies of the thirties. In Sinclair Lewis' *Babbitt* (RKO), Hattie was afraid of a toaster and other "new fangled" gadgets such as the telephone. In *The Bride Walks Out* (RKO), she exclaimed, "I don't see why white men don't want their wives to work. I went to work just as soon as I married." She played a maid in *The Singing Kid,* 1936, for Warner, with Al Jolson. Hattie did not have a speaking part in this movie. She simply widened her eyes when a man told a scary story—another racial stereotype, complained many critics.

Through the decade, her roles lost the flavor she had given in earlier performances. In Warner's *Over the Goal,* for example, as Hanna, throughout the movie, she was the superstitious, eye-rolling comic servant that so many black newspaper writers were coming to hate. The movie was, of course, about football and Hanna and her husband, William, were the caretakers at the college where football was so popular. The school's mascot was a large black bear. To keep the bear safe, William brought it home with him. During the night, while Hanna was sleeping, she rolled over to find that the bear—not her husband William—was in the bed with her. The ensuing ruckus amused movie audiences from coast to coast.

Racing Lady (RKO) definitely put Hattie into a black stereotype. She constantly spoke about the importance of working for "quality folks," and she used a rabbit's foot and voodoo charms to try to affect the outcome of a horse race. Hattie played the overworked maid Abby in this movie, and her favorite expressions were "Lawsy me!" and "Bless my soul!" and "Two Shakes of a Lamb's tail!" Her "chilluns" were sleepy-headed, lazy, and fawning. Her husband, Josephus Hezekiah, was almost as bad.[27]

In *Forty Five Fathers* (Fox), Hattie played Beulah, who expressed pleasure at the departure from the household of two uppity English housekeepers. The head of the household rebuked Beulah to control her tongue, and she replied, "Yessir, but ah hopes you gets some real white folks this time." *Everybody's Baby* was a 1938 Fox production, in which a young black child wandered into a room where a group of white people were talking. Hattie, apologizing for the child's entry, said, to the amusement of everyone present, "There was too much sun in the back where I'se hangin' out clothes, and I figure she's already tan enough."

29

In *Can This Be Dixie?* (Fox), Hattie played Lizzie, and sang in characteristic fashion:

Don't quit pickin'
Else you don't get no chicken.
Never get a moment to play
Take pick, pick Pickaninny, pick that cotton
Yo Mammy and yo Pappy so old and gray
Now they's so tired and you all's required
to pick away 'til judgement day.[28]

This song, plus other material in the movie caused many black editors to heat up their typewriters. One writer complained that Hattie, along with Louise Beavers, Clarence Muse, and Stepin Fetchit, repeated the same role endlessly—"devoted, dog-like servant, lazy, good for nothing, meek and happy."

As the decade drew to a close, Hattie had become a conspicuous (as opposed to leading) actress. Her ascendancy—once she did break into movies—was fairly rapid. In the thirties she played noticeable roles in forty different movies, averaging one movie a month in 1936 alone. True, each of her roles was as a domestic servant of some sort, but it was "being in the movies," and that's what she wanted. At this early stage of her movie career, Hattie came by her parts "pot-luck," and was the creation of her scripts. She had no continuity of writers, directors, actors, or "white friends at court," so to speak, to get parts for her. Later, after she became famous, producers such as David O. Selznick created parts specially tailored for her talents.

When a friend objected to her playing so many servant parts, or "handkerchief heads" as they came to be called, she replied "Hell, I'd rather play a maid than be one."[29] She certainly had had experience as a maid both in movies and real life, so she spoke authoritatively on the subject.

Her home on 31st Street, in a neighborhood of rambling bungalows in old white Los Angeles, became a magnet for aspiring young actors and actresses. She gave them board and lodging, sometimes for months on end, until they found work. Hattie loved children, and became godmother to the children of many friends. At one time Hattie had as many as thirty godchildren,[30] perhaps compensating her for a life-long dream to have a child of her own.

Hattie also became philosophical as the thirties drew to a close. She was glad, she said, that her father, Henry, had taught her early on to be an optimist about life. Through even her hardest times, she remembered his advice that if you want something badly enough, and are willing to work for it, you will be successful. Henry had always been fond of quoting the biblical proverb that "A man's gifts will make room for him," which she adapted to suit her own purposes. She was positive that neither Henry nor God would mind.[31] Also she came to feel obliged to pay back the world for its kindnesses. This tenet led her toward many acts of charity in the years ahead. She made generous contributions to charitable organizations and orphanages, and, busy as she was with the movies, found time to visit old people in nursing homes, and patients in hospitals, to cheer them up with her big, flashing smile and bubbling personality. (Her favorite charities were the Braille Institute, the Jewish Home for the Aged, the Home for Children in New York, and the Boys Home of the Los Angeles People's Independent Church of Christ.) All these activities showed that Hattie had not forgotten the lessons of her simple upbringing that one should be kind to everyone, and that her circle of friends went beyond her film life.

Hattie was not much of a reader, although she enjoyed poetry. Consequently Ruby Goodwin, a poet in addition to being a journalist, frequently sent her creations to Hattie, who enjoyed them immensely. Her favorite poet, however, was Paul Lawrence Dunbar. She found comfort and solace in words of poems like "We Wear the Mask," which must have struck Hattie with some force, given her screen personae.

But there was one book making the rounds in the late thirties that all of Hattie's friends recommended to her. There was a character in it, they believed, which was ready made for Hattie. Such a role might enable Hattie to merge her screen images. It would be fine, for example, for Hattie to be bossy, cantankerous, and sassy, *if* she could also be loveable about it, and "stay in her place" in the context of a white society. After so much persuasion, Hattie yielded and read the book. Yes, she affirmed excitedly, there was a part for her, and she sensed that she would have an opportunity to test for it. To be ready to portray the role of Mammy, and do it right, she read the book three times. The book, of course, was *Gone With the Wind*.

CHAPTER THREE

"I Did My Best and God Did the Rest"

One of the most memorable episodes in movie history was David O. Selznick's talent search for the film version of *Gone With the Wind*. When he acquired Margaret Mitchell's novel, Selznick let it be known that the casting was to be competitive; thus, he and his staff traveled through much of the United States, visiting colleges and little theatre groups, looking for suitable talent to play the various parts in his upcoming epic.[1] (Apparently the only part in the film that was not up for grabs was Rhett Butler. Though he reportedly did not want the role, Clark Gable was the unanimous choice.)

Many actresses and actors, famous and otherwise, tested for the roles of Melanie and Ashley Wilkes (Ann Sheridan, Margaret Sullavan, Lana Turner, Bruce Lister, Lew Ayres, Melvyn Douglas, Robert Young),[2] and the other players at Tara and Twelve Oaks. The part of Scarlett was not actually chosen until the filming was underway. Selznick's brother brought Vivien Leigh with him to view the first scene, and Selznick was entranced by her. The competition was quite keen for the black roles, and of these, that of Mammy received most of the attention.

The best Hollywood guesses pointed to the choice of Louise Beavers, who had gained fame in *Imitation of Life*. She and Hattie were long time friends, their careers and lives frequently crossing. (Many film anthologies even today list Hattie with roles that were actually played by Beavers, *Mr. Blandings Builds His Dream House* and *Reap the Wild Wind,* to name two.)

In 1937, Beavers was better known than Hattie, and possessed a wider range of experience in such films as *Bullets or Ballots* and *Imitation of Life*. She was thus favored by many important people for Mammy. Sol Lindser, an official at RKO, wrote a strong letter for Beavers to George Cukor[3] who later became the first director of *Gone With the Wind*. She had recently completed *Rainbow on the River* for RKO, and on her subsequent personal appearance tour, the public showed their immense fondness for her. As Lindser wrote: "It is our intention to publicize her name as being Hattie McDaniel, instead of 'the colored woman who was in *Imitation of Life*.' She will be as well known to motion picture fans as Bert Williams was to theatre goers. We have a feeling that Louise Beavers, cast in important pictures, can do much to enhance their entertainment value."[4] Lindser's opinions were underscored by dozens of letters arriving each day at Selznick International supporting Beavers for the role of Mammy. According to reports, though, Beavers walked in for her first interview at Selznick elegantly dressed, wearing her finest furs, an appearance not suggesting the role of Mammy.

Not all the letters, however, were for Beavers. No less a personage than the First Lady, Eleanor Roosevelt, a known champion of blacks, got in on the advice-giving, touting the White House cook, Elizabeth McDuffie (Mammy White House), as an excellent Mammy, saying she was "extremely capable and has a great deal of histrionic ability."[5] Selznick was uncomfortable with the White House connection because he feared the public would charge undue political influence if McDuffie got the role. Although McDuffie tested for the part, she did not, of course, get it. Mrs. Roosevelt was not alone in trying to get her cook into the movies. In Atlanta, it became commonplace for wealthy Georgians to show up with their servants at author Margaret Mitchell's home, for an "audition." The frustrated Mitchell had to tell the would-be Mammies that she had little to do with the movie production of the novel.

Then there were the longshot applicants for the role. One letter to Selznick came from a Mississippian, Bessie Mack, who wrote: "I believe I am your Mammy. I am fat, black, aged 36, born, reared Mississippi." Mack had toured the United States four times she said, singing black spirituals and reading dialect poems. Although she had two years of college behind her, she had fallen on hard times in the depression-ridden thirties. Mack wanted Selznick to send her a train ticket so she could come to Hollywood for a test.[6] If such ticket were against Selznick's policy (as indeed it was), Mack said she would borrow the money for the trip. There is no record that Mack ever received a screen test for Mammy.

Another candidate for Mammy was the veteran actress, Madame Sul-te-Wan, who had recently played the role of a slave in Frank Lloyd's *Maid of Salem.* Still other possibilities were two somewhat obscure black actresses, Hattie Noel and Bertha Powell. Selznick interviewed them on December 5, and tested a few days later.[7] Along with them was another black player who had numerous movies to her credit, but never the "big break." Her name was Hattie McDaniel. As Louise Beavers had worn her finest clothes to be interviewed for the part of Mammy, Hattie showed up authentically dressed as a typical Old Southern Mammy. Selznick was so impressed, he said he could "smell the magnolias." Her case was not hurt, either, by the fact that she was the favorite of leading man Clark Gable.

There is scant evidence that Hattie vigorously sought the role of Mammy in *Gone With the Wind,* though it is true that she had acquired an agent, MCA Artists of Beverly Hills. Even as Hattie read the book, she had the instinctive feeling that she would be sought out for the part, but it was as much a case of Selznick finding Hattie as it was the other way around.

Hattie may never have known it, but one of her early supporters for the role of Mammy was Bing Crosby. On January 15, 1937, Crosby wrote to Selznick:

Being loath to go down in cinema history as the only citizen not on record for sticking my nose into the casting for *GWTW,* I would like to suggest a Mammy. The little lady I have in mind played opposite Robeson in *Showboat,* and to my mind would be a cinch. I don't know her name, but your hirelings in the casting office could dig it up. Hoping you will pardon my guts.[8]

The "little lady," of course, was Hattie McDaniel. When they knew each other better Crosby gave Hattie a "motto" that she liked to repeat to her friends: "Always remember this; there are only eighteen inches between a pat on the back, and a kick in the rump." In any case, Selznick whimsically thanked Crosby: "Dear Bing, Thanks for the suggestion. And also for not wanting to play Scarlett. DOS."[9]

McDaniel tested for Mammy on December 6, 1938 with the scene from the beginning of *GWTW* where Mammy is lacing a corset onto Scarlett, and fussing because Scarlett had been "gobbling like a hawg," running the risk of gaining unwanted weight. Mammy also counselled the young Southern lass against making a fool of herself over Ashley Wilkes, object of her infatuation, at the upcoming barbecue at Twelve Oaks Plantation. "Mr. Ashley" was betrothed to Melanie Hamilton and Scarlett should, Mammy warned, resign herself to that fact.[10] Hattie outshone the other contestants as she emoted with her voice, shuffles, and a loud thick Georgian accent which she acquired for the occasion. As she said later, she just opened her heart and let the words flow. When she finished her audition that day, Selznick cancelled all others. He had found his Mammy in Hattie who exemplified all those characteristics Selznick wanted for the role, a Mammy who was more than a servant: "a confidante, counselor, and manager of the O'Hara household." (Later reviews of *GWTW* referred to Mammy as the "Emily Post of the O'Haras".)[11] Besides, Hattie was now far ahead in the public polling for Mammy. The tally for December 8 showed 106 letters for Hattie, one for Louise Beavers, and one for another black actress named Helen Wesley.[12]

Not all the Selznick personnel, however, were enamored with Hattie. At the beginning of production, Selznick brought in a dialect expert from Macon, Georgia, Susan Myrick, a reporter on the *Macon Telegraph.* Though she and Hattie ultimately became the best of friends, Myrick did not at first favor Hattie for the role, confiding in a letter to Margaret Mitchell, January 15, 1939, that in her view,

> Hattie McDaniel . . . is not the right Mammy. . . . [S]he lacks dignity, age, nobility and . . . she hasn't the right face for it.[13]

Fortunately, not many people listened to Miss Myrick's opinion on who should play Mammy.

Selznick offered Hattie a contract on January 27, 1939, borrowing her from Warner Brothers, with whom she had been affiliated for quite some time, though most of her movies in the thirties had been made for Fox. Her services to Selznick were to begin on February 1, and run for renewable fifteen-week periods at $450 a week for her work with Selznick International.

Hattie promised to give her entire time, attention, and best talents to Selznick productions. The producer had the right to dub Hattie's appearance, acts and voice. If for any reason her face were disfigured, or her voice impaired, or if her "present unique and unusual value as an actress" changed, the agreement with Selznick would become null and void. In emphasis of this requirement, the contract obliged Hattie to submit to any medical examinations the producer might want.

There was a "morals" clause in the contract Hattie signed. If she committed an offense under federal, state, or local laws, or if her manners "offended decency, morality, or social propriety," to the point that it caused a public scandal, the agreement could be terminated.

If Hattie had to travel (such as on promotional tours or to shooting locations), Selznick would pay for it. Otherwise, while working on *Gone With the Wind,* she would wait each day for the studio car to pick her up. One limousine was used to transport all the black players in *GWTW,* while the principal whites had his/her own private service, furnished by Selznick,[14] a reflection of the "star system" that dominated Hollywood at that time, not racism.

If Selznick wanted to lend out Hattie to another studio, he and that studio would negotiate a price. No matter how high the amount, Hattie would still receive only her contractual fee of $450 a week. (This was common practice; Warner did it when Hattie worked for Fox.) Selznick, who was infamous for penning memos to his staff, wrote many about filling up any of the "off-time" of Hattie and the other "colored" players. He suggested in a memo on March 29, 1939, right in the middle of filming *GWTW* that his assistant, Henry Ginsberg, hire an agent to see that Hattie, Butterfly McQueen, and the rest of the black players be hired out for other pictures, because such a practice "could save us a substantial amount of money."[15]

Of course, it could be asserted that this system of hiring out to other studios, aside from giving Hattie gainful employment, also offered her a widespread fame. Also, it is true that the movie industry was far ahead of the rest of the country in giving opportunities to blacks. After *GWTW*, Hattie signed another Selznick contract which started out at $500 a week and, if she worked steadily with Selznick three or four years, could rise to $1,500 a week.[16]

When the news spread that Selznick would produce *GWTW*, two dialect problems relevant to blacks cropped up. One had to do with Southern accents in general, and with black dialects specifically.

As early as October 1936, there were some misgivings about dialect. Carl Strange, Atlanta office manager of Macmillan, Mitchell's publisher, told Selznick that regardless of the stars for *GWTW*, the whole production could be ruined if a wrong selection were made for the black cast. He said, "If the parts of Pork, Mammy, Uncle Peter, and Prissy, are given to some of our bright Harlem products with harsh voices or to Negroes who know no better than to accept some director's word for it, that they are to use 'you all' in the singular, you will have missed by that much having a good picture, regardless of who plays the parts of Scarlett, Ashley, Melanie, and the others of the leading characters."[17]

Strange went on to complain about the recent stage version of *Green Pastures,* saying that it was an "absurdity." Marc Connelly, he said, imposed Pennsylvania Dutch accents on "Harlem harshness." (The angels, for example, wished De Lawd would *leave* them clean up his office.) Strange admitted that he did not know very many available black actors. He thought, however, that Stepin Fetchit would be "100 percent all right." He believed, too, that the characters in a recent movie, *The Gorgeous Hussy,* would be acceptable except for John Randolph's butler who spoke to him and used "you-all" with no-one else in mind. Strange begged Selznick "not to spoil what may be the greatest picture of the century" by the travesty of false dialect.[18]

Selznick assured Strange[19] that he and his production crews would be as faithful as possible to the original material, including dialects; and suggested that two people who had not read either the book or the script be placed on the stage to hear the rehearsals to make sure that "the Negroes" were "completely understandable." He wanted special attention paid to Pork's and Prissy's lines, as well as to Uncle Peter's and even Mammy's. Selznick thought it important that one of the two listeners be an Englishman, apparently believing that if someone from England understood Southern accents and black dialects, anyone could.[20]

The dialect problem did not cause as much public frenzy as had the casting contests. Nevertheless, there was some attention given to the matter. Birmingham, Alabama's morning newspaper, *The Post,* conducted a search over radio station WAPI, for one man and one woman with "true Southern accents." Tapes of the winners were to be sent to the Selznick studios, so that no one there would needlessly be misinformed.[21]

The United Daughters of the Confederacy also got into the dialect act. Mrs. E. Dolly Blount Lamar of the Alabama UDC, urged Selznick to put more emphasis on naturalness than local color. "The Southern intonations cannot—never have been—successfully reproduced by one not native to the section." If the dialect were false in *GWTW,* the movie would exasperate Southerners and be unconvincing to the general public.[22] Mrs. Lamar also wrote to Clark Gable in June 1938, imploring him not to try to imitate "socalled Southernisms. If you will speak naturally, guided by your own good judgment and flair for portrayal previously proven, you will present a satisfactory result."[23] Gable refused to take any dialect lessons, believing that his many fans would not notice whether he had a Southern accent or not, and wouldn't care. As it turned out, accent and dialect were not that big of an issue on the sets of *GWTW.* Whenever difficulties did arise, Susan Myrick was on hand, with her colleague, Will Price, to set things straight. As Myrick pointed out, all the black actresses and actors in *GWTW* "fell easily into the Negro dialect as it was written by Margaret Mitchell and carefully preserved in the script."[24]

A far larger problem than dialect dealt with race and *GWTW.* As the publicity for the movie widened, many black leaders feared extensive demeaning portrayals of their people. The argument raged from 1936, when Selznick first announced his purchase of *Gone With the Wind* until after its release.

When the book first appeared, not all of its reviews were favorable. In *The Daily Worker,* David Platt charged that *GWTW* glorified the Ku Klux Klan, the old Southern "slaveocracy," and lynch laws.[25] Just as the NAACP had objected to Thomas Dixon's novel and play *The Clansman* in 1906 and to its filming in 1915 by D. W. Griffith, as *The Birth of a Nation,* the contemporary generation of blacks rejected the racism and incorrect historical accounts to be found in *Gone With the Wind.*

Dona Popel reviewed the book for the *Journal of Negro Life.* She said, "In [Miss Mitchell's] array of Mammies, Cookies, Porks, and Sams, one sees only ebony black Negroes. One or two may be described as leather colored. The term of 'mulatto' is used disparagingly."[26] L. D. Reddick's review for *The Journal Of Negro History* ascribed honesty to Miss Mitchell's efforts, though limited by her "passion and sectional and racial bias."[27]

As the casting arrangements for the film continued, much of the Jewish community joined with blacks in expressing their misgivings. With Hitler's Germany looming in Europe, Cleveland's Rabbi Barnett Brickner told Selznick that "surely at this time you would want to do nothing that might tend even in the slightest way to arouse anti-racial feelings."[28] The Rabbi mentioned that many of the cast officials for filming *GWTW* were Jewish, including Selznick, and they would be upset if the racial slurs and historical inaccuracies of the book were perpetuated by the movie.

The black press scorched the book, and soon-to-be movie, as

did indeed some of the white press. Lewis Gannett, for example, of the New York *Herald Tribune* wrote to Walter White, executive secretary of the National Association of Colored People, that "I planned my vacation so that I wouldn't have to read *that* book. And then when it sold a million, I had to anyway. I've slurred it on every possible occasion since, but never reviewed it."[29] Earl Morris of the *Pittsburgh Courier*, alarmed at the prospect of having black stereotyping broadcast throughout the country and the world, campaigned against the book's adaptation into a movie. His most prominent article was a pamphlet, "Sailing With the Breeze," in which he urged his readers to contact the Selznick legal department in an effort to stifle if not rid the upcoming movie of the word, "nigger."[30] Ironically he seemed to go out of his way to give favorable publicity to Hattie McDaniel and ultimately was invited to California to see some of the filming, an invitation he readily accepted.[31]

The major black objection toward *GWTW* was its portrayal of slaves and the idea that for some slaves like Mammy and Pork, servility was preferable to freedom.

In the book, Scarlett had been attacked by a black (in the movie, it was by a white), and the Ku Klux Klan had gone off to "save" her honor. Big Sam, a gang boss, again in the book, had referred to "trashy niggers," and when Mammy herself set foot in Atlanta, one of her first utterances had to do with "no-good niggers." It was these slurs against the black race that activated so many people in late 1938 and early 1939, as filming moved ahead. One of the strongest participants in the matter was the National Association of Colored People, whose executive secretary, Walter White, suggested that Selznick employ a black person to view the filming of *GWTW*. There is no evidence that Selznick ever took this action, although he brought columnist Morris out to Hollywood for extended periods. Noted civil rights activist, Arthur Spingarn, suggested Professor Charles Wesley of Howard University as black advisor for the film, but this suggestion apparently never materialized. Also, White believed that all those in decisive positions on the film (screenwriting, directing, producing, etc.)

should be required to read W. E. B. Du Bois' *Black Reconstruction* as a source of knowledge to avoid numerous errors.[32]

At first the Selznick people claimed that they would not "dignify" black newspaper criticisms with replies. One of their representatives, Marcella Rabwin, however, wanted to send special portraits of the black characters to the leading black newspapers of the day, "treating these actors as stars of the picture. In other words, we would let our actors in *GWTW* do our work for us in the colored newspapers across the country."[33]

As time passed, though, the race question became increasingly important to Selznick and his associates. For instance, they began to take Walter White seriously because, said Selznick, he was a "very important man," and "his ill will could rouse a swarm of bad editorials in Negro journals throughout the country."[34] Selznick suggested that White be brought to the *GWTW* sets and given a red-carpet tour of the place.

Certainly, the black protests had their impact. Hattie herself objected to the word "nigger" and ultimately, all references to this slur were eliminated, although the word "darky" was used. While it was true that many of Hattie's film roles in the past had been of a servile nature, she did not carry her obsequiousness into real life. She was justly proud of her race and of her career, and would not lightly view slanders against either. Her opinions on the matter, along with the thoughts of her secretary, Ruby Berkley Goodwin, led to an extensive dialogue among the actors and writers connected with *GWTW* about usage of the word.

Margaret Mitchell did not object to removing the word "nigger" from the script,[35] despite her equal scorn for liberal "professional Negroes," and conservative "professional Southerners."[36] Nevertheless there was a widespread belief on the *GWTW* sets that it was common for black people to call each other "nigger," in either an affectionate or contemptuous manner; they objected only when a white person referred to them by that name. Was it not all right for Mammy, Pork, Prissy, Sam, and Uncle Peter to call each other "niggers?" Much was also made of the fact that several recent movies had used the word "wop" to refer to Italians, and that no widespread protest had occurred as a result.

All of these justifications and rationalizations notwithstanding, Selznick ultimately yielded on the word "nigger," and wrote to Walter White that he had gone further than the removal of "nigger" from the script. He had "left no stone unturned in our efforts to eliminate from our picture any possible objections which the Negroes of America may have had to portions of the novel, *GWTW*.[37] The important black characters in the movie, Selznick proclaimed, would be cast as "loveable, faithful, high-minded people . . . [who] . . . would leave no impression but a very nice one." In the movie, Mammy could not refer, as she had in the book, to "De Lawd," and could not exclaim, "Praise de Lawd!"[38]

Selznick continued that "Mammy is treated very loveably" (in the movie) and with great dignity. The only liberties, he said, that the movie took from the book were to "improve the Negro position. . . ." He asserted further that "We have the greatest friendship toward . . . [blacks] and their cause. We are not portraying Negroes as either mean or bad." The movie, exclaimed Selznick, was "free of anti-Negro propaganda."[39] He summed up his feelings by saying that "I think these are no times in which to offend any race or people."[40] He added that "I feel so keenly about what is happening to the Jews of the world that I cannot help but sympathize with the Negroes and their fears, however unjustified they may be about material which they regard as insulting or damaging."[41]

Principal photography of *Gone With the Wind* finally started on January 26, 1939, the first scene (actually shot on December 10, 1938) being the burning of Atlanta. On the sets, Hattie quickly became the informal entertainer. Typically one day at the noon hour, Vivien Leigh walked over to Hattie, and said, "Mammy, may I go to lunch?" Hattie replied in her Mammy-like manner, "Whea yo goin?" And then they both laughed, as they remembered they were not playing a scene.[42] One of Hattie's favorite scenes from the movie was of the defeated homeward bound Confederate soldiers stopping by Tara for rest and food. Everything on the set was authentic, right down to the food: real Southern corn pone, turnip greens, dry salt pork, and sweet potatoes. When the studio commissary sent out boxlunches that day of chicken and turkey sandwiches, the delivery man found the entire cast of *GWTW* dining on "soul food." Technical advisers Susan Myrick, Will Price, and Wilbur Kurtz joined Hattie, Vivien Leigh, and Clark Gable in the feast. Hattie exulted, "The old Southern standby had won out over a Hollywood diet and many of the boxlunches were returned to the cafeteria unopened."[43]

Another favorite scene had Mammy and Rhett Butler having a drink together right after Bonnie Butler's birth. In the scene they were drinking only colored water. As the takes multiplied, Hattie remarked, "I sure am tired of drinking this colored tea." Soon after she said this, Gable's valet left the set. He returned a while later, and since everyone was smiling at him, Hattie smiled too. When it was time for the next take of the drinking scene, the director yelled, "Lights, camera, action!" and Hattie took a big swig of her drink. Instead of tea, she had just swallowed a large quantity of scotch, bringing "whoops of laughter, and breaking up the scene entirely."[44]

Hattie said of the incident, "It was the real stuff, so they say, and they tell me it was good, but I don't know because it was burning my mouth so. The idea of him playing that kind of a trick on poor ol' Mammy! I'm telling you, it was the hottest afternoon I had seen in many a day, and the sun wasn't shining either. The next morning, he had the audacity to whiz past me and holler, 'Mammy, how's the hang-over?' "[45]

In the same scene, Mammy wore the red silk petticoat Rhett had bought for her but which she heretofore refused to wear because she disapproved of "Mr. Rhett's mean ways." But Bonnie's birth was a joyful time, and Mammy buried her old antagonisms. In the scene, her petticoat was supposed to swish loudly, and Rhett was to say, "What is that rustling noise I hear, Mammy?" Perhaps it was the mix-up in drinks but, inexplicably, Hattie forgot her lines. She stood still as the camera ground on. Finally, Gable, realizing what had happened, grinned and said, "What is that rustling noise I was supposed to hear if you had walked away, Mammy?"[46]

One day Susan Myrick found Hattie on the set with a pencil and paper, moving her lips, jiggling her feet, and laughing to herself. "What on earth are you up to, Mammy?" she asked. Hattie replied that she was writing an act for the time that she might go on a personal appearance tour for GWTW. Then, as Susan Myrick explained, Hattie "eased herself out of the chair and began demonstrating an act she did in vaudeville. . . . It was fine entertainment, too, I can tell you. . . . Mammy went into a tap dance, humming in her lush contralto voice, 'Way down upon de Swanee River.' She turned and she kicked, and she did limping steps and she rolled her eyes, and she demonstrated the ways in which a male chorus does its stuff in a dance routine."[47]

One day many of the cast came to work with colds. Myrick said she felt happier about her malady than she otherwise would because she was in such "good company" with Clark Gable and Hattie McDaniel, who were also suffering. Myrick thought that Hattie had played Mammy for so long in *GWTW* that she now wanted to play Mammy in real life, worrying about Myrick and Gable's coughing, and made them take a big dose of cough syrup every hour or so, which, said Myrick, was "made up according to an old formula which Hattie got from her mother." The medicine contained "linseed oil, lemon juice, and some of the best bourbon."[48] Under the circumstances, the cast suffered numerous "relapses."

While many viewers agreed that Hattie was excellent throughout the movie as Mammy, her fans acknowledged that there was one scene that cinched the Oscar for her. Even while the movie was still in production, it became known as The Scene. It came after Bonnie Butler's death. Everyone was trying to get her father, Rhett, to agree to her burial. Rhett was so upset that he refused to have the body moved. Finally, Melanie Wilkes came to the Butler household, and there she confronted a wildly emotional Mammy. Though, according to Carroll Nye (who played Frank Kennedy in the movie), Hattie kept forgetting her lines for the scene, she finally did choke out these words:

> Mistuh Rhett done los' his min' since Bonnie was killed trying to make her pony take a high jump. Den dis evenin' Miss Scarlett holler th'u de do' dat de fune'l set fer termerrer mawnin' and he says 'Try

45

dat an' Ah kills yer termerrer. Does you think Ah'm gwine put mah chile in de dahk when she so skeered of it?' Yessum, it's de Gawd's trut. He ain't gwine let us bury dat chile.[49]

All the while she poured this out to Melanie, Mammy wiped her big eyes and wept profusely. It was perhaps the movie's most touching moment.

Many people on the set the day that scene was shot realized that it would come close to winning an Oscar for Hattie. One person who was particularly impressed was Olivia de Havilland, who had visions of getting the best supporting actress award for her portrayal of Melanie. She knew, though, when the scene ended, that "Mammy McDaniel" had it. Olivia said afterwards, "That scene probably won Hattie her Oscar and that almost broke my heart too—at least at the time."[50] Later, too, *Variety,* the show business journal, also predicted that "Time will set a mark on this moment in the picture as one of those inspirational bits of histrionics long remembered."[51]

The movie was finished in the fall of 1939, and ready for the industry's censor, the "Hays Office." Will H. Hays, an attorney, former congressman, and one of President Warren G. Harding's postmaster generals, "ran herd" on all the movies put out in the thirties and on into the forties. He was chosen by the Motion Picture Producers and Distributors of America to "codify and enforce" movie morality. In *GWTW*, of course, the most debated line was "Frankly, my dear, I don't give a damn!" an innocent oath by Rhett Butler which violated the producers' self-imposed code.

Other minor offenses caught the eye of the Hays Office, and the words "diaper" and "belch" were stricken from the movie, (but later restored), though the phrase "wipe yo nose," was left in.[52] In addition to the Hays Office in Hollywood, *GWTW*, like all other movies, had to get clearance from many state censor boards and from numerous foreign governments before it could be shown in cinemas. It was a time consuming, often frustrating, process.

When the movie was finished, Selznick knew he had a racially touchy product on his hands and sought to avert controversy. Nevertheless, he praised Hattie: "I should like at this time to

46

congratulate and thank you for your brilliant performance as Mammy in *GWTW*. I think you will find it is universally acclaimed as one of the finest performances of this or any other year."[53] Margaret Mitchell also recognized Hattie and sent her a set of Wedgewood cups and saucers, each saucer hand painted with an Atlanta landmark of the Civil War era.

Selznick soon found himself confronted with two problems of racial etiquette in relation to Hattie McDaniel and the role of Mammy. One was the program to be used in the showings and major advertisements for *GWTW*. On the back of the program was a montage of all the movie's major players, with, of course, Hattie included as Mammy. Although Selznick himself responded that he would like to see the matter of "black and white" put aside, the staff worried about the inclusion of Hattie in the programs that would be distributed throughout the South. He argued that Southerners were more fond of blacks "in their place" than the much-vaunted Northern affection for them, and therefore begged the program makers to include the blacks, or at least Hattie, because "she really gives a performance that if merit alone ruled, would entitle her practically to co-starring."[54]

In the end the sales department recognized Selznick's protests about the program and compromised. When they were printed, Hattie's visage was included on the programs distributed in New York and Los Angeles, while the program in Atlanta and other Southern cities, featured Tara and only the white players.

This fear of alienating white Southerners continued far beyond the program, the most glaring example being the Atlanta premiere of the movie in December 1939. Selznick's initial reaction to the question was not to jump to any conclusions. It had not yet been shown, he said in November, that whites would object to the black stars' presence, especially Mammy, at the Atlanta premiere. Besides, he argued, the "colored" actors could circulate through the black sections of town, generating publicity for the movie and giving interviews to black newspapers. He reasoned that a short personal appearance at the premiere, would justify bringing the black players to Atlanta.[55]

Selznick's representative in Atlanta, Legare Davis, disagreed, arguing that if the black players appeared in the Atlanta premiere, especially Hattie, they would be obliged to stay in sub-standard rooms in the segregated section of town. Moreover, he said, their inclusion "might cause some comment and might be a handle that someone could seize and use as a club." Therefore, "while it was unfortunate to exclude Mammy," Davis thought it was the "wisest policy, to keep any opportunities from arising that would allow someone to cause trouble." Selznick regretted the situation, for he really believed that Hattie's performance in *GWTW* would cause her to be hailed as the "greatest Negro performer of this decade."[56] As with the programs, he did not push the matter, and he acquiesced in the decision not to bring any of the black players to Atlanta. Selznick was probably relieved when Hattie said that she could not go to Atlanta, because she was "otherwise committed." She wrote to Selznick just as he was leaving for the Southern city:

> I am writing to thank you . . . for the opportunity given me to play the part of Mammy in the epochal drama of the Old South. I have nothing but the highest praise for the cooperation extended by my fellow players and the entire studio staff. I am sure that the picture will live up to every expectation of the producer and preview critics, and I hope that Mammy when viewed by the masses, will be the exact replica of what Miss Mitchell intended her to be.[57]

Nonetheless, Hattie's diffidence notwithstanding, as Atlanta and America thrilled to the opening of *Gone With the Wind,* one of its principal stars was missing from the festivities. In late 1940, at a second grand showing of *GWTW* in Atlanta; the so-called "Second Premiere," Hattie did show up for a brief personal appearance and in Denver, Hattie's hometown, the Five Points cinema marquee read *Gone With the Wind,* starring HATTIE MCDANIEL and vivien leigh.

Did Hattie mind being shunned in 1939 by the Atlanta premiere? Of course she did. She was proud of her accomplishments without being "prideful." She also loved her race, and was loved by them, but felt that sudden jolts to the white community were not the way to change things. One of her favorite sayings was that in her life God came first and work came second.[58] Through hard work and gentle example, Hattie believed she could make life better, not only for blacks, but for whites as well. Probably her favorite saying was "Faith is the black person's federal reserve system."[59]

As soon as *GWTW* began to fill the cinemas, black and ultra-liberal reactions proliferated. The *Daily Worker's* first attempt to get a review was not successful. A $25.00 per week reporter, Howard Rushmore, was told even before he saw the picture to "blister it." Rushmore's review spoke of the "technical achievement" and "thematic sweep" of *GWTW*; however, he called the picture a "magnificent bore," and criticized what he thought were anti-black sequences.[60]

The *Daily Worker* editors rejected Rushmore's review as a "shameless glorification of white chauvinism and an affront to the Negro people." When Rushmore quit his job at the paper, he stated that its editorial policies were controlled in Moscow rather than New York, and that was why he had no choice in the content of the review he was assigned to write.[61]

The paper got what it wanted with freelance reviewer Carlton Moss. On January 9, 1940, he wrote, "Whereas *The Birth of a Nation* was a frontal attack on American history and the Negro people, *Gone With the Wind*, arriving twenty years later is a rear attack on the same. Sugar-smeared and blurred by a boresome Hollywood love story and under the guise of presenting the South as it is in the 'eyes of the Southerner,' the message of *Gone With the Wind* emerges in its final entity as a nostalgic plea for sympathy for a still living cause of Southern reaction."[62] Moss erroneously stated that in the movie, Scarlett was attacked by a black man. She was not; in the movie, she was saved by a black man, her gang boss, Big Sam. He described Mammy as "doting on every wish" of Scarlett as though Mammy loved her degrading position "in the service of a family that has helped to keep her people enchained for centuries."

The *Daily Worker* attacks angered Selznick, to the point of wanting to seek litigation in the courts. Its statements, Selznick said, showed a "clear, organized attempt to damage the picture." He pointed out that the Communists repeatedly claimed that the movie was a slander against Abraham Lincoln. Yet, there was only one direct reference in the movie to Lincoln; that was when Scarlett was at the Atlanta benefit for the Confederacy and she said she would not mind "dancing tonight with Lincoln himself."[63]

Selznick compared his travails with D. W. Griffith's *The Birth of a Nation*. Even though in subsequent pictures, Griffith unsuccessfully tried to prove that he was not anti-black, a quarter of a century later such charges were still being leveled. Selznick repeated his oft-made claim that he "cleaned up" the script of *GWTW* and presented no insults whatever to the black race. Yet he forecast that twenty-five years hence, the radical and Communist attacks against the epic would still be heard. If he were silent now in the face of these attacks, he "might give the appearance of truth to the slanders," so even if he lost a suit against the *Daily Worker*, "we cannot help but gain with the publicity through at least having defended ourselves."[64]

Selznick was ultimately dissuaded from pursuing the matter in the courts. His friend, attorney John F. Wharton, told him that any suit, no matter how worthy, would give Selznick the appearance of trying to strangle freedom of opinion. This would not be an auspicious image to acquire, given the political situation of the world at that time. Better, Wharton said, to count your friends rather than your enemies.[65] Selznick took this advice, and tended largely to ignore future negative comments.

Other protests came into the Selznick offices. Such political complaints issued from a variety of leftist sources, typified by an American Labor Party resolution that charged:

> Whereas the motion picture *Gone With the Wind* represents a falsification of U.S. history, and is an insult to President Abraham Lincoln and the Negro people, be it resolved that we go on record as condemning the picture, and urge our members and friends not to attend performances of it.[66]

The Washington District Council of the Maritime Federation of the Pacific, said the movie was "anti-labor" because it glorified the Ku Klux Klan, slandered the black people in the United States, and violated the spirit and intent of the thirteenth, fourteenth, and fifteenth amendments to the Constitution.[67] A branch of the Sons of Union Veterans of the Civil War protested the "false and injurious presentations of the union soldier as bestial," and misrepresented the burning of Atlanta.[68]

On and on the complaints ran, but after his first outburst at the *Daily Worker,* Selznick ignored them. Numerous black newspapers wrote initial negative reviews, but as time passed, they took a second look at the artistry of the black players, especially Hattie McDaniel. In early 1940 stories in the three leading black papers in the country, The Chicago *Defender,* the Pittsburgh *Courier,* and the Baltimore *Afro-American,* concentrated on the real possibility that Hattie might win an Oscar rather than any negative aspects of the movie.

If these black newspapers became obsessed with an Oscar for Hattie, they had much of the country as company. In early February 1940, for example, Sigma Gamma Rho, a black sorority, endorsed Hattie for an award, writing to Selznick that "We trust that discrimination and prejudice will be wiped away in the selection of the winner of this award, for without Miss McDaniel, there would be no *Gone With the Wind.*"[69] Selznick wrote back in full agreement about Hattie's talents, but advised the sorority that ". . . there is nothing that this studio can do about an Academy Award, since this is voted on by the entire industry. Naturally, we hope, as you do, that Miss McDaniel may be the recipient of an award."[70]

When in February the Academy of Motion Picture Arts and Sciences announced that Hattie had been nominated as the best supporting actress, the *Amsterdam News* joined the campaign with much of the black population in rejoicing over this turn of events.

On the big night, February 29, 1940, the Academy Award presentations were held in the Coconut Grove ballroom of Hollywood's Ambassador Hotel, before an audience of 12,000 people. As Hattie arrived late at the ballroom on the arm of Wonderful Smith many people jumped to their feet to applaud her. Hattie wore an aqua blue evening dress, an ermine wrap, and wore gardenias in her hair with a diamond clasp, her purse dappled with rhinestones. She sat through most of the ceremonies at David O. Selznick's table.

After a seemingly interminable wait, Hattie's name was called as the winner of the Oscar for Best Supporting Actress. When Frank Capra and Faye Bainter made the announcement, the crowd went wild. As one observer noted, "The ovation that . . . [Hattie] . . . received will go down in history as one of the greatest ever accorded any performer in the annals of the industry. En masse, the entire audience, stars in every place, stood and cheered their beloved Hattie McDaniel. Tears came to Mammy's eyes as she made her way to the stage to accept the award."[71]

Accepting the award, she said, "Fellow members of the motion picture industry, guests, this is one of the happiest moments of my life, and I want to thank each of you who had a part in selecting me for one of the awards for your kindness. It makes me feel very humble, and I shall always hold it as a beacon for anything that I may be able to do in the future. I sincerely hope that I shall always be a credit to my race, and to the motion picture industry. My heart is too full to express just how I feel, so may I say to each and everyone of you, Thank You and God Bless You."[72] She was barely able to finish her speech before she was overcome with emotion at being the first black performer ever to win an Academy Award. As she walked back to her seat, the crowd rose again, giving her another standing ovation. Gossip columnist Louella Parsons caught her by the arm and exclaimed. "See Hattie, you've made me cry!" That she was black had no bearing on their cheering. As one person put it, "Here was a tremendous actress, an outstanding personality, an American, and they were happy to have an opportunity to fully respond as they wished." Many in the audience, like Hattie, were weeping for joy. Olivia de Havilland, who herself had been nominated as the best supporting actress for portraying Melanie Wilkes, attributed Hattie's success to The Scene. She said later that "Hattie was entitled to that award. . . . I realized that. . . . But on Academy Awards night, I found I couldn't stay at the table another minute. I had to be alone; so I wandered out to the kitchen at the Ambassador Hotel and cried."[73]

For two weeks after the Academy Awards, de Havilland later asserted, she was "convinced there was no God." Then she changed her mind: "One morning I woke up in more ways than one, filled with delight that I lived in a world where God was certainly present, and where justice had indeed been done. . . . I suddenly felt very proud . . . that I belonged to a profession which honored a black woman who merited this [the Academy Award], in a time when other groups had neither the honesty nor the courage to do the same sort of thing."[74]

When Hattie got back to her seat, she was greeted by an exuberant Vivien Leigh (who won the Best Actress award for her role as Scarlett). Clark Cable, who lost out on the Best Actor award to Robert Donat for *Goodbye Mr.Chips,* vigorously shook one of Hattie's hands, while David O. Selznick kissed the other. Later, on her way out of the Ambassador Hotel, Hattie told Louella Parsons, "I love Mammy. I think I understood her because my own grand-mother worked on a plantation not unlike Tara."[75] When she got home that night, Hattie was deluged with huge bouquets, tele-grams, letters, long distance telephone calls, reporters, neighbors and friends. It was an evening that she thoroughly savored.

Hattie's award was hailed as an example of "democracy in action," because while much of the world was yielding to tyranny, it was asserted that the United States set an example of the dignity of all peoples. While this idealistic stance might not have been as true as some believed, it nevertheless created a marvelous image for the United States as the place where dreams came true. This thought was very powerful in Hitler-infested 1940.

The award showed, according to optimists, just how liberal and broadminded Americans were becoming. One person, ex-claimed, "Ten years ago no one would have dared to think about giving a colored person such high honor." (In 1935, for her sterling performance in *Imitation of Life,* Louise Beavers received an "hon-orable mention" from the Academy. That was as high at that time as any black performer had gone). "Today, it's a matter of merit and merit alone. Miss McDaniel deserved every honor she has received for her splendid performance in *Gone With the Wind.*"

The liberal *Atlanta Constitution* said Hattie's award delighted "all genuine Southern people. . . ." She is, the paper asserted, the "Southern Mammy," and her characterization was true to fact and to tradition. "She was, in short, a grand Mammy, and, the South, first to recognize this fact will be first to tell how much she deserves the honor she has won."[76] A few days after the honor, Hattie told a newspaper: "I hope that my winning the award will be inspiration for the youth of my race, that it will encourage them to aim high and work hard, and take the bitter with the sweet."[77] She was proud, she said later, to have played the role of a black woman "who was fearless, who cringed before no one, who did not talk in whispers, walk on tiptoe, who criticized a white woman's morals, and who showed real emotion."

What was her ambition now, after winning an Oscar? To win another one, of course. So she went back to work just as quickly as she could. (Later, she willed her cherished Oscar to Howard University in Washington, D.C. It turned up "missing" during the civil rights demonstrations of the 1960s and has not yet been found.)

Another result of Hattie's Oscar was that it temporarily ameliorated much black anger over the movie itself. Though some urged her to reject the award on the grounds that *GWTW* was racist, most blacks rejoiced in her triumph. A new round of showings of *GWTW* began in April 1940, and, if anything, the film enjoyed greater popularity than the presentations of the year before, in part, because it had lower ticket prices than during its first run. One notable absence in 1940, almost directly attributable to Hattie's award, was black picket lines wherever the movie was shown.

Although it was a quick jump from late 1938—when Hattie was a well respected, but not widely known movie actress—to early 1940, when she became a world renowned celebrity, she did not let her fame go to her head; indeed, she simply kept repeating one of her favorite phrases: "I did my best, and God did the rest."[78]

CHAPTER FOUR

Life After *Gone With the Wind*

Hattie was now permanently and irrevocably known as Mammy, much to her lifelong delight. When the cast and crew finished *Gone With the Wind*, Hattie wrote into Susan Myrick's diary: to lovely Miss Myrick whom I have been so happy to know. I trust we can get out for our Southern dinner—before she says adieu." She signed her message, "Mammy," Hattie McDaniel.[1]

Even members of the general public now called her Mammy. As long as it was clear that the reference was to her role in the movie, and not to any past or present condition of servility, Hattie not only liked it; she reveled in it. In fact, whenever people discussed the movie, Hattie McDaniel's part often got more attention than some of the players who had been billed as "stars."

In a proposed sequel to *GWTW*, much of the action was to revolve around the character of Mammy. Selznick wanted Margaret Mitchell to write the sequel, and thought a good title for it would be *The Daughter of Scarlett O'Hara*.[2] Mitchell, however, balked and would sell no right to a sequel, either to Selznick or to anyone else. Not even the Mother Country's wishes in the matter convinced the Atlanta author. Selznick, to no avail, told Mitchell that he had hundreds of letters from England demanding a sequel to the classic.[3] Finally, an exasperated Selznick exclaimed ironically to a friend that frankly, he didn't give a damn whether Mitchell wrote the sequel or not; he just wanted a sequel!

One far-fetched suggestion was that Frances Griswold's novel, *A Sea Island Woman,* be turned into a "Wind" sequel. Another proposal was from Hattie Owen Edge of Cullman, Alabama, who had already written a sequel, using all the characters of *GWTW, Give Us Tomorrow.* When she finished it she told Selznick that her sequel was set in the late Reconstruction period in the South with Scarlett "in the depths of despair" at Rhett leaving her, Ashley married again, and beloved old Mammy grown feeble and weary of the load she so faithfully shouldered all those years, and too weak "to live through another book."[4]

Selznick could only give Mrs. Edge an explanation of the fine rules of copyright. Despite his statements to the contrary, it seemed clear that if he could not get a sequel from Margaret Mitchell, he really did not want one.

Aside from her acting, Hattie also got much attention because of *GWTW* for her cooking ability. Hattie loved to cook, not by recipe, but by instinct and, as with so many other aspects of her life, she was a success at it. Thus when several magazines around the country wrote to Selznick International for Mammy recipes they had to wait until she finally put them in writing. She said she cooked by "grabbing a little of this and a speck of that, and throwing them all together until they looked right!"[5] (See Appendix C).

Hattie often spoke of wanting to open a fried chicken restaurant when she retired. She said she would call the main serving "Mammy's Fried Chicken à la Maryland."[6] She told her friends that when she prepared chicken, she just "chucked" it on the stove, and "went out and got hungry."[7] She obviously did not worry about calories because she told a friend one day, "As for those grapefruit and buttermilk diets . . . I'll take roast chicken and dumplings. When I was little, my mother taught me how to use a fork and knife. Now I'm not so little anymore. The trouble is that Mother forgot to teach me how to *stop* using them!"[8]

In addition to becoming known for her culinary abilities,

Hattie also got some publicity because of her washing machine. While *GWTW* was being filmed, the Selznick photographer snapped numerous photos of Hattie at home, one of them with a Maytag washing machine in the background.

The President of the Maytag West Coast Company, William John, wrote to Daniel O'Shea of Selznick to offer the newest Maytag to Hattie, a white deluxe model which was much more efficient, said the company official, than the old Model 18 that Hattie was currently using.[9] Well, of course, Hattie would be thrilled to have a new Maytag washer. ("I always have the best of everything," she smilingly said to the company official.)[10] At first Selznick International saw nothing wrong, but Maytag wanted some publicity, first in a house organ, *The Maytag News,* with a picture of Hattie receiving her new washing machine. Department stores then would get a copy of the photo.[11]

In all likelihood, if the Maytag offer had come before March 7, all would have been well. But, after Hattie won an Oscar neither her services nor her likeness could be squandered away, at least not on a washing machine that cost a mere $139.95. Hattie was a "hot property," and the Selznick people intended to take every advantage of that fact.

Hattie's managers did "feel out" the merchants in the "Negro belt," and there was "some chance" that they might promote the "Hattie tie-up." The Mammy connection would have to incorporate Hattie's achievement in *GWTW,* together with her Oscar award.[12]

Moreover, MGM, the distributors of *GWTW,* insisted a royalty would have to be paid to MGM everytime a Maytag washing machine was sold as a direct result of Hattie's advertising. Next, wherever *GWTW* played, Maytag dealers would be responsible for window and counter displays of Hattie and the Maytag, and other tie-ins of the washing machine and the movie.[13] The Selznick Corporation seemed pleased with the possibilities, even proposing to split the profits with Hattie 60–40.[14]

In the end the matter never came to any agreement. The Maytag officials needed a less expensive way of advertising their products than the "Hattie plan," which had grown far beyond the original proposal.[15]

Beyond washing machines Selznick continued his campaign to exploit Hattie's new found fame in other ways. He suggested loan-outs of her contract with Selznick to radio programs and movies that were likely to be interested in Hattie "Mammy" McDaniel. He brooded about the possibility that someone else would "get the benefit" of the "sensational impression" of Hattie as Mammy. Thus, there was a need to move quickly as he wrote to O'Shea, "I hope you are putting real pressure to bear on the Hattie McDaniel radio situation, since each day that goes by makes her a little less hot." Selznick wanted a starting price for Hattie's services of $2,000 a week, out of which she would receive expenses and perhaps a guaranteed minimum of thirty weeks of work at $500 a week, "with right or privilege during our time to rent her out to radio and personals."[16]

One suggested role for Hattie on radio was a reunion with Eddie "Rochester" Anderson ("Uncle Peter" in *GWTW*) on the Jack Benny program; another was to use her as "Aunt Jemima."[17] Selznick's idea was for a radio series named "Mammy."[18] He exuberantly wrote to William Paley, head of CBS Radio, telling of his plans for a "Mammy" show. Paley dashed cold water on the idea when he wrote back that his program directors thought the best way to promote Hattie was in guest slots. "There is a feeling that it would be difficult to sell her for a series of her own, largely because of the reticence on the part of the advertisers to make a colored character too dominating in a show."[19]

Despite the opinions against a radio serial for Hattie, the ideas kept rolling in for programs that at least gave her a major, if not dominant, though servile-to-white characters part. One such suggestion came from a New Orleans newspaperwoman. It was to deal with a family whose "welfare and future happiness" was determined by the sacrifices of their loveable old mammy. Another idea was for Hattie to play in radio adaptations of some of McKinley Kantor's short stories.[20]

Will Price, a dialectician for *GWTW*, suggested a series of programs to be called "Hattie and the Hambone Meditations," based on a short story by James Street, "The Crusader," which had appeared in the November 1939, *The Saturday Evening Post;* and upon the cartoons of J. P. Alley. Street's mammy, "Aunt Charity," would be "Aunt Hattie" on the radio. She would become the real power behind the *Weekly Crusader,* and through her, the editor would gather all the gossip and news trends for his paper.[21] Price told Selznick that "the show, because of its warm Negro humor . . . and its homey American scenes and situations, should be appealing to every type audience." It would even be well received, he believed, in the South, where the cartoon, "Hambone's Meditations, had been running in Southern newspapers for many years, and its homespun humor appealed to Southerners.[22]

Unfortunately, William Paley was right. The American public, at least as it was seen through the eyes of the frequently erratic world of producers, agents, networks and, most importantly, advertisers, was not ready for a radio program that featured a black person as the leading character. Even when the "Beulah" series started a few years later, the first two Beulahs were white men. When they left Hattie got the role. (It was, of course, not unusual for whites to play blacks on radio. Amos 'n Andy, for example, were played by white men. A white man playing a black woman, however, was unique to the Beulah show.) It was guest slots and special appearances that brought Hattie back to radio in 1940.

Her first appearance after the premiere of *GWTW* was in January 1940, on a program sponsored by Maxwell House Coffee, "Good News." It was a sort of test O'Shea told Selznick; "one of the reasons for putting her on the show was so you could make an appraisal of her radio work."[23] The premise of "Good News" was for Hattie and her old friend, veteran actor, Edward Arnold, to perform a few skits roughly based on *GWTW,* but definitely with no racial gags such as an idea for someone mistaking Mammy for Scarlett O'Hara. After convincing Selznick that the gag would be harmful to the radio show's popularity in the South, the offending bit of the script was deleted.[24]

Many times, however, it appeared that the producers used this ploy simply as an excuse for their action rather than as real reasons. All of which makes one wonder just how much programming was changed or canceled in those days to suit "Southern taste." Apparently not much effort was ever made by the producers to find out exactly what Southern "tastes" were. Selznick himself had said that probably Southerners, both black and white, would welcome a black dominated program—as long as the black "stayed in her place," and did not mix socially with whites; i.e., in fairly much the way the racial situation was in the North. Producers, however, were constantly refusing program ideas or canceling others because of the "Southern point of view."

In the dialogue between Arnold and Hattie, Arnold told her that he had recently seen *GWTW,* and thought her part in it was wonderful. Hattie responded, saying that she had never had so much fun in her life making a picture, and "Playing the Mammy of Miss Leigh was just about the biggest thrill I've ever had." Inevitably, the dialogue turned to Clark Gable, who was "just about" Hattie's "favorite actor."[25]

Toward the end of the program, Arnold announced that while millions would thrill to Hattie's performance as Mammy in the weeks ahead, he wanted everyone to hear Hattie "do something a little different from Scarlett O'Hara's Negro Mammy." He then presented Hattie who was allowed to do an old-time revival scene, singing some old-time Negro spirituals, and demonstrating the manners and methods of tent-meeting revivalists. Altogether, it was a grand performance, one that thrilled audiences from coast to coast.[26]

Hattie's appearance on the "Good News" program cost the sponsors only $350, but it caused a ruckus. The New York agency that handled her performance on "Good News" was Benton and Boles. They deducted about $35.00 from the check for social security and California taxes.[27] When the Selznick business office received the check, not for $350, as it had expected, but for $314.50, the reaction was forceful and swift.

The Selznick Corporation sent the check back to Benton and Boles, informing the agents that Hattie was not their employee. She was under weekly contract to Selznick, and "will not participate in the monies"[28] received for her services. Therefore, the agency's deductions were improper. The practice of lending players was a common one between studios, and the borrowing studio never made any deductions itself; the parent studio was always paid the full amount, and then it performed whatever payroll deductions were made. In emphasis of this point, Selznick International made it clear that though the agency might have been authorized to supervise Hattie's performance, it was the studio that had the right to "hire or fire" her. If there was any complaint about her services, it should be submitted to the Selznick studios rather than to Miss McDaniel.[29]

The people from Benton and Boles had apparently never heard of such a thing. Its representative, A. M. Davis, wrote to O'Shea that "You advance a new thought . . . to the effect that we did not engage Miss McDaniel's services, but rather you loaned her to us." Davis stated that he would comply with Selznick's request in the matter, but only upon a statement "that should our client or ourselves ever be called upon to pay the taxes, you will indemnify us."[30] Selznick furnished such a statement.

In April 1940, Photoplay Magazine picked *GWTW* to receive its "Gold Medal Award." Plans were made to present radio skits of the movie on the "Kate Smith Show" with Vivien Leigh playing Scarlett and her husband, Laurence Olivier, in the role of Rhett. Naturally, the skits would require Mammy, and Selznick was eager for Hattie to perform.[31]

Another radio appearance came in July, a black program originating in Cleveland, "Wings Over Jordan," featuring the "Happy Am I" choir and Reverend Glen Settle of the Gethsemane Baptist Church, singing spirituals.[32] The program, purely inspirational, full of good, old-fashioned spirituals featured a five-minute spot "by a distinguished American Negro on how the white and colored races can best get along." Hattie appeared on Sunday, July 7, 1940. A part of her presentation went:

I want to take this opportunity to thank each and every one of you for the many lovely and kind things you have said about me from time to time, and for the many kindnesses shown to me . . . for I realize you were showing recognition for my work in the movie version of *Gone With the Wind*. I want you to know that I feel no great personal pride for my contribution to the world of art. Rather, I feel that the entire fourteen million or more Negroes have all been raised a few notches higher in the estimation of the world. Each one of us is an ambassador now, either for good or ill for our race. The entire race is usually judged by the actions of one man or woman. Therefore, if I am proud at all I am proud of the fact that Hattie McDaniel has been able to add something which I hope will be a lasting credit to our race.

Many of you may think that Hollywood has been exceptionally kind to me, and it has; but not before I had spent a few heartbreaking years learning to give Hollywood the thing it demanded. And you ask, what is that thing that Hollywood demands most? It is sincerity. No place in the world will pay such a high price for this admirable trait. We all respect that trait in our friends and acquaintances, but Hollywood is willing to pay for it.

It is not necessary for me to speak of the picture, as I know most of you have seen it. But I would like to say that every actor and actress is possessed of the absorbing passion to create something distinctive and unique. He or she desires a role which will challenge his capabilities and send him searching for new mannerisms, and latent dramatic power. Such a role was given Louise Beavers in *Imitation of Life,* and the veteran actress Madame Sul te Wan in *Maid of Salem.* My desire for the part of Mammy, which I played in *Gone With the Wind,* was not dominated by selfishness for, as I have said before, Hollywood has been good to me and I am grateful. In playing the part of Mammy, I tried to make her a living, breathing character, the way she appeared to me in the book. There was an opportunity to glorify Negro womanhood; not the modern, streamlined type of Negro woman who attends teas and concerts in ermine and mink, but the type of Negro of the period which gave us Harriett Tubman, Sojourner Truth, and Charity Still; the brave, efficient, hard-working type of womanhood has built a race, mothered our Booker T. Washington, George W. Carver, Robert Moton, and Mary McLeod Bethune.

So you see, the mothers of that era must have had something in them to produce men and women of that caliber. I knew that she [Mammy] would have to wear a handkerchief on her head, but I felt that would not be objectionable since head rags of all colors are quite the vogue with the younger, perfectly groomed women of today. To you young people who are aspiring to succeed in some line of endeavor, in spite of the troubles that many of us have experienced, let me say this: *There is still room at the top.*[33]

Despite her radio successes, Hattie's "hottest" possibilities in early 1940 were for other movies. One suggestion was "The Little Orvie" series, for RKO. Another possibility was *Down Went Mc-Ginty,* for Paramount. Neither of these films was "sufficiently worthy," according to Selznick and Hattie's agents, the Music Corporation of America.[34]

Hattie made only one movie in 1940, to a great extent because she was so busy promoting *Gone With the Wind.* Her single movie for 1940 was *Maryland,* in which she played a cook named Carrie, who amused audiences by "scrapping" with her "no-account" screen husband, Shadrack, played by Ben Carter. Hattie was loaned by Selznick to Fox for four weeks at $500 a week. At the end of filming, Fox paid Selznick $1,500 for the loan of Hattie, who made $2,000 out of the deal, and Selznick almost as much.[35] (Hattie's earnings from July 1, 1940, to December 28, were $11,000).[36]

Hattie's underemployment stemmed from being caught between offers of conventional black roles, and on the other hand Selznick's fretting that Hattie's part in *Maryland* might be too close to Mammy of *GWTW,* and he disliked the idea of having a movie other than his own to project the Mammy image. The dialogue was certainly similar to *GWTW.* Carrie told Miss Charlotte that "I don't know what I gwine ter do with this Shadrack. When ah reforms him ob de gambling,' he's backslid on de lying.' When I reforms him ob de lyin' he backslid on de gamblin."[37] Worse yet, Selznick felt it was entirely possible that vast numbers of cinema patrons might see *Maryland* before *GWTW,* and conclude that *Maryland* was the real progenitor of Mammy.[38] Hattie herself agreed, writing her childhood friend, Ruth (Collamer) Dermody, "Last week I finished working in another picture, *Maryland,* at 20th Century Fox. The role is similar to that of 'Mammy' in *Gone With the Wind,* but it is more comical."[39] Finally, however, Selznick was convinced that there was no direct competition between the two movies, and he allowed Hattie to work for Fox.

Hattie mentioned her personal *GWTW* tour planned for the following month. Ruth had written to Hattie earlier, urging her to come to Denver. Hattie was positive Denver would be included in the cities she was to visit.[40] (It was not, at least in 1940. The following year she did go back to Denver.)

Many years had passed since Hattie and Ruth grew up together in Denver. And the passing of time, Hattie feared, might produce a problem: "You have the advantage of me in that you know how I look after our few years (smile) since childhood. I don't know that I would recognize you but won't you please come up to me when I get to Denver and say 'Hattie, I'm Ruth Dermody who wrote to you. We used to go to school together and you taught me, 'one two, button your shoe.' "[41]

Planning for Hattie's tour, including cities like Chicago, Pittsburgh, Cleveland, New York, and Baltimore, started in February, even before Hattie won the Oscar. Most of Selznick's advisors wanted her engagements to be solely at "colored" theatres and cinemas. They reasoned that Hattie would be received in the black districts "like a visiting monarch."[42] Black people would storm the theatres to see her, and perhaps they might arrange for honorary degrees from black colleges in the cities she visited.[43]

All of these activities, of course, were at no risk to white sensibilities. Perhaps, Selznick thought, they might appoint a black tour manager—a black educator, or newspaperman to be her advisor. She would go on tours through each city's black district, give talks to neighborhood meetings, present awards to children and parents for some meritorious services they might have performed, and make commercial tie-ins with black businessmen.[44] In towns where *GWTW* was showing, toward the end of the film's run Hattie might appear in person at another movie outlet in town. Such an arrangement would certainly draw an audience; how could anyone resist seeing Mammy in person?

By mid-March, three weeks before Hattie's tour was to begin, an unsettling report reached Selznick that advance sales in black theatres were not going well, but he brushed his fears aside by asserting that "I doubt that colored people are used to buying seats in advance."[45] He was "fully aware" of the "limited means" of most "colored people," and of the "poor nature" of most black cinemas, and he thought that perhaps a ticket price higher than usual at places where Hattie was to perform would convince the blacks that her personal appearance was indeed a special treat.[46]

Hattie made a "trial run" for her tour on April 12, when she performed in a Glendale, California, theatre, which was only twenty-five percent full. The people who were there fully appreciated her talents and gave her much applause. A piano was the only musical instrument to accompany her in the Glendale performance, allowing her managers to say wishfully that in the big cities where full orchestras were available, her acts would go over better.[47] Hattie sang "Comes Love," read a few excerpts from *GWTW*, first the book and then the movie, including three or four lines from the scene where, as Mammy she is tightening Scarlett's corset just before the Wilkes barbecue. Then she did the scene between Mammy and Rhett on the occasion of Bonnie's birth.

After her recitations, she sang some Mammy songs. These songs, or "Mammy Meditations," proved to be the most endearing of all her performances. She thrilled her audiences by dancing the juba and the cakewalk, and singing:

> *You can talk about your Mammy, dear old Mammy;*
> *yes of yore.*
> *Dear old Mammy with her corn cob pipe, sitting 'round*
> *her cabin door.*
> *But things are changin' nowadays, and Mammy's gettin'*
> *bored.*
> *She wants to have a good time, and sway it and swing it.*
> *Mammy's tired of being found 'round her kitchen door.*
> *She wants music, not just 'weep no more.' Mammy must*
> *have rejuvenation, razz-ma-tazz, and syncopation. I want*
> *somebody to cling to me; I want somebody to sing to*
> *me!*

And then came the "sexy" part which brought a rebuke from Selznick:

> *I saw you last night and got that old feeling;*
> *When you came inside I got that old feeling,*

The moment that you danced by I felt a thrill,
That's what Mammy wants.

Selznick feared that some women in the audience might take offense at: "I saw you last night and got that old feeling . . ." and he did not want Hattie to deprive herself of stature as a performer by "stooping to things that might be offensive." Selznick's spokesman, O'Shea, wrote to Hattie on the eve of her departure for the East: "I know I need not tell anybody with as fine a sense of showmanship as you, or anybody with a fine sense of taste that you have already demonstrated, that it is of the highest importance to you and your race that your act be a dignified one, and on the highest possible plane."[48] The lines were stricken.

Perhaps it was just as well to strike the lines because they really were not what audiences applauded. Rather, they preferred when Hattie sang a sentimental version of a song made famous by Al Jolson (with whom she had been in movies):

"Mammy, Mammy, I'd walk a million miles for one of your smiles, My Mammy . . ."

Then Hattie went into a dramatic monologue:

"Why, just those last words, why, they mean something. No, I won't be blue; I won't be sad, I won't wish for things I've never had. I'll be content just to think about that S'wanee Shore. Forgive me. I don't want 'swing' no more.

"I want my children I nestled to my breast, black and white, with so much zest. Why, I've been foolish, a fancy dream; give me back my babies, my babies, yes, of yore."

"But let me say this before I go, before I take my pipe to my cabin door. Why, I can see my own Mammy dressed in snowy white. I'm comin' Mammy! I'se comin' so you can tuck me to bed in my old 'tucky home, and let me lay there, stay there, never more to roam."

Just when Hattie had the audience thinking she'd always rather be a Mammy than anything else, she took a deep bow and in the best style of Sophie Tucker, and borrowing some from Cab Calloway, began to belt out:

66

"Well, folks, I've changed my mind. I guess I'll have one little fling before I go back home."

Jump and jive
The jim jamb jump is the jumpin' jive
Makes you get your kicks on the mellow side.
Hep, hep, hep, hep. The jim jamb jump is the
solid jive.
Makes you nine foot tall when you're four
feet five.
Hep, hep, hep, hep. Don't be the ickaroo.
Get hep and follow through. . . .
The jim jamb jump is the jumpin' jive.
Makes you like your eggs on the Jersey side.
Hep, hep, hep, hep. Jim jamb jumping jive
Makes you hep on the mellow side.[49]

By the time she finished this song, Hattie had the whole audience clapping their hands and some even dancing. It was easily the highpoint of her performance.

Hattie received an extra 25 percent of her $500 a week salary for expenses while traveling, along with expenses for her hairdresser.[50] Before Hattie left Los Angeles for Chicago on April 22, she had received a movie offer from her old boss, Warner Brothers, which she couldn't accept, and less than a week into her tour, Fox Studios called her back for re-takes of *Maryland*.

Nonetheless, before the re-takes she performed at the Chicago Theatre and the Stanley Theatre in Pittsburgh. Her tour was to be limited to the big cities, where she would cater to both black and white audiences. As her shows began, the orchestra played "Mammy," and she came on stage and said:

"Oh, how do you do folks? And thank you. Thank you very much. It sure looks good to see an honest-to-goodness audience after looking at you all for so long from the silver screen. You know, it's been many a year since I've been before the real footlights, but just to see your happy faces just does something to me in here, or should I say 'smiling faces?' " Then she sang "Smiles," after which she went into her recitation of the *GWTW* excerpts, a rendering of "Comes Love," and ended with "Mammy's Meditations."

Early in May 1940, Hattie left Chicago, taking an express train back to Los Angeles, where she took a day or two to shoot the scenes Fox wanted,[51] and then in haste, despite her fear of flying, she boarded a TWA plane back to Chicago.

On the renewed tour, Hattie played the black Royal Theatre in Baltimore, where chorus girls came onto stage, and sang, "We're the Hattie McDaniel Girls!" Then a singer, Edna May Harris, sang the "McDaniel Swing," all in preparation for Hattie herself.

She also played the Lincoln Theatre in Washington; the Paramount in New York, where she was accompanied by the Harry James Orchestra; the Riverside Theatre, Milwaukee; the Palace Theatre, Cleveland; and then back to the State-Lake Theatre in Chicago, the tour lasting well into July, frequently with two shows a day.

In mid-May, E. G. Smith who represented a black "Coordinating Council" in South Bend, Indiana, thanked Selznick for "making it possible for the remarkable achievements of Miss Hattie McDaniel" to be broadcast throughout the country. "We feel," the Council continued, "that if more producers would give Negroes the chance to show their ability, they would prove to the public that they could play even more important roles than maids or cooks."[52]

Claude Barnett in Chicago mounted an American Negro Exposition to be held in the coliseum from July 4 to September 2. The Exposition was to be national in scope, with exhibits to show the remarkable progress made by the black race in the previous seventy-five years. Emphasis was upon the place the black person had occupied in American history.[53] First were the murals surrounding the balcony of the coliseum, depicting important events, individuals, and achievements of the black in the United States. Next, there would be a huge stage upon which the progress of black music and drama since emancipation would be highlighted.[54]

(The Exposition was financed through a grant from the State of Illinois for $75,000, and a similar award from the federal government. The Rosenthal Fund contributed another $15,000, as did the Illinois General Education Board.)[55]

One of the productions at the Exposition was the "Cavalcade of the Negro Theatre," written by playwrights Langston Hughes and Arna Bontemps. To this performance were invited many notable black entertainers of the day, including Duke Ellington, Paul Robeson, Ethel Waters, and, of course, Hattie McDaniel. In fact, as Barnett said, since Hattie had gone "to the highest in the film world," the writers of the Cavalcade planned the climax of the whole performance around her act.[56]

The Selznick people claimed not to be opposed to Hattie's participation in the American Negro Exposition (or the A.N.E.). Selznick, however, invoking issues of laying off Hattie during the week, and the lost profit, would agree only if it appeared that her performance in the A.N.E. was likely to attract additional bookings for her tour.[57]

Selznick maintained a similar posture in regards to any other black invitation on which he would not make a profit. John Turner of Bennett College in Greensboro, North Carolina, hoped to dedicate two new buildings, one a memorial chapel and the other a little theatre. For these dedications, Bennett planned a pageant with the theme of "The Negro Woman in Retrospect and in the Future."[58] The main attraction at these ceremonies, Turner hoped, would be Hattie McDaniel. He wrote, "I am positive that this favor (the loan of Hattie McDaniel) on your part will go a long way for better relations with the theatre goers. We are justly proud of Miss McDaniel, not only for her recent award, but for her genuine spirit of service to her art and to her race."[59]

But, as with the A.N.E., Selznick had no objections to Hattie helping dedicate these two college buildings as long as conflicts in scheduling did not occur. Too, Hattie had to agree to relinquish her Selznick salary while she worked for other people.

These arrangements for both the A.N.E. and Bennett College came to nought. On July 17, Hattie telegraphed O'Shea from Chicago: ". . . I am ill and I want to come home for a rest. I am positive there will be no hard feelings with my race, as I understand them."[60] O'Shea wired his regrets to Barnett of the A.N.E. and to

Turner of Bennett College, promising that if Hattie returned to the East before the summer ended, he would make arrangements for her to accommodate their wishes. Hattie took a train back to Los Angeles.

Her one vaguely black political appearance was in the fall of 1940 to receive a certificate of merit at the New York World's Fair for being "an outstanding member of the colored race in the field of theatrical entertainment." It was awarded by Mrs. Roosevelt, who at the same time, presented Hattie with a block of one hundred new postal stamps commemorating the Thirteenth Amendment.[61] While she was in New York on this occasion, Selznick Studios tried to book her into various theatres, without success. She went back to the West Coast in October, and stayed there for the rest of the year.

Hattie's *GWTW* appearance tour in the summer of 1940 had not been a great success, and perhaps that is why she could get no bookings later on in the fall when she went to New York. There had been some black pamphlets against the election of Wendell Willkie in the presidential race that year and some of the Selznick people surmised that New York theatre managers, trying to avoid politics, were not booking any black acts until the election was over.[62]

On her *GWTW* tour, Hattie earned from $100 for a single performance to $1,500 for a week's work. At one stop, however, the Lincoln Theatre in Washington, the owners were unhappy with Hattie's performances, and complained to Phil Bloom, Hattie's agent at MCA, that they had lost money on Hattie. She brought in less than average for the week she performed at Lincoln's, perhaps because, said the manager, that in the context of the theatre's usual features of show business and world affairs, Hattie McDaniel "meant nothing."[63]

Bloom expressed surprise at the assertions, claiming Hattie had played quite successfully at her other engagements. He wondered if Hattie were not more successful, despite her color, before white audiences than black.[64] It seemed that, with few exceptions, black patrons of the arts did not acquire seats in advance, pay prices raised for special purposes, or see too many live performances.

Thus, Hattie's managers decided that in the future she would play mostly to all white, or mixed audiences, rather than to exclusively black audiences.

In any case, Selznick would not entertain a notion of adjusting the Lincoln bill. O'Shea wrote to Bloom: "I regret that the Lincoln Theatre in Washington did such poor business with Hattie Mc-Daniel, and I also regret our inability to make any adjustment. As you are aware, if we gave the Lincoln Theatre any adjustment, it would have to come out of our own pockets. We can't start that at this late date."[65]

Politics aside, her personal appearance tour also proved that despite her vaudeville years, Hattie was more at home on movie sets than before live audiences. The public perceived her through her cinematic abilities, as opposed to stage performances. Millions of people remembered her for her pictures; few indeed for "Mammy's Meditations."

Her stage tour showed that despite her fame as Mammy in *Gone With the Wind,* she was still subject to exploitation and manipulation. Regardless of her happy speech in accepting an Oscar, and her inspirational oratory on "Wings Over Jordan," success for a black person in 1940 simply was not the same as success for a white person. She found that though she was good at her profession, she had to perform better than a white person to get to the same place. *GWTW* gave Hattie only fleeting fame and fortune; it by no means guaranteed that she would be widely accepted in a white-dominated world. Perhaps some black artists would have called it quits under the circumstances, and not tried to gain any more movie or radio roles. They might have reckoned that the crowning achievement of the role of Mammy was as far as they wanted to go, for they would be well remembered. But not Hattie; it was a mark of her fortitude that in the face of being snubbed in Atlanta for the *GWTW* premiere, and then used primarily as a creator of profit for her studios, she increasingly sought to improve her acting capabilities.

Many of her friends and acquaintances began clamoring for her to do some more movies. That is where her talent lay, they told her, and the place where she set the best example for her race. Her reputation was now secure as a character actress.

Hattie's friend, Etta Moten, wrote from Chicago that America was entering a "new era" in pictures, and that Hattie was "the fortunate person" who had the versatility to fit into either the dramatic or the comic situation. "There is nothing like being ready when opportunity knocks."[66] And Hattie, as always, was "ready!"

Throughout 1940, Hattie savored her reputation as a character actress which, for all practical purposes, was new-found, despite the fact that she had played in movies for almost ten years before *GWTW*. She was hailed as a great performer, as someone who brought joy to millions of people around the world. As the personification of dreams come true for black people she knew the responsibilities these images of her entailed, and she tried to set proper examples. Also, for the first time Hattie was making enough money to enjoy a few luxuries. She had, as she said, "grubbed" for a living for a good part of her life, and perhaps now she should begin to enjoy some of the fruits of her labor, and starting in 1941, that is exactly what she set out to do.

CHAPTER FIVE

The War Years: 1941–1945

J ack Warner allegedly predicted that *Gone With the Wind* would be the flop of the century. When events proved him wrong, he turned heaven and earth to get Hattie McDaniel back into one of his pictures. At first Selznick was reluctant to let Hattie be loaned to Warner, claiming that Warner had not given him enough "favors" with stars Warner controlled.[1]

The film Warner wanted Hattie for was *The Great Lie*, from the novel, *Far Horizons*, by Polan Banks. Selznick relented in return for the sizeable fee of about $10,000.[2]

Selznick wanted assurance that in the advertising for *The Great Lie*, no reference be made to *GWTW*, and that Hattie not appear in the promotions in her Mammy garb. As with *Maryland*, Selznick was afraid that cinema patrons might see *The Great Lie* before seeing *GWTW*, and conclude that the latter copied off the former.[3]

Hattie's role as Violet was much more extensive than any of her pre-*GWTW* performances. In fact, she was a Mammy to Maggie, played by Bette Davis whom she shielded from Mr. Pete, a scoundrel, portrayed by George Brent. Hattie's accent in the movie was definitely *GWTW* vintage: "I'se a comin! I'se a comin!" And, as in *GWTW*, her laughing and her crying usually sounded alike. (If she had to cry in a movie, she said she thought of the "bad days" when she was a struggling actress, and the tears flowed.) Her brother Sam played Jefferson in this movie. He and Hattie resembled each other so much that they might as well have been twins, and he referred to himself and Hattie as the "Dark Barrymores."[4]

Hattie had some trouble with her lines in *The Great Lie*. One line that should have read: "Nobody is going to stop yo with no force, Mr. Pete, but if yo conscience don't stop yo . . . your manners should," stymied her three times in a row. On the fourth try, it appeared that she was going to make it. But when she got to "But if yo conscience don't stop yo," she faltered, as she rolled her big eyes in frustration, and added, "my blowups sholy will."[5] Her humor cleared the air, and soothed the feelings of several Warner executives who wanted to get on with things. (One line that she did get through with no difficulty was "Just like a man, thinking of his pleasure." This line, plus the word "gigolo," because it would offend British audiences, were deleted by the Hays Office.)[6]

Critics panned *The Great Lie*, emphasizing its "sappy" plot, made bearable only by expert acting.[7] One paper said that Hattie performed so well that she was apparently going after her second Oscar. Studio gossip had it that Bette Davis, fearing a coup by Hattie, demanded and got extensive cuts in the role that Hattie played.[8] Though she did not win an award for *The Great Lie*, it was widely agreed that Hattie's role deserved star billing.

On the set of *The Great Lie*, Hattie told reporters that she was writing her memoirs, to be entitled *Help Yourself*, and she said that her "good friend" Bette Davis would get the first copy (despite rumors that Davis had wanted to curtail Hattie's role in *The Great Lie*). There is no evidence that such memoirs were ever published. The major theme of her work, she said, was that an aspiring actor or actress, or anyone for that matter, should be willing to start at the bottom and work their way to the top. Too many young people, she felt, were not willing in today's world to put in the time and effort to get the "big break." Luck, she often said, comes mostly from "helping yourself."[9]

Another of Hattie's 1941 releases was *Affectionately Yours*. She played the maid, Cynthia, in this rather silly situation comedy starring Merle Oberon, Rita Hayworth, Frank Morgan, and Ralph Bellamy. Hattie's old friend, Butterfly McQueen, played Butterfly in the movie, and for all her coquettish behavior and dialogue, she might as well once more have been Prissy in *GWTW*.

Hattie also appeared in *They Died With Their Boots On*, a 1941 epic about General George Armstrong Custer, starring Errol Flynn and Olivia de Havilland. Hattie was a highly superstitious household worker, Callie, who played matchmaker between Flynn and de Havilland. When General Custer wanted to visit his sweetheart without letting the father know about it, Hattie, or Callie, would make a sound like an owl to show that the way was clear. (Hattie's earnings for 1941 were $31,400, a far cry from the $5.00 per movie she started out with.)[10]

The biggest event for Hattie in 1941 was not a movie, but her marriage to James Lloyd Crawford whom she had known from her old TOBA days. Crawford was a real estate man originally from Detroit. Described as a "handsome, broad-shouldered rancher with a pleasing smile, and intimate knowledge of world events,"[11] Crawford was purported in the early forties to be a well-to-do cattle and land speculator in several western states.

She met Crawford on a trip to Wyoming, and their old friendship was rekindled. Lloyd followed Hattie back to Los Angeles, where they began to be seen together, much to the delight of the sensationalist Hollywood tabloids. Two months after arriving in Los Angeles, Lloyd proposed, and Hattie accepted.

Despite Hattie's dislike of flying, she and Lloyd took a plane to Tucson, Arizona, and on March 21, were married by the Reverend B. Cornelius at the Union Baptist Church. On arrival in Tucson, Hattie discovered that she had left her bridal bouquet of gardenias and orchids in Los Angeles. The ceremony was delayed for four hours until the precious bouquet arrived by a later flight.[12] Hattie wore a white crepe gown with gold bead trim, a juliette cap with gold sequins, and gold slippers. Crawford wore an oxford gray frocked coat, with striped trousers. Bobby Brooks, a twelve-year-old tenor, sang "Because," and "I Love Life." As the ceremony ended, Hattie told reporters, "I personally intend to stay married forever this time."[13]

After the wedding, Hattie and Lloyd headed east, where Hattie was scheduled to do the Eddie Cantor, Count Basie, and Rudy Vallee shows in New York. Throughout the tour the couple reveled in the publicity of their marriage. Eddie Cantor gave them a "whopping" check for $50 as a wedding gift, and David O. Selznick favored them with a "warm" letter of congratulations.[14]

Married or not, Hattie discovered that her New York schedule was incredibly busy. She spoke at the Reverend Adam Clayton Powell's church, where she said that she "had the congregation rolling in the aisles." She did a program for Greek War Relief and at least three shows a week for Cantor. New York friends hosted the newlywed couple at innumerable dinners and teas. While in New York, Hattie and Lloyd stayed at the Theresa, the city's most elegant black hotel. In one of her letters back to Ruby, Hattie signed it "Hattie Crawford," but underneath it, wrote "McDaniel," and then in parentheses, "smile."[15]

One result of Hattie's "honeymoon-tour" combination was that she was dislodged from any further consideration in a Cecil B. DeMille film, *Reap the Wild Wind*. She was to have played the part of Maum Marie, but the uncertainty of Hattie's availability because of her travels caused DeMille to sign Louise Beavers for the part. It seems to have been, however, more a case of DeMille trying to get Hattie than Hattie wanting the role. She was still "hot property" because of *GWTW, Maryland*, and *The Great Lie*, and producers were very eager to receive her services. Though *Reap the Wild Wind* was a sea adventure, the dialogue was definitely in the mode of *GWTW*. The heroine, played by Paulette Goddard, even said "Fiddle dee dee" when she was annoyed. To this day, many movie anthologies still list Hattie McDaniel as playing in *Reap the Wild Wind* instead of Louise Beavers.

Toward mid-April the couple left New York by train, Hattie having rejected Cantor's offer of a long-term contract with his radio show; she was still bound to Selznick. They stopped off for a night in Chicago to visit Hattie's friend, black columnist, Harry Levette, and then went on to Denver, for a long awaited visit to her hometown.

Hattie's entry into Denver resembled that of a conquering empress. The beloved Mammy was coming to see her "own" people. "Denver is the only real home I ever had, and I hope to be able to stay here again some day."[16] Mayor Ben Stapleton presented Hattie with the keys to the city, and Governor Ralph Carr awarded her a "declaration of appreciation from the people of Colorado." She was feted in the Tea Room of the Blue Parrot Inn, where her visitors included her old dear friend, Professor George Morrison. Hattie and Lloyd stayed with her nephew, Lorenzo Lawrence, during their Denver stopover.[17]

A new acquaintance in Denver was a young hatmaker, Leon Bennett, who, when he heard that Hattie was coming to town, made a hat for her. From then on, Bennett was her "official" hatmaker. Each time Hattie appeared in public after 1941, she wore a Bennett hat, and the more "outlandish" it was, the better she liked it. Later, Bennett moved to Hollywood, where he became a hatmaker, not just for Hattie, but for numerous other stars as well.

On Sunday, April 13, Hattie, along with Lloyd and Morrison, attended services at the Shorter African Methodist Episcopal Church. The Reverend L. P. Bryant asked Hattie to speak. Hattie wept before the large congregation when she reminisced upon her early life in Denver. She asserted that she wanted to "see to the fixin' " of the graves of her brother, Otis, and her mother and father. "My pa's there in the circle with the veterans of the Civil War," at Riverside Cemetery, she said, and she wanted to arrange a suitable headstone for him.[18] As she spoke, she closed her eyes, swayed her head like a willow in a soft breeze, and talked about the necessity of loving, so that one would be loved in return. The audience responded with "amens," and "ain't it so?" It was like a revival scene from out of one of Hattie's movies. It was definitely Mammyesque, as "Miss Mac," as she was lovingly called, mesmerized her people.[19]

The couple left Denver on April 14, heading for Hollywood, where dozens of friends waited to honor them. While Hattie was away, the household help (a maid and a gardener, and a hairdresser) planned an elaborate "at home" get-together for the couple's return. Hattie had a reputation of being a lively party thrower, and this event was no exception. About 500 guests came to the afternoon affair, which filled up not only her house, but the front and back yards as well, and even some of the street, with 100 staying for a buffet dinner. Hattie's living room was converted into a "flower bower," of gladioli, larkspur, calla lilies, peonies, gardenias, smilax, and cantius palms. There was a huge three-tiered wedding cake, which Hattie and Lloyd cut amid the bravos of their guests. Messages, gifts, and telegrams arrived throughout the afternoon, all received by members of the Sigma Gamma Rho sorority.[20]

During the festivities, which caused such a jam on nearby streets that uniformed policemen were called out to regulate traffic, Hattie and Sam showed off with some of their old time dances such as the cakewalk and juba. Ernest Whitman and Eddie "Rochester" Anderson joined in with songs and dances. Toward the end of the day, Lloyd wanted to make an announcement: as a wedding present to his beloved Hattie, he intended, he said, to give her the deed to 160 acres of prime farmland in Montana. To Hattie, everything was as a dream. Unfortunately, as events unfolded in the years ahead, that's exactly what it was: too good to be true.[21]

For the rest of 1941, Hattie stayed mostly in Los Angeles, exhausted from her whirlwind tour of the east, grateful for an opportunity for a long rest. She was, of course, on call to the "stujo" twenty-four hours a day, and she also made a few public appearances such as the time she presided over ground breaking ceremonies of the Pueblo del Rio, Los Angeles' first housing project primarily for blacks. She also remodeled her house on 31st Street, adding a breakfast room, an upper deck for outdoor parties, and a half bath for her "husband's suite," an indication that the two were living separately in the house.[22] Already, it seemed, just a few months after they were married, Hattie and Lloyd began to drift apart.

On December 7, 1941, Pearl Harbor Day, Hattie and Lloyd were once again en route to New York, for another tour on Broadway, again under Selznick sponsorship. On one Saturday in her exhausting schedule, she did five shows. She sang and danced to "Smile," and at every performance, audiences demanded and got lengthy skits from *Gone With the Wind*.

Hattie again stayed at Hotel Theresa, and on December 14, she wrote to Ruby: "Well, New York is jumping. The streets are crowded with Christmas shoppers. . . . Well, the war is on . . . I can understand now why the British want to go home. Be it ever so bombish, there's no place like home. On our way here [to New York], the soldiers were watching the bridges at night."[23]

Apparently, Hattie had been shopping for a house before she left Los Angeles, because she grumbled in this letter that Ethel Waters "bought the Dempsey place." She also wanted Ruby to "write me a paper" for Reverend Powell's church, and send a poem, "Building Bridges," that she wanted to use in her various presentations.

By December 20, Hattie had moved on to the Earle Theatre in Philadelphia. She told Ruby, or "Goody," that "when you folks are eating your Christmas dinner, think of me. We've had only one decent home cooked meal" on the tour.[24] In early January, Hattie fell ill, and missed a few shows. The doctor said it was "almost pneumonia," brought on by Philadelphia's highly changeable weather.[25] When she got well enough to travel, she and Lloyd (who was apparently able to take extended trips away from his businesses) once more made their way back to sunny California.

In October 1941, several weeks before her Eastern tour, Hattie had been invited by Jack Warner to test for a part in a movie he planned to make. He wrote to Hal Wallis about the matter:

"I ran about twenty-five tests in my house last night. . . . I am sure we are wasting your time, effort, and money, looking for someone to play this part when we have the greatest colored actress in the world, Hattie McDaniel. I am not worried about her getting laughs, for they played her seriously in *Gone With the Wind*, and I remember her part very vividly. The other women [tested for the part by Warner] were very amateurish in my estimation, and we should definitely set McDaniel for the part."[26]

The part was that of Minerva Clay, and the movie was *In This Our Life*, the first of Ellen Glascow's novels to be filmed. Although no-one realized it while the movie was being shot, it was to become revolutionary in the context of the time in which it was made. Shooting of *In This Our Life* was completed in the fall of 1941, and the movie was released early in the following year.

The story revolved around the antics of a spoiled young woman named Stanley (Bette Davis). Stanley carelessly hit a person with her car, and to exonerate herself, blamed the deed on a young black man, Parry Clay. Stanley's sister, Roy (Olivia de Havilland), suspected Stanley's story from the beginning, and ultimately proved Parry's innocence.

In the movie, Parry Clay (Ernest Anderson, who was a studio service attendant at Warner Brothers, and went back to being one when the movie was over)[27] spoke continuously of his ambitions to become a lawyer when he grew up. This was the first time, according to much of the black community, that Hollywood had portrayed a black person as real, honest, human, and ambitious, and depicted the intolerance of white people toward those ambitions.

Another significant factor in *In This Our Life* was that Minerva and Parry commuted each day to and from their work at the Timberlake household. They were not *live-in servants*, as all previous films had depicted. Moreover, it was Roy, a white woman, who came to the Clay house (instead of summoning them to the Timberlakes), to find out the truth about the tragic accident. In just one line of this movie, Hattie disspelled much of the fawning image she acquired from the thirties. When Roy asked Minerva, Parry's mother, why she didn't tell the arresting officer that Parry had been home when the accident occurred, Minerva replied, "Well, you know those policemen. They won't listen to what a colored boy says."[28]

There were a few black criticisms of *In This Our Life*. One was that when Parry was in jail, all the other inmates were also black, although jails throughout the country were segregated. There was also a scene where a black took off his hat while talking to a white, a throwback to the old stereotypes. Furthermore, there was talk that numerous scenes showing Parry and Minerva's "boldness," had been cut in several Southern localities.[29] One person wrote to Walter White of the NAACP that "surely the producers must know that the picture of the enlightened colored race doesn't end with one struggling law student."[30]

On the whole, however, black response to *In This Our Life*, was overwhelmingly favorable. The letters of approval poured in. Jack Warner basked in the glory of *In This Our Life*. His advertising director, S. Charles Einfeld, exuberantly told the NAACP's White that, "It is always Warner Brothers' purpose to present the spirit of our country and its people in the most forthright and intelligent manner."[31] Herbert King wrote to director John Huston that "the challenging utterances both of Minerva and Parry Clay were faithful to the spirit and the feeling of Negroes in contemporary American life."[32] Inez Wilson thanked Warner Brothers for "such a straightforward and honest approach in the development of a great story." It was something "for which we American Negroes are deeply grateful and proud."[33] Darius Johnson, Jr., asserted that "one reason I liked the picture was because it showed that actors of my race can act other than the minstrel role or have to be laughed at. . . ."[34]

Edith McDougal lauded *In This Our Life* because for the first time in cinema history, "A Negro is depicted as a normal, intelligent, clean living human being." She said that for too long the movies had depicted blacks as a "pitiable burden of society." Thousands of people were working in a world at war to maintain American civilization. "We only ask an opportunity to learn and to be judged on merit. In *In This Our Life*, you have taken a step in democratizing film land. We are grateful."[35] John Holley told Warner that "your example here is worthy of emulation by other major Hollywood companies, who by their portrayal of Negroes and other racial types have long contributed to the misinformation and narrow-mindedness which forms the basis of American race prejudice."[36]

Walter White, executive secretary of the NAACP, had begun a campaign to obtain more dignified roles for blacks, and some producers had already shown an interest in his proposals. These interests were loosely referred to as "The Pledges," and many people thought that *In This Our Life* was a direct result. White said this was not so, but the movie was indeed what he had in mind when he talked about dignified roles for blacks.

White wrote to Olivia de Havilland about the movie:

"The treatment in that film, and the honest sincerity of your handling of the role marks one of the greatest experiences we have ever had in the moving picture theatre. In addition to our joy with the treatment of Negroes as human beings, instead of as menial comic figures, we were further thrilled by the spontaneous applause which swept over the . . . theatre at the conclusion of the scene between you and Parry, and again when you believed him to be telling the truth instead of your screen sister. You have made a great contribution to human relations, and I want you to know how grateful we are."[37]

Miss de Havilland wrote back to White:

"Several of us who were associated with the film felt that it would have been a more interesting picture if it had been a less conventional story of romance and trouble, and had dealt more deeply and extensively with the story of Parry and Minerva and their relationship with the principal characters. I hope someday Hollywood will produce a really significant and penetrating film concerning your people and their special and wonderful contributions to the human race."[38]

Some forty years later, however, Miss de Havilland was uncertain about the thoughts of those who played in *In This Our Life*. "Since actors are generally sympathetic to all people who are unfairly treated by life, or by their brothers, I am not sure that when we made *In This Our Life,* we were aware that the film was regarded as a breakthrough for black performers, or that we were setting a trend with this movie."[39]

Unfortunately, *In This Our Life* was not followed by other films that portrayed blacks in a realistic fashion. Its uniqueness derived more from accident than design. One would have thought that after its release White and Hattie would henceforth be on better terms, but such was not to be. The bitterness between the two dragged on for the remainder of the decade. Hattie believed that she was professionally obliged to take whatever role *she* desired, and not have that option decided for her by "outside" forces. Thus, while her mendicant image faded somewhat with *In This Our Life,* many subsequent movies revived it. She believed, as did White, that blacks should get improved roles in movies, but she was not willing for such ideology to put her out of work completely. It would be like burning down your barn to get rid of the rats, Hattie felt, if she and her colleagues failed to heed the pragmatic aspects of their lives and careers. Ideology was fine, she felt, but you can't eat it.

Nonetheless, in Hattie's next movie, *George Washington Slept Here* (definitely anti-climactic after *In This Our Life*), she not only did not speak in dialect; she quite frequently told off her boss played by comedian Jack Benny. Perhaps this reading of "modern household worker" as opposed to "menial servant," was a spin-off from her experiences in playing Minerva Clay. In *The Male Animal,* however, she reverted to dialect as she asked Jack Carson, "Is you got a pain?" causing one reviewer to say that *GWTW* characters never quite got over being *GWTW* characters.

For the war effort, Hattie, along with much of the Hollywood community, spared no effort in contributing to the success and well-being of servicemen. The war effort increasingly took up her time and attention, but she gladly gave both, for she felt it her patriotic duty to entertain members of the Armed Forces, and build up their morale. She even announced plans—which were never fulfilled—to sponsor a school in Los Angeles for illiterate black soldiers.

She became a captain in the American Women's Volunteer Service, and headed a black subcommittee of the Hollywood Victory Committee which regularly met at Hattie's house. At the meeting of May 15, 1942, Hattie appointed Leigh Whipper and Eddie Anderson as "fact finders," Louise Beavers to "ways and means," and Lillian Randolph, as recording secretary.

Edward Arnold, President of the Screen Actors Guild, spoke to the group at Hattie's house about the lack of funds for adequate entertainment programs. He urged the black community to merge its activities with the overall USO and Victory Committee, and play to mixed audiences. Mixed groups, he said, would reflect the democracy for which we were fighting, and would bolster the morale of the black servicemen.

Randolph suggested that the black entertainers put on a mammoth fund-raiser to pay the necessary expenses in getting programs to mainly black military units. So, Hattie arranged for the use of the Shriner auditorium, and Fayard Nicholas assembled the available talent, and in July 1942, the event brought in enough funds to sustain the black part of the Hollywood Victory Committee.[40]

Hattie traveled to numerous "out of the way" bases, such as Camp Haan, in a remote part of the state, where the soldiers were mostly black, and always welcomed Hattie and her entourage. She posed with the cook at Camp Haan, and with several GIs. She tried her hand at driving tanks and heavy trucks, all to the pleasure of the servicemen. She was described as an "excellent driver."[41]

In addition, every weekend, it seemed, she entertained GIs at home. She told Ruth:

"With so many soldiers stationed in or near Los Angeles there is always the call to go out and entertain at a USO center or at an army camp. I always enjoy doing this, but I cannot help but feel sad when I look over a large crowd of our fine young men and realize that the world has found no better way to solve its problems than by taking so many of these young lives."[42]

In August 1942, Hattie was selected by the Hollywood Victory Committee to go to the Mid-West on a bond selling tour. She told an inter-racial rally in Indianapolis that "putting a little time aside for clean fun and good humor" was "very necessary to relieve the tensions of our time," because we could not live twenty-four hours a day with news commentators "without a Bob Hope, Red Skelton, or Eddie Cantor to help us keep our balance."[43] Looking out over the Indianapolis crowd, estimated at 40,000, she addressed them not as "colored Americans," nor as "white Americans," but as "fellow Americans." She continued that:[44]

"My work with the Hollywood Victory Committee and as a participant in many camp shows has taken me into . . . camps where our boys are stationed. I have talked with these boys. They are fine and clean and brave. Their lives have been interrupted. They have put aside professions, college careers, love affairs, all the things that make up a rich, full life; the way of life that has always been

called 'The American Way.' I have not found a grumbler in the
bunch, whether draftee or enlisted man. All are anxious to do their
part to right the wrongs of the world, and to return home to live
in peace under the protection of the star spangled banner."[45]

This speech (probably written by Goodwin), always well received, led to the sale of a considerable number of bonds. She
became one of the most called upon public personalities to work
for the war effort. Hattie told her audiences, "It's not how much
can I spare; it's how much have I?"

Hattie showed that she was really serious in her war effort
when she "sacrificed" one of her most treasured possessions: her
good luck rabbit's foot, which she brought with her when she first
came to Hollywood. With the help of Olivia de Havilland, Hattie
turned over the rabbit's foot to Lt. Commander Gene Marky, and
he placed it in his ship's trophy room. "That's a powerful lucky
rabbit's foot," Hattie said. "I got the part in *Gone With the Wind*
because of it. I got my Warner contract, thanks to it. . . . I've had
my share of good luck, and now it's someone else's turn."[46]

Hattie's big war movie was the tender drama, *Since You Went
Away,* adapted from the novel by Margaret Buell Wilder. She got
star billing in this prestigious David O. Selznick film, directed by
John Cromwell. Her contract required that whenever the other
featured players were mentioned in promotional advertising, so
would Hattie. Not only that, but her name would be mentioned
first among them.[47] If this requirement was indeed carried out, this
may well have been the first time in film history that a black person
got a star billing.

The only drawback the studio people could see in giving Hattie
star treatment was the often invoked but rarely documented
"Southern problem," which would undoubtedly raise questions
about the inclusion in printed ads of a black woman with white
people. The ads were run anyway, and, at least on this occasion, the
"Southern problem" was an empty threat.

Hattie played Fidelia, a maid, in this movie about a family
whose man had gone off to war, and had subsequently been listed
as missing in action. She ran strong Academy Award competition
with the other stars (Claudette Colbert, Jennifer Jones, Shirley
Temple, Joseph Cotten, and Monty Woolley). After one scene, so it

was reported, director Cromwell walked seriously up to Hattie, and said, "Well, Hattie, I see you're at your old tricks again."

"What do you mean?" asked Hattie, concerned. "What have I done?"

Cromwell broke into a big laugh, and said, "I mean you're up to your old tricks again of stealing scenes. You must be planning to carry off another Academy Award this year."[48]

Since You Went Away was the most prestigious film dealing with the homefront during World War II, and it was Selznick's biggest production since *Gone With the Wind*. The movie dealt with the fortitude of women who are left behind during conflict. Claudette Colbert was the strong wife in the face of adversity, Jennifer Jones and Shirley Temple were the daughters who balanced their lives between missing their father and finding their own independence, and Hattie McDaniel was the non-dialect speaking maid who proved to be a comforter, confidante, and counselor during the family's time of troubles. *Since You Went Away* was a marvelous foreshadowing of changed attitudes toward the role of women in American society.

At producer Selznick's insistence, Hattie was made to look like Mammy in *GWTW's* "The Scene." Her challenge was to *look* as Mammy did in the last part of *GWTW* but *act* about ten years younger than Mammy.[49]

A leading black newspaper, *The Pittsburgh Courier*, hailed Hattie's performance, and congratulated her for insisting that her part be free of dialect. "There was no eyeballing or kawkaw stuff on her part;" yet, she "succeeded in running the gamut of emotions in a manner not exceeded" by any of the other stars. The *Courier* felt, therefore, that instead of criticizing Hattie for her roles, the black community should uphold and honor her great acting abilities.[50]

Hattie seemed to be making it "bigtime" in Hollywood. Her name was on all the marquees and in the newspapers, and she was highly sought after by producers, but she still had a sense of foreboding, as though she was not meant for such a high-powered life, and that somehow her happiness would come crashing down about her. She seemed to become increasingly pensive as time passed.

Hattie expressed joy, however, at the ending of the war. As she wrote to Ruth in Ft. Collins, Hollywood was prepared for the heroic return of the servicemen. "Weren't you happy?" she asked Ruth, "when you heard the news . . . we won't have to rack our brains with rationing points much longer, but thank Heavens we had them, or else some would have eaten and others wouldn't have, but the system of rationing made everyone equal."[51]

In her private life, Hattie stunned Hollywood and indeed much of the country, when she announced in May 1944, that she was an expectant mother, a condition kept secret during the movie *Janie's* (Warner, 1944) filming. When Warner Brothers heard about the blessed event, the film company began to take her back and forth to the studio in a private limousine.

Hattie wanted her good friend, columnist Louella Parsons, to be the first to know of her pregnancy. She told Louella that "Betty Grable, Lana Turner, Maureen O'Hara, Gene Tierney, and the rest of those glamor girls have nothing on me. I, too, am taking time out to welcome the stork."[52]

Hattie exulted in quoting to her friends the 92nd Psalm about "bringing forth fruit in one's old age."[53] (She was now 49 years old.) There had been talk of sending Hattie on a grand tour of South America, where she had thousands of fans, especially in Brazil. One of Hattie's friends, Alexander Keeland, wrote to Ruby in April about the proposed tour, that it "should be a remarkable experience" for her, and one she should never forget.[54]

Hattie gleefully canceled all preparations for her proposed South American tour as she waited for her baby to arrive. She also turned down several movie offers, not minding in the least the huge loss of income. Throughout the summer and fall of 1944, Hattie's entire life was absorbed with her impending motherhood. Nothing else mattered.

Keeland wrote to Goodwin delightedly, "Will wonders ever cease? I made every guess imaginable regarding Hattie. But I must confess that motherhood escaped my list. Really, dear, I am too happy for words, learning about Hattie's coming event."[55]

At home, Hattie set aside two "baby" rooms; one to be the nursery, and the other to hold the avalanche of gifts that began to arrive. Already she had received anticipatory gifts from Clark Gable, Vivien Leigh, and Claudette Colbert.

To Hattie, all of this was a dream. On top of her great movie successes, she was now to have a baby of her own.

"Yes, my dear," she told Dermody, "I'm expecting this very month and it's due any minute and I am thrilled—it is really a gift from God!" She had been a god-mother to so many of her friends' children, "and never got to cuddle them for long—it is such a thrill to think I'm going to have my very own baby!"[56] Indeed, she told Ruth, "By the time you receive this letter . . . probably the 'little stranger' will be here."[57] Oddly enough, Lloyd was silent on the impending birth; he made no statements, at least in public, about his feelings on the matter.

But time passed, and there was no birth. Hope grew into public disappointment. Hollywood specialists were brought in to determine why the baby was taking so long. At last, Hattie heard the hateful news: hers was a false pregnancy; there was to be no baby. Hattie was a large woman, the doctors averred, and that was why they had gone so long in misreading Hattie's condition.

Ruth Dermody believed that Hattie's "pregnancy" in 1944 was an ominous symptom of precarious health, which began to decline in the late forties.[58] Hattie was soon diagnosed by various doctors as suffering from diabetes and heart problems.

Needless to say, Hattie was thoroughly crushed by this turn of events, and no one, not even Ruby or Clark Gable could comfort her. She was so absolutely depressed that she refused to see anyone for weeks; she frequently spoke of not wanting to live anymore. "The Old Man upstairs has deserted me," she said. "It's damn hard for me to believe in God or anything." A remark from a well-meaning but tactless friend that at Hattie's age, maybe God carried the matter off for the best brought only a sad shake of the head.[59]

Her health and state of mind, coupled with changing conditions in Hollywood limited her work the following year to the "Billie Burke" and "Amos 'n Andy" radio shows. It was not entirely her depressed state, however, that kept her from making movies in

1945. The offers simply were not there. (She had become a free lancer in 1943, severing her contracts with Warner and Selznick, so she was no longer guaranteed any work by these studios.)

To compound her problems in 1945, many of Hattie's white neighbors tried to nullify the contracts by which she and other blacks had moved into the area, claiming "restrictive convenants" inserted in residential deeds, limited the neighborhood to whites only. Hattie had moved into a house on Harvard Boulevard in the spring of 1942, and this was her home during most of the war years. The two-story, thirty-room mansion had a huge American flag adorning the vestibule, a safe where the previous owners had secreted their money (which Hattie used for storing canned goods), and a white baby grand piano in Hattie's living room.[60] According to Butterfly McQueen, Hattie didn't know how to play the piano, but did have her picture taken several times sitting at one. Hattie was fairly good at the drums.

In fact, Hattie was not the only black person to move into the West Adams Heights area known as "Sugar Hill." Ethel Waters, at 2127 S. Hobart, lived next door to a white women's club; Louise Beavers acquired a house that belonged to a previous mayor of Los Angeles; Louis Belsen, white, but married to Pearl Bailey, and Juan Tizon, a member of the Duke Ellington band, settled in, as did Norman Houston, president of the Golden State Insurance Company, Ben Carter, businessman Horace Clark, actress Frances Williams, actor Joel Fluellen, and many others.[61]

An ostensible reason for Hattie's and many of her friends' moves, was that a freeway was planned in their neighborhood on 31st Street. It was clear, however, that the blacks were motivated by the fact that they had become quite wealthy because of their success in the movie and radio industries.

Clearly, someone in the Los Angeles city hall drew up a map, and designated separate parts of the city for specific nationality and ethnic groups. The blacks—at least those who had not become wealthy and influential—were planned to live in the Watts area.

Thus, if a black person wanted to move into an area not "designated" for him, he'd usually have to pay a higher market price than ordinarily, until the restrictions had been shattered by enough pioneering blacks like Hattie. Even the higher prices did not ameliorate the fears of the white racist conservatives that their property was being "invaded" by "outsiders," and that its value would drop as a result.

Consequently, a number of whites brought suit against any further sale of land to incoming blacks. Moreover, the whites argued that the blacks already there were in violation of the city's restrictive covenant system, created years before, by which white owners were limited in their right to sell to whomever they pleased. This development, of course, meant that Hattie and all of her neighbors were faced with the possibility of being evicted from their houses. (To be sure, Los Angeles was not the only large city with a restrictive covenant system. St. Louis, Cleveland, and Philadelphia practiced the same policy. Denver, Hattie's hometown, had had such a system, since the early part of the century.)

Frances Williams took the lead in fighting restrictive covenants by organizing Saturday workshops to talk over strategy, and make plans for court appearances. Williams hoped that everyone would pool their efforts, and fight this case, "one street at a time." She was not at first successful in this endeavor, because the lawyers for the blacks wanted to handle the matter on a case-by-case basis, obviously a better financial deal for them than if they collectively fought the battle.[62]

In time, however, the situation changed. Loren Miller, a black attorney, began to consolidate his defense of those who were fighting the restrictive covenant system into a class of fifty blacks, including Hattie, Ethel Waters and Louise Beavers in a suit brought by an association of white property owners.[63] The whites wanted the city of Los Angeles to enforce the restrictive covenants.

The arguments were heard before Superior Court Judge Thurmond Clarke, who gave his decision on December 6, 1945. "This court is of the opinion that members of the Negro race are accorded, without reservations and evasions, the full rights guaranteed them under the 14th Amendment of the Federal Constitution." It was a ruling that sent shock waves throughout the country; it was an index of things to come. Lest anyone misunderstand, Judge Clarke went on to spell out the message of the 14th Amendment: "rights of citizens shall not be abridged because of race, color, or previous condition of servitude."[64] There it was, in black and white, so to speak, and all the chagrined plaintiffs could do was take their biases home with them.

The judge located the heart of the case in the war ethos. "Certainly," he emphatically asserted, "there was no discrimination against the Negro race when it came to calling upon its members to die on the battlefield in defense of this country in the war just ended."

A bubbling Hattie told a reporter as she left the courthouse: "That's one fine judge." She was, she said, "mighty happy I've still got my home."[65]

Judge Clarke's ruling was one of many that built an imposing body of law against restrictive covenants in the immediate post-war period. A new sense of democracy allowed blacks of all walks of life—not just movie stars—to penetrate heretofore exclusively white establishments. In 1948, the U.S. Supreme Court gave its famous decision of *Shelly v Kramer*, which definitively legally barred the practice of restrictive covenants. One may say, therefore, that Frances Williams, Hattie McDaniel, and a host of their friends materially helped build the case for fair housing practices in the United States.

Sadly, the victory did little to buoy Hattie's declining fortunes. Her happiness over the restrictive covenant ruling was short-lived, for a few days later, she obtained her divorce from Lloyd Crawford. A few months before, in September, she had told Ruth, "I have had to file for my divorce. I cannot stand conditions any longer. I do not intend to trot all over God's creation when my home is here. Can you blame me?"[66]

Apparently, Lloyd's speculations on the real estate market had fallen on hard times, despite the housing boom of the immediate postwar period. Unfortunately, his "vast holdings" of property in the West, as reported when he married Hattie, were as imaginative as real. His "wedding present" to Hattie of 160 acres of Montana farmland, either was bogus from the start, or had to be re-claimed to take care of future financial emergencies. He apparently wanted

Hattie to bankroll some new real estate ventures, and then travel with him to their various locations.

Part of the problem between Lloyd and Hattie was that he constantly lived in the shadow of her status as a star. She made much more money than he, and this probably produced jealousy. Moreover, when the couple socialized, it was generally with people from Hattie's profession, with conversations that frequently left Lloyd stranded.[67] Lack of common interests led to a drifting apart, ultimately producing an estrangement.

According to Hattie, Crawford was without a job, and made little or no effort to get one. She told the judge, "He thought because he married me, he shouldn't have to work." Belying the reports that Crawford was an astute manager, Hattie exclaimed that "he never showed he could do any kind of business." Based upon Hattie's testimony, Superior Court Judge Goodwin J. Knight, granted her divorce on December 20, 1945.[68] Soon thereafter, Lloyd who still claimed to love Hattie, moved east, first to Wyoming where his real estate holdings purportedly were, and then, for some unknown reason, to Minnesota.

One news service, the American Negro Press (ANP), of Chicago, thought it had ferreted out the real reason for Hattie's departure from her marriage. One of its late December stories read:

"A Lt. Booker of the Armed Forces is the swain whose name is being coupled with that of the 1939 Academy Award winner."[69] The report angered Hattie, and she had her lawyer, Clore Warne, demand a retraction. Warne stated that the ANP had unduly exaggerated her divorce from Lloyd Crawford. Hattie, the attorney claimed, "had no knowledge of any such rumors."[70]

Claude Barnett of the ANP hastily retracted, claiming that the writer of the story "evidently succumbed to the urge to build up a yarn unusual in interest because he was writing about a star. Through the years our efforts have been devoted to building Miss McDaniel up. We would not willingly do anything which might have a reverse effect."[71] There the matter dropped, although Hattie and Booker were good friends for several years. In April 1951, Hattie and Booker—now a Captain just back from the Korean front—posed for photographers in the foyer of the Pantages Theatre on the occasion of the Academy Awards presentations for 1950.

On a rare occasion when she let down her defenses, Hattie admitted that she was not happy and, for all her successes and triumphs, did not know if she ever had been. It seemed that she even possessed a sense of guilt because of her great accomplishments. It was as though she constantly asked, in reference to success, "Why me?" She held to the Puritan ethic that success is God-given, and felt a huge responsibility to God and her public, and worried about her capabilities to meet it and, indeed, her worthiness to possess it. On the one hand, she was a mere human being with all the frailties attendant thereto; on the other, she was a public institution, who had to seem happy and contented whether she was or not. It was the conflict of what she privately conceived herself to be, and her image projected by the public that gave Hattie her doubts and fears.

Hattie McDaniel at fifty: married three times, widowed once, divorced twice. Loved and respected around the world for her images of Mammy. Always smiling in public, her flashing teeth lighting up her round, plump face and big, rolling eyes. But in private, lonely, depressed, and inflicted with a bitterness that seemed to grow on a daily basis.

Her failure to bear a child in 1944 seems to have been the starting point of Hattie's decline; her depressions certainly did affect her physical health, and under this condition, her movie career suffered. The question of legality concerning her home, and her divorce from Crawford, further unsettled her mind. Then, too, there was the long simmering quarrel with Walter White of the NAACP. In the immediate postwar years, their fight with each other broke out in a raging fury.

CHAPTER SIX

The Crusade Against "Mammyism"

Two entertainers in the twentieth century rose to fame on one word: "Mammy."[1] The first was Al Jolson, whose Mammy from Alabammy endeared him to generations of theatre goers. The other was Hattie McDaniel, whose portrayals of Mammy brought her to grief more than once. Jolson, of course, was white, and played in blackface. His performances were related to the minstrel era, when black opposition to stereotypes was not strong enough to make an impact. Thus, white audiences—and even black audiences—continued to enjoy Jolson's acts.

By the mid-point of Hattie's career, the late thirties, things were changing. Black newspapers had grown in quantity, and many of their reporters were young, sophisticated, and educated, and would not follow what they considered to be the meek, fawning ways of their ancestors. The liberalism engendered by World War II furthered this feeling of black independence. Anything that smacked of "Uncle Tomism," or "Mammyism," came under attack by the black activists. The "Uncle Tom," actors like Ben Carter, Stepin Fetchit, and Clarence Muse, caught the brunt of the assault, as did Louise Beavers, Ethel Waters, and above all the others, Hattie McDaniel, for "Mammyism." Hattie was singled out for playing

Mammy in *Gone With the Wind,* and the household servant who "yassired" and "yes'med" her way through 82 other attributed movies. The black attacks against her became so severe that at one time Hattie sadly proclaimed that her worst enemies were her own people.

Walter White, executive secretary of the NAACP, spearheaded the drive to get more sophisticated roles for blacks. In 1940, as White explained in a letter to Edwin Embree, President of the Julius Rosenwald Fund, White was approached by a number of wealthy, influential Republicans, who were violently opposed to a third term for President Franklin D. Roosevelt. This Republican group maintained that it had made an exhaustive study of the political situation in the country, and had found seventeen states, primarily in the industrialized North, with 281 electoral votes where the blacks held the balance of power.[2] This Republican group told White that he had more influence over the blacks in these states than anyone else. Apparently, in return for delivering these electoral votes to their presidential candidate, Wendell Willkie, in November 1940, the Republican group would use its power in Hollywood to achieve better roles for black players.

White vehemently denied that he had anything to do with this scheme. ". . . I told them [the Republicans] that under no circumstances would the NAACP or I engage in partisan politics." White also declined to meet Willkie before the election, "for I know that such a meeting would be interpreted as politics."[3] The Republican offer to White during the campaign of 1940 nevertheless opened some doors for him. For one thing, it ultimately brought him into close, personal contact with Wendell Willkie. White was on his way in early 1941 to make a speech at the University of Southern California, and Willkie was slated to address the dinner for the Academy Awards presentations. White suggested that the two visit producers and discuss the black situation with them.

At a luncheon held for White and Willkie, Daryl Zanuck told White, "I make one sixth of the pictures . . . in Hollywood," and the problem of black stereotyping had never even occurred to him until White brought it up. Along with Walter Wanger, Zanuck and several other producers gave "The Pledges" (discussed in Chapter

5, in reference to *In This Our Life*), for fair, reasonable treatment of blacks in their movies.[4]

White told a friend some months later about meeting the Hollywood producers. He said that after "The Pledges," Hollywood agents "started scurrying around for stories in which Negroes played principal roles. . . ."[5]

White was not so naive as to believe that Hollywood producers would eschew certain roles for blacks, especially if those roles kept the cash registers ringing. "The Pledges" may have been well intended, but he wasn't going to hold his breath for them to be honored. Every picture made had *majorities* in mind rather than minorities. Thus only pressure groups and fan clubs flooding Hollywood with complaints and ideas might make any dents in the *status quo*. Black movie fans in the past had not written very many letters to black movie stars. (Hattie had received some for her role in *GWTW*.) White wanted to engineer huge amounts of publicity for blacks who played roles other than menials.

He was somewhat encouraged by letters to the NAACP from the Negro Motion Picture Players Association, which represented most of the black extras in Hollywood. These "bit players" produced the mob scenes, street wars, parades, dock workers, sports events, and dozens of other situations "that depict American life." The group asserted that in 1941 the studios spent three million dollars for black extras as atmosphere players; yet less than $10,000 in salaries ever reached them. The association wanted to enlist the NAACP's help in getting the motion picture industry to pay ten percent of its expenditures for extras to the association for disbursement to its members.[6]

White took up the extras' cause, but did not get very far with it. The NAACP received a letter from a studio representative, Samuel Bischoff, that "you can . . . rest assured of this fact. In Hollywood there is absolutely no prejudice of any kind or description against the colored extras. . . . Twenty-five or thirty percent of our actors are colored people. Such colored actors and actresses as Paul Robeson, Clarence Muse, Hattie McDaniel . . . are kept working most of the time, and they are treated with the same respect as their fellow players. . . ."[7]

White's campaign started a debate among newspapers—primarily black—that reached national proportions before the end of 1942. He frequently told the story about meeting a white woman "who didn't like Negroes." She had never known any blacks personally, but she had "seen them in the movies," and knew them to be "lazy, shiftless, crap-playing, gin drinking ne'er do wells."[8]

The movies, he asserted, were powerful instruments in determining public opinion. As White's co-worker, Roy Wilkins, put it, the main idea of the NAACP was to get blacks into movies in some capacity other than clowns or servants. "One would never guess from a review of the movies of today," Wilkins said, "that thirteen million Negroes live in America."[9]

Several newspapers also suggested that black movie goers "teach Hollywood the value of a letter," to commend or condemn, as the situation demanded. It was widely held that most blacks did not own radios, and could not get nightly entertainment as the whites did. The black saved up his money and enjoyed his only form of entertainment about once a month—or at the most every fortnight—and that was the movies. If he didn't like what he saw, he should let the Hollywood studios know.

White told *Variety* in June 1942, that Hollywood should not make a hero of the black, "because not many Negroes are heroes, just as not many white people are heroes."[10] He did want the movies to give blacks their normal place in the world and "quit portraying them as fearsome of spooks, and rolling their eyes." In this same vein, he mentioned to *PM* Magazine: "There are Negro sharecroppers, and there is no reason . . . their existence should not be acknowledged. But there are also Negro artists, doctors, lawyers, scientists, teachers, businessmen, and others who have made and are making very material contributions to their own and the country's advancement."[11]

White did not want to destroy the old black actors, but he did want them to change their ways. More and more, White came to believe *Pittsburgh Courier* columnist, George S. Schuyler, that Hollywood must get rid of the "grinning darky stereotype, the slew-footed, liver-lipped, swivel-eyed cretins, male and female, who shuffled, jigged, and dropped consonants throughout the films that reached not only America, but the whole world, white and colored."[12]

And who did Schuyler and many other blacks believe these "grinning darky stereotypes" were? White had asked Archer Winsten of *The New York Post* to send him the names of black players who had been treated in comical ways. Winsten suggested that White simply get a list of movies "in which Eddie Anderson, Mantan Moreland, Stepin Fetchit, that Twentieth Century Fox specialist in the bug-eye, Hattie McDaniel, Sam McDaniel, and the *Imitation of Life* woman [Louise Beavers] have appeared. . . ."[13]

Next, White asked another friend to compile a list of movies that were excessively "anti-Negro," resulting in three movies: *Gone With the Wind,* with Hattie McDaniel degrading herself and her race as Mammy, *The Little Colonel,* with Hattie McDaniel spouting off niceties about the Old South, and *Maryland,* with Hattie McDaniel grinning, scraping, and bowing to her white masters. It became increasingly likely that White would sooner or later come to blows with Hi-Hat Hattie "Mammy" McDaniel.[14] These two lists certainly did explain the bitterness between Hattie and Walter White.

Hattie's friend and secretary, Ruby Goodwin, had begun writing a syndicated column, "Hollywood in Bronze." In one of her articles, Ruby set the tone by which the older black players would respond to White's overtures. "I have no wish or intention to try to discredit Mr. White's venture," she wrote, arguing that what many people hailed as "new" wasn't new at all, but only seemed so because White's activities received wider publicity than previous efforts by blacks to "clean up" the stereotypes.

For example, one reform-minded person, Leon Washington, editor and publisher of the *Los Angeles Sentinel,* had recently led a black picket line at Loew's State Theatre where *Tales of Manhattan* was shown. Both he and his colleague, Almena Davis, editor of the Los Angeles *Tribune,* believed there were unwarranted anti-black sequences in the movie, and they publicly protested it as a result.[15] Moreover, it was pointed out that Hattie herself had removed some unacceptable parts of the script for *Can This Be Dixie?* Clarence Muse also made news when he refused to kiss the hem of his mistress' dress in a movie, and Louise Beavers demanded that the word "nigger" be eliminated from *Imitation of Life,* just as Hattie had done with *Gone With the Wind.*

Much of the black Hollywood community had formed the "Fair Play" Committee to urge studios to create better parts for the black performers. (Ironically, when White started his campaign, the Hollywood Fair Play Committee was diverted from its original objective, and spent an uncommon amount of time combatting the NAACP offensives.) Thus, there had already been numerous efforts to improve the black situation in films long before White appeared on the scene.

For her part, Hattie's first major reaction to White's program was, "What do you want me to do? Play a glamor girl and sit on Clark Gable's knee? When you ask me not to play the parts, what have you got to offer in return?"[16] She suggested, according to Hedda Hopper, that wealthy blacks should invest in the film industry or, better yet, the NAACP should "drop some coin into film production; then they can make pictures suitable to the organization," and Hattie said that she'd "be only too happy to play in them."[17]

She, along with most of the other veteran black players, resented what they called "outsiders" coming in and trying to tell them what to do in reference to the movie industry. White and his colleagues were well-heeled, according to Hattie, and they didn't have to worry about earning a living. Of course, Hattie was well heeled, too—at least at this time—but she knew as well as anyone that wealth in Hollywood can be as fleeting as fame. Also, she never forgot her lean days; it was as if she had a fear of being plunged back into her earlier conditions of indigence, a condition common to many Hollywood stars. Perhaps thoughts like these made Hattie act as though Walter White was trying to grab the bread right out of her mouth.

Hattie held a meeting at her home in August 1942, to discuss the black film problem. In attendance were Lillian Randolph, Theresa Harris, Clarence Muse, Leigh Whipper, Mantan Moreland, Nicodemus Stewart, Charles Butler, Ernest Whitman, and Jesse Graves. They discussed how difficult their lives had become—

walking a tightrope between giving what the producers wanted on the one hand, and pleasing race leaders on the other.[18] This meeting produced two proposals. One was for the black players to explain their situation to the Producers' Association. The other was to petition the Screen Actors Guild for a meeting of its board of directors, where the black problem could be discussed. Unfortunately, neither of these proposals ever came to fruition, because in a few months the situation was so rancorous that it seemed for a time that no rational solution was possible.[19]

At Hattie's meeting, Clarence Muse steamed at the NAACP for interfering with his and his friends' careers, and vented his anger at the national organization in a lengthy statement. Although he himself was a member of the NAACP, and at one time headed its west coast branch, he felt that the NAACP leaders back east were doing irreparable harm to the black community out west. His statement was later published by newspapers—black and white—under the title, "The Trial of Uncle Tom."[20]

Like thousands of other members, Muse knew little of the national board. Each year, local chapters were invited to attend the national meeting which was always held in New York, so only those nearby could afford to come. With only seven at these meetings constituting a quorum, the entire organization was run according to the whims of a few people, with the executive-secretary dominant. Therefore, according to Muse, White had become a "majority of one."[21]

Muse lamented the NAACP's treatment of William Pickens, the organization's leader for thirty-three years, who apparently crossed swords with White on the Hollywood black problem, and was drummed out of the Association's leadership group. "I sat a few days ago at my dinner table with Mr. Pickens and read the soul of a man crushed by his own group. . . .[22] Muse bitterly complained that White and his cohorts had by-passed and ignored the black players altogether, going directly to the producers to be "wined and dined by them" in the "usual Hollywood fashion," without the courtesy to inform the Fair Play Committee or the Screen Actors Guild what he planned to do. "It is evident that we [the Fair Play Committee] have been more conscious than Walter White that

101

Negroes should have better roles. . . . We feel that if an organization like the NAACP is sincere in its fight, they should work it out with the moving force of Hollywood: the actors through their guild. . . ."[23]

Muse and the Fair Play Committee suggested ways to lessen the screen image of blacks as a "bunch of careless, illiterate porters, mammies, waiters, and sharecroppers." First, there should be no dialect unless the person using it is noble and ambitious, is a part of the plot, and "wins at the end." More light-skinned blacks, even mulattoes, should get roles. Black boys should have their hair straightened. Producers should be encouraged to make more films like *In This Our Life,* showing black ambitions, not just for the legal professions, but for architectural, medical, and professional careers as well. These pursuits, argued Muse, had been in existence before White began his crusade, and Muse resented the inference that White had "invented" the program for better black roles.

Muse welcomed a nation-wide opinion on the matter of "crucifying actors when they speak the lines as laid out before them. . . . Hattie McDaniel won the Academy Award because of her great artistry in portraying a character as written. Not Hattie McDaniel, but the part. . . ."

Muse agreed with Hattie that numerous white players had become associated with certain roles they played, yet their screen image did not merge into their private lives. Arthur Treacher was a perfect screen butler, but few people thought of him as a real-life butler. Jack Benny's image was one of miserliness; yet everyone knew that he was one of the most generous men alive; Gracie Allen was a nincompoop on radio and the screen, but in reality it would be difficult to find someone more intelligent than she. The roles of these and other people did not inspire those who saw them to act likewise. Why, then, Muse added, was the black community singled out, and the criticism made that it erred when playing the parts given to it? "My experience has been wherever a Negro character is glorified, be he . . . lowly . . . or a highbrow, the entire race reacts with enthusiasm. The actor must play the part as written, and his talent is unlimited when the opportunity presents itself. Negro actors of experience love their business and they want to protect it against selfish ambitions. Negro actors have progressed, and parts are better each year."[24] Though Muse got much praise for his diatribe, the black press of the day usually went against him. Reporter Fredi Washington (who played Peola in *Imitation of Life*), said in the *People's Voice* that the Fair Play Committee had dragged its feet for years on the matter of dignity for blacks in films. She believed if the FPC would cooperate with the NAACP instead of fighting it, "the kind of results we all want would be forthcoming." Miss Washington's viewpoint was widely shared throughout the country's black community.

Undaunted by Muse, Hattie McDaniel, and the FPC, White increased his activities. A friend, Almena Davis, had told him that, beyond the Muse-McDaniel group, there were several other blacks in Hollywood who predicted failure for his program. Like a commando going on reconaissance, White asked Davis to provide names, but she refused on the grounds of confidentiality.[25] The incident marked a point where White grew increasingly militant in his stance, even to campaigns against those who disagreed with him.

In early 1943, the famed composer, William Grant Still, became involved in the Hollywood black controversy. He wrote the score for Fox's *Stormy Weather*, only to have it discarded as "too polite and refined," the studio apparently wanting "erotic and sexy" music to portray the history of the black. Fox's decision immediately brought cries of protest from the black community, that the studio presented the black man not as he actually was, but as the white man wanted to see him.[26] Still walked off the set of *Stormy Weather* in disgust, an action that brought laudatory remarks about him from the black community. Still had honored his entire race, it was asserted, by disassociating himself from the bigots making *Stormy Weather*, and had vindicated countless others who put integrity in front of money.

Still wrote to White about his troubles with *Stormy Weather*, and he suggested something to White that was to have an important bearing on subsequent events dealing with the Hollywood black question. Still expressed his belief that movie scripts involving blacks should be subjected to some form of censorship, including plot and dialogue, proposing a movie about Dr. George Washington Carver, in which "they don't have him talking in dialect." Also, he felt that pressure should be applied to casting directors to include all shades of black people—all the way from the very light to the very dark and argued for some form of control over black music and costumes in movies.[27]

White agreed with everything Still said. He demanded that a black person be appointed to the Hays Office. He felt this action would cause studios to be more careful than in the past about how they depicted black life. This person in the Hays Office might require changes in unacceptable movies, and in extreme cases, could even keep movies off the market altogether.

White's idea of a black in the Hays Office was rejected by the Muse-McDaniel Fair Play Committee as censorship, which would lead the Hollywood studios along a path of resentment rather than cooperation. Undaunted, White promised additional forays in the years ahead into the complicated workings of Hollywood movie sets, and continued to seek advice from Still and others on the best approaches to the problem.

For example, White wrote to his friend Norman Houston in Los Angeles, about the "hard-core" black Hollywood players, led by Muse and McDaniel. He wondered if he were to meet formally with the Los Angeles branch of the NAACP, or even with its executive committee, whether or not the air would be cleared. He proposed to explain his position and show that he held no personal rancor toward the older set of black Hollywood actors.[28] Houston advised White not to meet the blacks through the NAACP. "The whole thing is very messy," he asserted, "because of the personalities involved." Although he believed that the members of the FPC had "made a mountain out of a molehill" over White's activities, he did concede that White probably should have consulted black players involved, instead of going directly to the producers. Some of the affected players, Houston said, acted out of a sense of jealousy or an inferiority complex—and these characterizations were compounded by White's friendliness toward Lena Horne.[29]

In all these controversies, Miss Horne was looked upon as symbolic of the "new" or "eastern upstart" black actress.[30] In her

Hattie McDaniel *(second row, third from left)* at the 24th Street Elementary School in Denver, where she was a student in the early 1900's. *Courtesy of the Denver Public Library.*

A view of the 24th Street Elementary School in Denver, which Hattie attended as a child. *Courtesy of the Denver Public Library.*

Sam *(third from left)* and Otis *(fifth from left)* McDaniel, Hattie's brothers, are among the "Cakewalk Kids" at Walden, Colorado, on October 4, 1902. *Courtesy of the Academy of Motion Picture Arts and Sciences.*

A 1910 photograph of fifteen–year–old Hattie on the occasion of her gold medal award for her emotional recitation of "Convict Joe" before the Women's Christian Temperance Union at Denver East High School. Shortly after receiving the award she left school to begin touring and entertaining full time. *Courtesy of the Academy of Motion Picture Arts and Sciences.*

Old East High School in Denver, where Hattie studied and recited "Convict Joe" in 1910. *Courtesy of the Denver Public Library.*

An advertisement, circa 1910, of Hattie's brother, Sam McDaniel *(left)* and his partner (named Mr. Brown, *right*). *Courtesy of the Academy of Motion Picture Arts and Sciences.*

Henry McDaniel, father of Hattie, about 1910, the time when he formed the Henry McDaniel Minstrel Show with his sons, Otis and Sam. *Courtesy of the Academy of Motion Picture Arts and Sciences.*

An autographed 1930 photo from Hattie's brother, Sam McDaniel, wearing minstrel attire, to his sister. The inscription reads, "10/17/30, From Sam. R. McDaniel Brother to Sis Hattie McD., Los Angeles, Calif." *Courtesy of the Academy of Motion Picture Arts and Sciences.*

An autographed 1936 photograph of Hattie wearing white ermine. The inscription reads, "With Sincerest Best Wishes to Bus and Sis. 11/23/36." *Courtesy of the Academy of Motion Picture Arts and Sciences.*

Clark Gable, as Rhett Butler, pours Hattie McDaniel, as Mammy, a drink of colored water "scotch" in *Gone With the Wind*, right after Bonnie Butler's birth. During one take of this scene, Gable's valet substituted real scotch in Hattie's glass as a practical joke. *Courtesy of the Turner Entertainment Company.*

This scene with Olivia de Havilland in *GWTW* is widely believed to have won Hattie the Oscar for Best Supporting Actress. *Courtesy of the Academy of Motion Picture Arts and Sciences.*

Hattie McDaniel, as Mammy, and Vivien Leigh, as Scarlet O'Hara, argue over the proper dress to wear to Ashley Wilkes' barbecue at Twelve Oaks. *Courtesy of the Turner Entertainment Company.*

A publicity photo of Hattie McDaniel in her Mammy costume from *GWTW,* 1939. *Courtesy of the Turner Entertainment Company.*

Hattie McDaniel and Wonderful Smith arrive at the Academy Awards Presentations, February 29, 1940, at the Coconut Grove, in the Ambassador Hotel in Los Angeles. *Daily Variety* wrote that "Not only was she the first of her race to receive an [Academy] Award, but she was first Negro ever to sit at an Academy banquet." *Courtesy of the Wisconsin Center for Film and Theater Research.*

Hattie McDaniel poses on February 29, 1940 with actress Fay Bainter who, earlier that evening, presented her with the Oscar for Best Supporting Actress for her 1939 role as Mammy in *GWTW*. *Courtesy of AP/World Wide Photos.*

Hattie McDaniel is filmed speaking a few days after she was actually presented with the Academy Award for Best Supporting Actress for her role as Mammy in *GWTW*. *Courtesy of the Wisconsin Center for Film and Theater Research.*

Hattie, the night she won her Oscar, February 29, 1940. *Courtesy of the Hearst Newspaper Collection at the University of Southern California Library.*

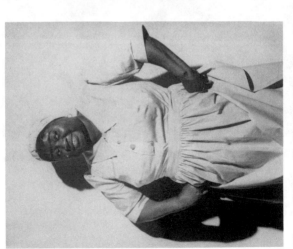

Three publicity stills for the 1940 release, *Maryland*. (*Copyright 1940 Twentieth Century–Fox Film Corporation.*) *Courtesy of the Wisconsin Center for Film and Theater Research.*

Hattie stands next to her Packard in 1940. She had previously owned a Chevrolet. *Courtesy of the Academy of Motion Picture Arts and Sciences.*

Hattie cuts the cake at a festive "at–home" party given in celebration of her 1941 marriage to Lloyd Crawford. The 500 guests caused a traffic jam in their Hollywood neighborhood. *Courtesy of the Academy of Motion Picture Arts and Sciences.*

Autographed photo from Hattie to Ruby Goodwin, dated May 4, 1941. Hattie McDaniel and her new husband, Lloyd Crawford, pose together at their wedding celebration. *Courtesy of James Goodwin, son of Ruby Berkley Goodwin, Hattie's lifelong secretary and friend.*

Hattie and her third husband, Lloyd Crawford, to whom she was married from 1941 through 1945. She attributed their divorce to the fact that "He thought because he married me, he shouldn't have to work." *Courtesy of the Academy of Motion Picture Arts and Sciences.*

Hattie sells a war bond at a Los Angeles bank in 1942. She was selected in August of that year by the Hollywood Victory Committee to go to the midwest on a bond selling tour. Hattie told her audiences, "It's not how much can I spare; it's how much have I?" *Courtesy of the Academy of Motion Picture Arts and Sciences.*

Hattie, in Mammy attire, and assisted by soldiers, serves Edward G. Robinson at a World War II USO show in the Hollywood Bowl. *Courtesy of the Hearst Newspaper Collection at the University of Southern California Library.*

The cast of radio "Beulah." Seated are Hugh "Harry" Studebaker, Henry "Donnie" Blair, and Mary Jane "Alice" Croft. Standing are Hattie "Beulah" McDaniel and Ernest "Bill" Whitman. *Courtesy of Marian Morrison Robinson.*

Hattie stands in her Beulah costume with the show's announcer, Marvin Miller.
Courtesy of Marian Morrison Robinson.

Hattie "Beulah" McDaniel poses with her radio and television boyfriend, Ernie "Bill" Whitman, whose shortcomings Beulah constantly forgave. *Courtesy of Marian Morrison Robinson.*

Hattie poses with Clarence Muse sometime during the forties. *Courtesy of the Wisconsin Center for Film and Theater Research.*

Hattie polishes mammy–esque figurine in the living room of her home. The portrait on the mantel is of her father, Henry McDaniel. *Courtesy of James Goodwin.*

Hattie McDaniel and her husband, Lloyd Crawford, at June, 1944 premier of *Since You Went Away*, at the Carthay Circle Theater in Hollywood. *Courtesy of the Wisconsin Center for Film and Theater Research.*

Hattie McDaniel wipes away a tear as she leaves a Los Angeles Superior courtroom December 5, 1950 after winning a default divorce decree from her fourth and last husband, Larry Williams. *Courtesy of AP/World Wide Photos.*

Hattie plays and smiles in her Beulah costume, 1951. *Courtesy of the Billy Rose Theatre Collection at the New York Public Library.*

Police hold back crowds as pallbearers carry Hattie McDaniel's casket from the Los Angeles People's Independent Church of God in Christ, November 1, 1952. *Courtesy of the Hearst Newspaper Collection at the University of Southern California Library.*

book, *Lena,* however, Horne credits Hattie with teaching her several important lessons about survival in Hollywood. Lena said Hattie was "an extremely gracious, intelligent, and gentle lady." Hattie invited Lena to her home, where she gave the younger actress "some perspectives" on the black problems in Hollywood. Hattie was "realistic and had no misconceptions of the role she was allowed to play in the white movie world." The meeting with Hattie "helped tide" Lena "over a very awkward and difficult moment."[31]

Houston ultimately proposed an informal get-together between the NAACP and the black players but it was put on hold, for a variety of reasons, the principal one being that in 1944, White went to the Far East as a war correspondent. Though he denied it to his dying day, and she believed it to her dying day, Hattie accused White of encouraging black soldiers to write condemnatory letters about the movies in which she played.

Platoon Sergeant Terry Francois wrote the NAACP that much could be done to discredit the blacks who continued to take degrading parts. He exclaimed that "Hattie McDaniel, Louise Beavers, Willie Best, and their kind should be relegated to the exact places in our hearts where resides the likeness of Joe Stearns, Eugene Talmadge, and Cotton Ed Smith. . . ."[32]

Corporal James Jackson, another example, complained from New Guinea about "thoughtless individuals of our race" who classed themselves as actors and comedians. He had in mind people like Willie Best, Clarence Muse, Mantan Moreland, and—as much as he hated to admit it—Hattie McDaniel,[33] particularly by Hattie's 1944 picture, *Three Is A Family,* in which she played, the Corporal said, a "laughing lunatic." She forgot her name in the movie, and was referred to by her white employers as "colored Mammy" or "What cha ma call it?"[34] In the mixed audience where *Three Is A Family* played, "The white fellers laughed their heads off, while every man of the Negro race burrowed [sic] his head in shame."[35] Most of the blacks at the movie got up and left, "feeling just as low as a group could after a shameful performance by one of his own race. I never hope to have to undergo such an ordeal again."

Many Australians saw the movie, according to Corporal Jackson. "The Australians are inclined to believe [movies like *Three Is A*

Family] because the motion picture is their only conception of life in the United States."[36]

Even on into the occupation period, the letters kept pouring in. Sergeant Paul W. Byers wrote that Hollywood producers must somehow be convinced of the harm inflicted in stereotyping a race in ridiculous roles.[37] Corporal Robert A. Brown wrote from Honshu, Japan, that "a soldier pulls occupational duty, drills the fields all day, does guard duty, and then when he goes to the movies he sees the old plantation picture with a Negro in it playing the part of a servant or maid and acting crazy." Brown went on to say that the American occupiers were trying to sell the Japanese on democracy, "and they respect the Negro soldier. . . ." But when they saw pictures of blacks playing stereotyped roles, the Japanese might very well conclude that the black in America was as subdued as Japan itself. He said that Hattie and others who played the comical, illiterate roles, lowered the black soldiers' morale, "and make them wish that they were sometimes never even born. . . . I am proud that I am a Negro, but I don't like to see my people act as though they were just in America to take up space."[38]

White saved each of these letters, and dozens more with similar themes. He was confident he could put them to use in his crusade against "Mammyism." He returned to the United States in early 1945, and was eager to take up where he had left off the year before. As for Hattie, the hurt grew with each letter received and publicized by NAACP. She did not deserve this kind of treatment, she felt, because her wartime efforts were many, such as her work with the AWVS, her constant USO tours, and her numerous trips to bond rallies. She suffered what she called "Walter White's indignities" mostly in silence.

She did, however, make at least one response. She wrote to Lt. George V. Byrnes of the 234th Anti-aircraft Batallion, who had asked her to defend herself against charges that her movie roles hurt the war effort by demoralizing black soldiers. Hattie replied that statistics indicated that in real life, 7 percent of American black people belonged to the artistic and professional groups, while the other 93 percent were cooks, butlers, streetsweepers, sharecroppers, porters, maids and washerwomen. Thus, perhaps she could argue that her roles were more "life like" than not.[39]

Byrnes had said that Hattie "grinned inanely" in all of her movies. Hattie asked, "Does the mere fact that a Negro is called upon to smile during the filming of a picture come under your definition of 'grinning inanely?' " Hattie did not know of a single Negro comedian with a deadpan expression, "and I am certain that my broad smile could never be termed an inane grim. Are we to forgo all comedy parts because we are Negroes?"[40] Psychologists, Hattie told the Lieutenant, assert that a sense of humor shows a sound mind.

Why, she asked Byrnes, did he single out black movie stars, whose images fleeted across the screen in just a few moments, and apparently not ask any other blacks—such as himself and his fellow soldiers—if they were doing anything constructive in race relations. His and all the other criticisms hurt the black acting community to the point that some producers in the mid-forties had gone back to a practice in vogue in the mid-twenties; they had become so fearful of black reactions toward black roles that they once again used whites in blackface. Hattie mentioned that Warner's was presently filming *Saratoga Trunk*, whose leading supporting actress was "being played by a white woman in brown makeup." She continued that "one informer tells me that makeup men are busy trying to perfect a makeup that white actresses and actors can use in an effort to offset the misunderstanding caused by using Negroes." Thus, if people like Lt. Byrnes and Walter White had their way, the comic roles would not be done away with at all; only the black actors who had heretofore played them.[41]

Hattie closed her long, impassioned letter to Lt. Byrnes by saying that "you can best fight any existing evil from the inside." She assured him that black actors and actresses were "speaking out against lines and types that we think objectionable, and both directors and producers are cooperative." She asked Lt. Byrnes to circulate her letter among his comrades in the batallion.[42]

Hattie, no doubt with Goodwin's help, had spent herself working on this letter. When it was done, she resumed her practice of trying to ignore all additional letters about her, feeling that she was patriotic, and did not need to apologize to anyone.

Though Walter White disavowed any encouragement on his part for the GIs to write anti-Hattie letters, it is nevertheless true that he made full use of them as he continued his crusade against "Mammyism." His big post-war venture was to establish a "Hollywood Bureau of the NAACP" to serve as a "source of information" in respect to black people in films, to be financed through special donations by members of the NAACP, and chaired by civil rights activist, Arthur Spingarn. (Other members were to be William Hastie, Marshall Field, Edwin and Walter Embree, Langston Hughes, Andrew Weinberger, Bette Davis, John Hammond, Lena Horne, and Buell Gallagher.)[43]

White let it be known that the Bureau wanted to check out the scripts of movies in which blacks would play, to have power to bring pressure on directors and producers to alter or eliminate unacceptable movies from the "new" black viewpoint. Needless to say, the "Hollywood Bureau" caused a storm of controversy. Again, White was accused of "meddling," trying to be the "big man from the east," who "wanted to save all the waifs who had come out west to Hollywood."[44]

White hoped he could strike an ameliorative note with the persons affected by the Hollywood Bureau. In January 1946, the Los Angeles branch of the NAACP sponsored a dinner, and invited "all the Negro movie folks" to attend. It turned out to be an affair to remember, with, as White described it to Wilkins, virtually the entire black community out for the event. The one notable exception was Hattie McDaniel, who would not "break bread"[45] with White because she blamed him for all the hateful letters she had received from GIs in the Far East. Hattie asked Louise Beavers to do the talking for her that night, and she blistered White. Not only was he responsible for the negative mail, he was also prejudiced, she said, against dark-skinned blacks.[46] White himself, Hattie proclaimed, was only one-eighth black, and was not qualified to speak for the race. Moreover, White knew little or nothing about the internal workings of Hollywood. He was simply a spoilsman, according to Hattie, who was willing to ruin any number of careers to have his way.[47]

White did not get off very easily from the other black performers. "Virtually all of them came with hatchets," he explained. "I presented briefly the plan for the Hollywood Bureau, and invited comments. And did they come!"[48] Led by Clarence Muse, the performers agreed that the Hollywood Bureau should be run by committees of actors rather than by people from back east. They struck out at "self-ordained do-gooders," who actually set back black reforms, because they frightened producers into using whites in makeup.

White played to the galleries, his critics charged, and wanted to be sure that the spotlight was on him. One of those attending (probably Louise Beavers) told White that "she was determined to stage a comeback," and that if she "had to play maids or any other kinds of roles," to do it, then that's what she would do.[49] White had "agitated" the black press against the Hollywood black community, and had unfairly ordered the editors of the *NAACP Bulletin,* sent out monthly to 565,000 members, to continually show non-cooperative black actors and actresses in a bad light.

White quipped that, "I laughed at their cracks, some of which were to say slightly less than good taste. . . ."[50] The dinner's saving grace, said White, were Lena Horne, and a young script writer, Carlton Moss, who by their moderate statements of support for the Hollywood Bureau "reflected the new type out here."[51]

White's feelings were ruffled by Hattie's remarks about complexions. It was a shock for him to be accused of such a bias "after working for twenty-eight years against color prejudice." It was apparent to White that Hattie and her colleagues were "going to play up the color line for all it's worth, with the hope of using that as a red herring." He had never been, he said, "quite so disgusted in all my life as I was by the sheer selfishness of some of these people. . . ." They seemed solely to be interested in saving their jobs irrespective of the "effect their actions would have upon the future of Negroes as a whole."[52] The issue of the Hollywood Bureau, White insisted, was bigger than careers for a few individuals. He promised that "if a choice has to be made, the NAACP will fight for the welfare of all Negroes instead of a few."[53]

By and large, the black press supported White. *The Chicago Defender* said that the "West Coast crowd" was so used to playing the menial parts "that they can no longer conceive of getting respectable roles on the screen."[54] Fredi Washington, in *The People's Choice*, lamented Hattie's resurrection of the color differences in the race. This issue was distasteful, and one that was thought dead, said Miss Washington, until the fateful dinner.[55]

The only major black newspaper to criticize the Hollywood Bureau, and White's actions at the dinner, was the *Pittsburgh Courier*. Its columnist, Lily Rowe, said "there is not a Negro artist in Hollywood who isn't a hundred percent for the advancement of his people. They, too, have ideas and ideals and deserve the right to be consulted. . . ."[56]

Two additional events in 1946 delineated the great schism between the black players and the NAACP. The first concerned a resolution that some blacks, led by Joel Fluellen, wanted to push through at a meeting of the Screen Actors Guild, calling for better roles for blacks,[57] which might have had the effect of beating White at his own game, by taking the fight out of his hands. When the resolution was initially presented, Hattie and Louise were among the first to sign, but the resolution did not pass at its first presentation, because it was identified—wrongly so—with "Walter White-ism." The next time the resolution was to be presented, Fluellen could not get Hattie's and Louise's continued cooperation.[58] At the same time as this resolution was to be presented to SAG, there was another one, to the effect that the black actors disassociated themselves from any Communist sympathies. Many people actually began to believe that if they voted against the *status quo* for black actors, they would somehow be identified as a red—in the witch-hunting late forties in the U.S.—and would be totally blacklisted from Hollywood.

White got wind of the proposed SAG resolutions, and wired the acting group for information. SAG's executive secretary, John Dales, Jr., denied that any resolutions had been made by the black actors but did say that a large number of blacks wanted SAG's help in meeting the producers. SAG as a labor union, Dales said, devoted itself exclusively to the economic welfare of its members, and did not become involved in politics.[59]

The other event of 1946 was the American Federation of Radio Announcers (AFRA) convention where Lillian Randolph (of the *Great Gildersleeve*) "pitched a fit" against White and the NAACP for throwing so many black performers out of work. Her tirade "went on and on," reported one witness, as she tried unsuccessfully to filibuster against an AFRA resolution supporting White's position.[60]

Actually, the Hollywood Bureau turned out to be largely moot, as did the SAG and AFRA resolutions, for things would have changed without them. This is not to say that the Bureau had no influence whatever; only that it cannot be credited as the major catalyst in the treatment of blacks in films.

A part of the liberalism produced by World War II was the end of segregation in the armed forces. Once soldiers began to know each other personally, old racial barriers started a slow process of erosion. After the war, television began to compete with radio, and along with the screen industry, increasingly presented shows with themes of social change.

The big studios began to break up in the late forties, giving way to other, smaller companies with new, often liberal ideas. The "star system" which had prevailed for so long began to decline in the face of the new liberalism and the advent of television.

Companies sprang up to make black films for black people, giving black audiences what they wanted in reference to "cop-slapping," and "talking back to whitey."[61] The major film companies, with a new generation of liberal directors such as Stanley Kramer and Carl Foreman, sought to regain this black patronage. They largely succeeded through films that depicted blacks as they had depicted whites (i.e., as covering the entire gamut of human experience rather than being placed into narrow stereotypical roles.) Ralph Ellison said in *Invisible Man*, that the black race was "young," just as though it were just now starting out, and there were many legends to be made.

111

The black image in movies changed with the convergence of new ideas with the developing technology of the day. Out of step with the new image was Hattie's 1946 role of "Aunt Tempey" in Walt Disney's *Song of the South*. It was as if Hattie tempted the fates. Although she had said repeatedly over the past few years that dialect was out of place in modern movies, *Song of the South* negated that premise as Disney resurrected the "Uncle Remus" stories of Joel Chandler Harris. Hattie explained that this dialect had to be used to stay faithful to the picture's purpose.

As early as the summer of 1944, when production of the picture was just beginning, the very words "Uncle Remus" sent shock waves throughout the NAACP dominated black community. Disney, sensing trouble ahead, contacted White for advice on how to handle the black aspects of the movie,[62] but White was too busy to respond fully to Disney's request, but did say his opinions would be forthcoming.[63]

As the release time for the movie neared, in the fall of 1946, Disney announced to a few insiders a "surprise switch" upon which the story was based.[64] It would deal primarily with a white family moving away from a Southern city because they had been ostracized for objecting to the white population's treatment of blacks. Live action consumed about 70 percent of the film, while cartoon sequences (in which B'rer Fox, B'rer Bear, and B'rer Rabbit definitely did talk in black dialect), took up the remaining 30 percent.

In early September, June Blythe of the Chicago based Council on Race Relations wrote to White that she had not yet seen the film, "and therefore do not know just how bad it is." She felt that some effort should be made to protest the film, and she believed the NAACP was the best prepared to lead the way.[65] In mid-November, Disney arranged a special screening of *Song of the South* at the RKO Studios in New York, for numerous black leaders around the country. Those attending included Arthur, Amy, and Hope Spingarn, Lillian Scott, Fredi Washington, Charles Collier, and representatives from the Urban League, and the Council Against Intolerance. Conspicuous by his absence was Walter White, though he had been invited. Gloster B. Current saw the special screening, and described the movie to White. It was an "excellent technical picture," he said, combining the movie media of live action and cartoon. He explained the plot to White, praising the "Uncle Remus" theme that adversity can be triumphed over by the use of brains. The "Uncle Remus" folklore belonged to the entire population, both black and white, and on the whole, Current believed that "it is doubtful that even Negroes throughout the country will find much wrong with the movie. . . ." He did object, however, to the stereotyped "docility, unusual happiness, and witticism interwoven with the motif of satisfaction with slavery." Also, he found the use of dialect to be unsatisfactory. Nevertheless, in the movie, "Uncle Remus," played by James Baskette showed great wisdom and sensitivity in dealing with the young white boy's wishes and emotions.[66]

Hope Spingarn largely echoed Current's opinion about *Song of the South*. She said that black pressure had not stopped Disney from making the film, but it did "put the fear of God into him." Thus, the stereotypes were handled "with kidgloves." She gave her opinion that "the story, while it should never have been filmed," was done in a "most gingerly fashion." Like Current, Hope Spingarn objected to the dialect, but she did believe, along with the Disney people, that James Baskette did a "beautiful job" as "Uncle Remus," and that he deserved an Academy Award for this, his first film part.[67] (He went on to win the award for best supporting actor. Baskette earlier had been known best as the voice of the lawyer on the "Amos 'n Andy" radio show.)

It was as though White never even heard from people like Current and Spingarn, who did at least find some redeeming features in *Song of the South*. He chose instead to listen to Carl Phillips from Brooklyn, who said that the movie was "openly anti-Negro." He believed it was time "that Disney and Hollywood learned what the people think of such movies." A picket line in front of New York's RKO movie palace, he argued, would cause other cinema owners to think twice before they booked the film. If the pickets led to a black boycott of the movie, perhaps this would hurt Hollywood where it was most vulnerable; in its pocketbook, and thus produce the changes the blacks desired.[68]

Though he had not seen the movie, White gave this statement to the press:

"The NAACP recognizes in *Song of the South* a remarkable artistic merit in the music and in the combination of living actors and cartoon techniques. It regrets, however, that in an effort not to offend the South, the production helps to perpetuate a dangerously glorified picture of slavery, making use of the beautiful Uncle Remus folklore."[69]

The major reviews criticized Disney for largely abandoning that which he could do best, the cartoon, in favor of nondescript live action. "Ideologically," reported *Time*, the picture was "certain to land its maker in hot water. . . . 'Uncle Remus' is a character bound to enrage all educated Negroes and a number of damn Yankees," but predicted the movie's success in the South, because it "unabashedly dotes on the 'good old days.' "[70] Bosley Crowther in *The New York Times*, chastised Disney for forgetting that his "art and forte is entirely in fanciful cartoon." Crowther fumed that the master and slave were "so lovingly regarded in Disney's yarn with Negroes bowing and scraping and singing spirituals in the night that one might almost imagine that Abe Lincoln was a mistake."[71]

In her part as Aunt Tempey, Hattie was the large, good-natured cook of the household, and co-confidante, along with Uncle Remus, of all the children on the plantation. She did speak in some dialect. She also sang a song in the movie that became a popular hit with teenagers in the late 1940s. It went, "Sooner or later, you're gonna be comin' around and want my lovin' again!"

Hattie made a public relations tour for the Atlanta premiere in the fall of 1946. Perhaps producers now realized that her presence at these events, even in the deep South, led to larger box offices for their movies. Accompanied by Clarence Muse, she stayed for a day in the Georgia capital, then traveled on to Nashville, Tennessee, where, among other things, they were treated to an exhibition black baseball game, where she was the guest of honor. Hattie's stature was then international, and she was greeted by both blacks and whites for the star she was. Of course, her stance against Walter White and the NAACP made her quite popular with hundreds of black and white Southerners. And, as in the North, it was primarily the educated Southern black who had opposed Hattie for the roles she played in movies.

Indeed, Hattie was so enamored of Tennessee that she said if Denver were not her hometown, then surely Nashville would be. She felt an affinity with Southerners, she said, all the way from dialect (she frequently asserted that both poorly educated white and black Southerners talked very much alike), to diet. Nothing was better, she believed, than Southern cooking done right, including, of course, her "fried chicken à la Maryland."

While Hattie basked in the Southern glory of *Song of the South*, White became increasingly angry, especially when the prestigious *Parents' Magazine* awarded *Song of the South* its Family Film Medal for 1946. He fired a message across town to the magazine's Vanderbilt Avenue offices, that he was "shocked" by the award to a movie which "virtually justifies slavery by picturing it as an idyllic system."[72]

The motion picture editor, Katherine C. Edwards, corrected White's impression that *Song of the South* was set in antebellum times. In fact, it was post Civil-War, and the black people in the film were not slaves, but farm laborers. There was no idyllic master-slave theme in the movie. What *was* idyllic, though, was the "bond of understanding" between old age and childhood, providing a unique happiness for Uncle Remus and the young white boy.[73]

An un-mollified White asked Spingarn and Current to give him some ideas on how to reply to editor Edwards. He told his friends, "I have not seen *Song of the South*, but even not having seen it, I can spot several errors in Mrs. Edwards' reasoning which are typical of the well meaning but un-informed Northerner."[74]

Hattie on the other hand said *Song of the South* was not "subtle propaganda" to maintain the *status quo*. While she expected not to be relegated to the "yassir boss" type of film for the rest of her life, she did at the same time resent "alien" or "outside" influences trying to run her life.[75]

In August 1947, Dr. Stanley Bates, of Rock Island, Illinois, believed the time had come for peace between the NAACP and the black Hollywood community. Surely there was some solution to the problem other than the "constant bickering, innuendoes, and open letters to the press."[76] Bates called Hattie in his self-appointed role as peacemaker, and the result was disastrous. What was intended to be a "friendly chat," turned into a "complete denuncia-tion" of White and the NAACP. Hattie accused White of having the attitude, "I'm going out there to Hollywood and see how those black niggers can live so fine." For the first five months of 1947, Bates told White, Hattie had had only two weeks of movie work, and she "was one of the lucky black performers;"[77] most did not get any employment at all and they blamed their plight on Walter White.

To some extent, they were correct. The continual, unrelenting attacks by White against stereotyping were having some effects by 1948. The Omaha *World-Herald*, for example, said that "financially, the NAACP pressure was almost disastrous for Miss McDaniel." She was going around Hollywood, the paper said, doing her best not to let the word "gwine" accidentally fall from her lips. Whether the crusade against "Mammyism" had led to racial understanding, the paper editorialized, was debatable, "but there is no doubt that it hurt the career of Hattie McDaniel."[78]

There was another reason, though, for black film unemploy-ment in the late forties. The House Un-American Activities Com-mittee (HUAC) began to probe the movie industry to ferret out what it referred to as Communist sympathizers. Walter White, alarmed that primarily those blacks active against stereotyping were singled out for investigation, warned the Committee against such practices.[79] In fact, however, the Committee tended to lump black performers into one category, and not consider them as "stereotyp-ical," or "non-stereotypical." The words and deeds of the activists, therefore, frequently affected the attitude of the Committee, and subsequently Hollywood producers, so that the *entire* black acting community would be affected.

Hattie told Hedda Hopper that she "loathed" Communism and regretted that a "few prominent members" of the race had acquired the red tag. "Because of the publicity they receive," she said, "outsiders may get the idea that many more of us are Com-munists. And that is not good for the race."[80]

Author Lisa Mitchell said, "McCarthyism was hanging heavier in Hollywood than the smog that would follow later. If producers heeded the demands of the protestors on the left [i.e., Walter White and the NAACP] they ran the risk of being ruined by oppressors on the right [i.e., McCarthyism]. So, by stalemate," Hattie found herself on a "black list," which put her and dozens of her fellow performers out of any work for the movies. It was an embittering experience for "Her Haughtiness, Hi-Hat Hattie."[81]

Even while her movie activity was at a minimum, the hate articles continued. One particularly vitriolic piece came from Carl Cain, writing for the *California Eagle*, claiming that Hattie once made a speech where she lauded the intelligence of white people so much that her predominantly black audience threw sticks and stones at her.[82]

Poor Hattie found herself "damned if you do, and damned if you don't." If she played a menial, dialect-speaking servant, she got into trouble with the NAACP; if she didn't, she became the object of scrutiny by HUAC.

Finally, almost in desperation, she contacted State Senator Jack Tenney, who was a member of the California Committee on Un-American Activities. "I have spent my life in entertainment," she told the Senator. During the war, her patriotism was unquestioned, as she went from one base to another, entertaining soldiers and had raised millions of dollars in U.S. war bonds, to say nothing of winning the Academy Award, and "here I am without a job," she plaintively told the Senator.[83]

Tenney had some influence with Hollywood—or at least, that is what Hattie believed. Shortly after her letter to him, she received a telephone call from Universal offering a role in its forthcoming *Family Honeymoon*, from the novel by Homer Croy, starring Claudette Colbert and Fred MacMurray. She played Phyllis the cook, who was a grumpy sourpuss. Hattie told reporters, "It's a mistake to portray rotund persons as always cheerful, gay, and often obsequious," when in real life, sometimes the reverse is true. She welcomed, she said, the realistic approach to her role.[84] On the other hand, she lightly told Hedda Hopper that "maybe I'll get criticized again. But since when has it become a sin to laugh?"[85] It was as though HUAC was watching over one of her shoulders as she made these remarks, and Walter White the other.

Though Hattie did not get star billing in this picture, movie fans still lauded her performance, and let her know that she was endeared to the American public. A part of this endearment could have been caused by her recent radio introduction as "Beulah." (In fact, she made *Family Honeymoon* during a seven-week recess of "The Beulah Show".)

Her other movie role for 1948 was in *Mickey*, as Bertha, the housekeeper, who commuted each day to her work, where she gave advice and counseling on teen-age problems to Mickey (played by Lois Butler). She had to go home every night, she said in this Eagle-Lion production, because she didn't want to leave her children with her husband, "a man."

These two movies, *Mickey* and *Family Honeymoon* brought Hattie, at least for a while, back into the mainstream of Hollywood filmmaking. As long as three years after *Mickey*, Hattie still received congratulatory mail for her part. Pola Grinsfaun, for example, wrote from far-away Rio de Janeiro that *Mickey* was the best movie she'd ever seen.[86]

The White-McDaniel feud tapered off in the late forties. Though she did play in one or two more movies, she increasingly buried herself in her role as radio Beulah. Walter White spent much of his time in 1948 and 1949 in a dialogue with Daryl Zanuck in reference to the movie *Pinky*, adapted from the novel *Quality* by Sid Ricketts Sumner. It was about a mulatto mixing into a white society. The movie, banned in Texas and Ohio,[87] starred Ethel Waters and Jeanne Crain.

Zanuck believed that pro-black movies should be shown in the regions "where injustice and racial prejudice are the strongest." If the public could feel and experience great wrongs via the movies, Zanuck felt they would begin to find solutions to racial problems through the democratic process.[88] White disagreed, saying that this viewpoint was too ideological for the times. Southerners would not correct racist wrongs by seeing them in movies, he pessimistically averred; they would merely be confirmed in long-held beliefs. Pro-black movies, then, according to White, should be shown, at least initially, in areas friendly to black people, and then hope that the process spread into other places.

Assessing the NAACP-black community struggle, as exemplified by the White-McDaniel differences, who was right and who was wrong? And, of course, the answer is "neither," and "both." Apparently, the "old time" Hollywood producers thought that literature in the form of novels, plays, scripts, and short stories, reflected life, and that movies reflected literature. Why should movies with black characters simply avoid the stereotype? Why shouldn't they go forward and deliberately show the worthiness of the black person in America? Definitely, White was within his boundaries when he tried to improve the roles for Hollywood blacks. His work in this respect was the only thing that black actors and actresses saw about the man. They never emphasized the fact that at the same time White had his Hollywood reactions, he was also doing everything he could to stop the worst aspects of racism in its other manifestations, the most detestable of which was the widespread lynching of blacks in the American South. Perhaps it only seemed that his total obsession was with Hollywood, when that was not the case at all. White knew it was the Hollywood producers who had the power of life and death over scripts that came to their attention, and that is why he thought they were the logical sources of change. Perhaps he underestimated the producers' commitment to box-office receipts; he was, in effect, asking them to lead a revolution, but as long as they could not see the cash at the end of the rainbow, their interest was minimal. It was the producers' job to give the movie-going public what it wanted, and this formula very often included stereotypical roles for blacks. White was ideological in trying to change the system; the producers were pragmatic in retaining it.

Unfortunately, White chose not to attack the producers as much as he assaulted the old-time black acting group who played the scripts as handed to them. This regrettable cleavage between White and the black players probably held back reform. The *real* culprit—if "culprit" is the right word—in this entire ordeal, was the producer. But he was the man with the money, and he constantly kept in mind the old American adage that "he who plays the fiddle calls the tune."

For their part, the black players approached the problem with a mixture of idealism and reality. The idealism made them believe that slowly things would improve if they prodded the producers here and there. White, though, was in a hurry, apparently wanting instant gratification. Realistically, Hattie and her colleagues were aware that entrenched systems cannot be changed overnight. The most lasting reform, the black players apparently believed, is reform that comes gradually, one step at a time.

The unhappiest aspect of the whole problem was the personality clash between White and the black community—especially with Hattie McDaniel. This struggle, which led nowhere—except to more struggle—exhausted the energies that could have been spent more profitably against script writers and producers. It was as though the old rule of "divide and conquer" was invoked as the NAACP and the black actors flailed each other.

White's motives were noble, but his means sometimes misplaced. The black actors' objective was to inculcate change and reform, and at the same time hold on to their careers. After all, most of them, like Hattie, had been performing in Hollywood for more than a dozen years—since the early thirties—and they knew best, they believed, how to get improvements in black movie roles. White's and the black players' actions had an accumulative effect, which merged into the liberal thought of the post-World War II era. The combination of liberalism and the advance of technology heralded changes ahead, changes that both Walter White and Hattie McDaniel helped to create.

CHAPTER SEVEN

"Somebody Bawl for Beulah?"

Though Hattie's movie career was on the rocks as the forties drew to a close, she was far from being an unknown in the entertainment world. She was a featured performer, for example, at the Million Dollar Theatre, in Los Angeles, singing with the Erskine Hawkins Orchestra, and showed that she was no "footlight neophyte." Her songs were "put over in a jovial manner, and Hattie seems to enjoy herself fully as much as her audience enjoys Hattie."[1]

Then, on November 24, 1947, radio history was made when Marvin Miller stepped to the microphone on a national CBS hookup, and announced, "Time for "The Beulah Show," starring Hattie McDaniel!" And then, Hattie, nervous about once again being in front of a mike, bellowed out, "Somebody bawl for Beulah?" to the thorough delight of the studio audience,[2] and, as it turned out, to the delight of millions of fans all over the country. The Hooper ratings, an audience sampling system, indicated that "The Beulah Show" was heard each week-night by 7 million people, and before the end of 1948, that number had increased to 15 million.[3] (When "Beulah" first aired, it was once a week for thirty minutes, then nightly for 15 minutes, becoming episodic, hooking millions into staying tuned, causing one critic to grumble that "Beulah" was a comic soap opera.)[4]

Proctor and Gamble sponsored "The Beulah Show," with competition keen for its principal role, including Hattie, Louise Beavers, Ethel Waters, and Lillian Randolph. Though this quartet constantly vied with one another for radio and movie parts, they remained friends. There were times, however, that the competition became so tough that words passed among them, especially from the fierce-tempered Ethel Waters.[5]

The character, Beulah, dated from 1939, when a white man, Marlin Hurt, played her in a program called "Hometown, Unincorporated." Then in 1943, Beulah became a major part of "That's Life." Beulah's next job as radio-writer, John Crosby reported, was to open doors on the "Fibber McGee and Molly" show. Hurt's "perpetually distressed voice" caught national attention, so much so that in 1945, "Beulah" became a separate program, continuing until 1946 when Hurt died.[6] For twelve months after Hurt's death, a nationwide search occurred for a new Beulah, only to come up with another white man, Bob Corley, from Alabama, who said he'd had a "Negro Mammy" who sounded just like Beulah. Sponsored by "Tums for the Tummy," the Corley "Beulah" lasted for only a few months because it lacked the attraction of Hurt's performance.

Producers searched for a new Beulah and through force of habit looked for another white man to play the role. Finally, the idea occurred to one of the program's script writers, Adrian Smith, that since Beulah was a black woman, why not seek a black woman for the part?

"Beulah" was the first sponsored radio program about a major black role.[7] Hattie had been on many radio shows in the past, but when in 1940 David O. Selznick tried to get a program for her in the wake of her *GWTW* popularity, networks and sponsors would not go for it. Seven years later, radio management had changed, helped along considerably by World War II, and Walter White. The American public, the radio moguls believed, was ready for a black star to play a black part. Hattie signed her first "Beulah" contract on October 31, 1947, agreeing to fifteen consecutive weeks of programs. Her salary started at $1,000 a week and rose by incre-

ments to $2,000 weekly, over a seven-year period. She had written
into the contract that she was to speak no dialect,[8] and demanded
and got the right to alter any script that did not, for any reason,
dialect or otherwise, meet with her approval. She told a reporter
that she thought a black playing the starring role in a sponsored
radio program, "even if it seems to be stereotyped here and there,"
was a beginning in the field for younger members of her race.[9]

The NAACP and the Urban League both praised the new
"Beulah" show with Hattie McDaniel.[10] In the past, the two
organizations objected to Beulah played by a white person. They
hailed Proctor and Gamble's decision to award the part to Hattie.
The National Parent-Teacher Association recommended it for family listening, and the Inter-racial Unity Committee awarded it with
a scroll for its contributions to race relations.

Beulah was a pivotal figure in the radio Henderson household.
She could beat Harry Henderson (Hugh Studebaker) and his wife,
Alice (Mary Jane Croft), at radio quiz games, help Donnie Hender-
son (Henry Blair) do his history homework and in fact, solve
everybody's problems but her own. Her boyfriend was Bill Jackson
(Ernest Whitman), who was described as a "swaggering hedonist,
a compilation of all the worthless but loveable Negroes of fiction."[11]
"Love dat Man!" became a popular catch-phrase nationwide, as
Beulah constantly forgave Bill for all his shortcomings, frequently
at the advice of the next door cook, Oriole, played by Ruby
Dandridge. When he came onto the program each night, he'd
proclaim to Beulah, "It's Bill, baby! Big, broad, and breathtaking!"

Before long "Beulahisms" became a part of the national jargon.
Beulah described herself as "a happy gal, who's never sulky; who'd
be twice as happy if she weren't so bulky," a real "standout," and
explained, "no matter which way I stand, too much of me is out."
If anyone asked her if she were ever going to get married, she
replied, "fat chance!" In just about every program, Beulah would
disagree with somebody, and she'd let them know about it by
exclaiming, "On the con-positively-trary!"

Beulah frequently spoke of "industrial typhoons," and defined
a promissory note as "I promise, you note it." The program was
sponsored by Proctor and Gamble's Dreft dishwashing liquid, and

after her introduction each night, Beulah declared, "You ain't lived 'til you've tried washing your dishes with Dreft!" Once when Harry said he should give Beulah a bonus, she asked, "You don't mean in the form of cash, do you Mr. Harry?" Henderson replied, "No Beulah, I don't plan to insult you in the form of money," where-upon Beulah asked, "Well what do you plan to insult me with, Mr. Harry?" Later, when Beulah was alone, she figured out the "bonus." "Well, Beulah, you don't need three guesses to figure out what Mr. Harry's got in mind. Sure looks like you're goin' to have a White Christmas again this year. Another box of handkerchiefs."

Beulah once told Alice about the need for controlling one's weight. She'd have to go through her cookbook, she said, and make some changes. "What kind of changes?" asked Alice. "I'll throw out all the recipes that require food," croaked Beulah. Her boyfriend, Bill, came up with his own solution for dieting. Instead of buying whole wheat bread, get halfwheat bread; instead of buying pum-pernickel, get pumperpenny. Beulah asked Bill how, when he drew his master's bath, he would tell if it were too hot. That was easy, said Bill: "If he screamed." The loveable, ne'er-do-well Bill was also a charter member of the "Order of Mismatched Socks."[12]

In the early "Beulah," the sound effects people had trouble simulating the noise of frying eggs. *Time* reported that "they tried everything . . . from crumpling cellophane to popping corn." At last someone got the bright idea of actually frying eggs and holding the skillet close to the microphone.[13] That did the trick, and caused a parking lot attendant outside the studio to yell at Hattie that "you're the hottest thing around here since hell!"[14]

As the "Beulah" ratings soared, so did Hattie's fan-mail. While it may have been true that black movie viewers did not write very many letters to black stars, this situation certainly did not prevail with radio's Beulah. Hattie received hundreds of letters a day, many of them addressed to "Beulah McDaniel." Most of her fan mail came from whites who said they were glad to see the black family finally getting radio recognition. Maxine Hampton of Dixmoore, Illinois, along with her brother and sister, "adopted" Beulah as their aunt; "We will always love you dearly."[15]

Beulah's letters were full of advice, mostly in the form of the relationship she had with Bill. Many fans requested that a recording be made of Beulah and Bill's conversations.[16] Apparently, no such recordings were ever made, although a "Beulah doll" did hit the market for a short time in 1950.[17]

Gaynell Tipton wrote from Frostburg, Texas, that she named a litter of puppies after the "Beulah" cast. Gaynell said that "Beulah" was the "best and funniest program I ever listened to."[18] Dora Bart of St. Louis said, "Every night at six I just have to listen to Beulah McDaniel."[19]

One fan in Georgia wanted to know if Beulah was white or black. She had a bet with a friend that Beulah was a white woman dressed like a black, and didn't "mean to make Hattie mad" by asking, or at least she didn't think Hattie "would get mad at her listeners."[20]

From San Diego came a letter sentimentally reporting that "I were in bed this morning feeling downhearted and sad, but your picture brought joy to my soul." She cried when she read Hattie's letter to her, and said, "as long as I live, I will always love you and will always listen to your radio show."[21] Beulah Bass of Chicago echoed these sentiments, as she wrote, "Your voice really do make anyone happy that hear it. It sound so real and happy and your laughter is so pure and cheerful."[22] Clara Frison of Tallahassee, Florida, said she'd have to "write a book" to tell Hattie how much she enjoyed "The Beulah Show."[23]

These were the tones of the majority of letters to Hattie in reference to Beulah. As might be imagined, many letters came from people wanting Hattie's help in getting started in show business. One writer even told Hattie how to let her know that Hattie would help her. She wanted Beulah to say at the end of the program, "and now I have a message for that lucky girl from Pittsburgh, W. S. Come on out to Hollywood, darling. You're in!"[24]

Several people asked Hattie for financial help. A woman from Mississippi wrote, telling Hattie about her poverty. She enclosed a card with her letter, for Hattie to check off the amount she intended to send! When Hattie did not respond, the woman wrote back, asking for the return of the card because she "had uses for it elsewhere." Hattie had Ruby send it back, without comment. It was well known that Hattie was a "soft touch" when it came to helping down and outers, and even those who weren't for that matter, but the Mississippi woman carried things too far.[25] In one such case, Hattie sympathized with a young lady from Kansas City, who fell victim to "Hollywood tunesmiths" who promised to write tunes to several lyrics she wrote, but took her money, without producing the music. The woman told Hattie that she had spent most of her money on the "tunesmiths," and was now in economic need. Hattie collected size 13 dresses and other apparel and sent them to the victimized lyricist.[26]

Another young black woman—from Caspar, Wyoming—did not fare so well with Hattie. In a beauty contest the candidates got votes according to the amount of monetary donations they could raise. Hattie rebuked the beauty contestant, saying it was hard work that led a person to success, not donations received, especially for something as frivolous as a beauty contest.[27]

Several letters came from abroad, their writers wanting Beulah to sponsor them for trips to the United States, where they could be auditioned for the movies. Though Hattie regularly wrote back— she had to hire an extra secretary to take care of all her correspondence—she never really held out any encouragement for these people. To have done so would be unrealistic and unkind. In addition to her voluminous correspondence, Hattie sent out Thanksgiving and Christmas cards, 5,000 of them each year.

It was inevitable that poets—some good, some bad—would write to Beulah. Mickey Malone of Victorville, California, called herself the "Shanty Irish Gal," and penned this poem to Hattie:

Dear Hattie McDaniel, I take my pen in hand to say
I enjoy your radio show for its joy to the end of the day.
Now there's one fault with it that I find,
The Beulah Show should have lots more air time.
There's just a good every day human touch in your plays,
Which so many people have gotten away from in these days,
So I want to wish the best to you and yours,
May your life never hold any hard chores.[28]

Another poem, which "scanned" a bit better than Mickey's, was Freddy Johnson's "Beulah Boogie."

Beulah is a lovely, lovely lassie, with a jazzy chassie,
Boy, she's really a pip; Beulah's neat and sweet and
  all reet.
That gal ain't no drip.
Beulah treats me fine, we go out to dine
And brother, that's not all.
Her eyes are blue and they twinkle too; man, she's really
  on the ball.
Beulah likes to dance in the dark and walk in the park
Now who am I to object.
Beulah's not so slim, but shakes a lovely limb,
And she really knows how to neck.
I know I sound sappy, but I'm so darn happy
Because that gal belongs to me.
Beulah's so fine, can't get her off my mind,
That's one gal you really ought to see.[29]

Because of her role as Beulah, Hattie could hardly stop at a traffic light without someone yelling, "Hi Beulah!" and to walk along the street without being asked for autographs dozens of times was impossible; she changed her telephone number every few weeks because some enterprising fan was always finding it out and calling her at all hours. Goodwin wrote a "Hollywood in Bronze" column about Hattie, entitled, "Riding the McDaniel Special," and likened keeping up with Hattie with "riding the tail of a jet plane."[30] Whether speaking to a large audience, emoting before the cameras, or singing a torch song, Hattie was equal to the occasion. It was almost as though Hattie was only now being discovered, after being in Hollywood for nearly twenty years!

Larry Walters wrote in the *Chicago Tribune* that Hattie was "battling the zooming cost of living by way of her radio scripts. She wrings a laugh, as Beulah, out of almost any sort of situation."[31]

The first performer out on the stage was, of course, Hattie herself. Her appearance always brought loud huzzahs and laughter from the audience. After Hattie's "Somebody Bawl for Beulah?" Hugh Studebaker, Mary Jane Croft, Henry Blair, and Ernest Whitman, and the other cast members entered and, script in hand, stood before their respective microphones. If a player had several minutes between speaking his lines, he would back away from the mikes, and sometimes initiate the applause or laughter from the audience.

"The Beulah Show" was a good example of how actors on the stage can interact with their audiences. Though all of the "Beulah" shows were noteworthy for their continuing quality, every now and then a particular performance (such as the one featuring Bill's Order of the Mismatched Socks) would catch on between performers and viewers, and produced a truly memorable occasion. Though there was a prompter on hand for applause and laughter, his services were rarely needed.

Since "Beulah" was performed before an audience, the players dressed for their parts. Hattie's personal maid, Florence Jacobs, designed all of Hattie's costumes. Sometimes Beulah, as Bill said, "put on the dog," and wore a modish Persian lamb ensemble, to the thorough delight of the audience. Most of the time, though, she wore regular street clothes, along with her modest maid's attire.

One thing that endeared "The Beulah Show" to so many millions of people was that the cast members liked and respected each other. Their sincerity for one another was conveyed to the listening audience, and became one of the program's great pluses.

In over three years of steady work on "Beulah" (six 15-week cycles), Hattie did not miss a single program. Only during summer recesses did she take vacations to Wyoming and various parts of Mexico, mostly Tijuana. She did no socializing during the week while she played Beulah. Hattie said about Beulah: "I live the part. I live the role. I feel I really am Beulah. I try to make myself a plain, down to earth servant. Loveable, I mean. I think I'm doing a good job."

Hattie loved to throw week-end parties for the "Beulah" cast and others. Sometimes she'd stay up half the night cooking things herself. Certainly, she could afford to have things cooked for her, but it was the love of the culinary art that made her do it. She baked prune pies, fried chicken, devilled eggs, and prepared summer squash boats, tamale pies, and macaroni delights.

After her guests from the cast ate, they'd dance and sing the evening away. Frequently, Hattie and brother Sam performed, while the onlookers—who sometimes included Bette Davis and Esther Williams—sat on the plush carpeted living room floor, while lavendar incense smouldering on a big tray in the downstairs powder room gave a pleasant smell. In addition to dinner parties, Hattie enjoyed having several people over to her house on Harvard for early morning breakfasts. One guest described his meal at Hattie's house as "succulent slabs of Southern fried ham, scrambled eggs, biscuits, and three steaming cups of coffee."[32]

Everybody, including Hattie, came away from her parties a pound or two heavier. In the early "Beulah" days, Hattie and her dog, a "man-hating" dalmation named Danny, both had to go to Dr. Gaylord Hauser, to be put on his reducing plan. Nevertheless, Hattie always told reporters that she was a "svelte 44." Her weight stayed in the 200 area, give or take a few pounds, with an accent on the give.

Clearly, Hattie's effervescent personality did much for the show's success. Director and producer of "Beulah," Tom McKnight, said that success did not go to Hattie's head. "She is the only star I have ever worked with . . . who, with the measure of success that has come to her, has remained the same. She is just as cooperative and understanding as when we first started on the air. Believe me, this is a rare and priceless attribute."

Mary Jane Croft, who played Alice Henderson, said that everyone on "Beulah" got along, and this was directly credited to Hattie. "It's been three years of good fun."

Hugh Studebaker, "Mr. Harry" on the show, said, "We don't think of race, creed, or color. We're simply good friends." And Beulah's man, Bill, reported that "Hattie is a grand trouper, and it's . . . fun working with her."[33]

If "Beulah" made so many millions of people happy—certified by the NAACP, Urban League, PTA, Inter-racial Council, and a number of localized groups—why then was the radio program suddenly, without any advance warning, banned on Armed Forces

Radio in the Far East? Good question, Hattie thought, as she pondered anew her old problems of censorship. A few months after the Korean war started, a newsman for *The California Eagle,* Milton Smith, visited Korea. When he returned to Los Angeles, he wrote a letter to Major W. N. Tarrance, director of the Armed Forces Radio Services (AFRS) in the Far East, stationed in Tokyo. Smith protested "The Beulah Show," saying that it violated the spirit of the AFRS.[34] He said many black GIs had complained about "Beulah," frequently asking, "when are they going to get rid of that damn program?" On the whole, claimed Smith, the black soldiers regarded the "Beulah" program as humiliating and offensive, leading one of them to say that "If Negroes would quit selling their birthright for a mere pottage, there would be no more 'Beulahs.' "[35] Strange words, these, especially not long after the Inter-racial Unity Committee had presented Proctor and Gamble with a special award for sponsoring "Beulah," "for its promotion of great relations of racial and religious understanding."

Yet, once more came the sickening charges that Hattie was not doing right by her race. They made her angry, and ill.

She had more defenders of her Beulah role than a few years before when she was fighting off Walter White and the NAACP. Reporter S. W. Garlington stated that only one person, Milton Smith, had actually criticized "Beulah." Even when he encouraged protest letters from the black GIs, not many were forthcoming. At home, the program was still at the top, edging out "One Man's Family," and "The Tide Show." Plans were also afoot, said Garlington, to expand Beulah into the newly developing field of television. If "Beulah" was good enough for home consumption, Garlington argued, then she was suitable for our GIs abroad. If that were not true, black leaders would have been protesting for the past three years.[36]

Hattie became the victim of a mean-spirited, sensation seeking, newspaperman. In combination with the naive, gullible Major Tarrance, Smith's agitation worked, at least for awhile, and put Hattie off the air in the Far East. Hattie characteristically wanted to steer clear of this latest controversy, to put herself above such petty doings. The more she thought about it, though, the harder she found it to go to sleep at night. Necessarily, she decided that she would have to defend herself one more time. She took a deep breath, and wrote a letter to Major Tarrance, arguing that "Beulah" had been brought to the Far East *at the request* of black soldiers. "It is true," she said, that "The Beulah Show" was done in a light vein, "but so is 'Lum and Abner,' 'The Judy Canova Show,' 'Fibber McGee and Molly,' and several others," all of them comedies with white casts.

Besides, she said, the "Beulah" cast was a model in friendship and good race relations, and she mentioned the strong support of "Beulah" in all the black organizations around the country. Despite what Smith said, the words "sepia," "darky," and "brown skin" had never been used on "The Beulah Show".

She reminded the Major that a few years back, in the NAACP assault on black movie roles, "Many beautiful young girls who had been used" for choruses and atmosphere, "lost their jobs, and are now elevator and bus girls, getting per week what their daily salaries on a studio set would be." The "reformer" should beware lest he make things worse for the person whose lot he wants to improve.[37] Her letter had a significant impact on Major Tarrance. The first part of his reply to Hattie was defensive: "It is true that Mr. Smith's request was taken into consideration when we discontinued the 'Beulah' broadcasts. But quite coincidentally we were faced at the same time with a problem of discontinuing a 15-minute package show to make way for a locally produced information series. You will understand that since our primary mission is troop education, the local program had top priority."[38]

Major Tarrance found "The Beulah Show" to be "highly entertaining and in no way objectionable," he said, but in view of Smith's accusations, Tarrance "thought it advisable" to take "Beulah" off the air, because it was "offending some of our troops." The more the Major wrote, the more he seemed to realize that he had been duped by a few ill-tempered "crusaders." He had looked further into the matter and discovered that Smith "greatly misrepresented the facts." More black GIs wanted "Beulah" than otherwise.

"It appears that in an honest effort to avoid embarrassment to

131

anyone," the Major wrote to Hattie, "I have unwittingly caused it by allowing myself to be duped by a newspaper man in search of a sensational story." He begged Hattie to accept his apologies, "for permitting this to happen." Major Tarrance rescheduled the program and sent Hattie an AFRS schedule, listing the times for "The Beulah Show."[39] Hattie forgave Tarrance, and in a letter invited him to attend one of the "Beulah" shows, and also to visit the Warner Studios as her guest. Though this episode in Hattie's life and career ended happily, it did take something out of her.

For one thing, Hattie had begun to lose weight. She ascribed this flagging health to a number of things. First was her rigorous radio and film schedule. She "used up an extra share of nervous energy."[40]

The trouble with AFRS, despite its happy outcome, saddened and depressed her. The depression put her off her food, along with her declining health in the early fifties.

She also lost weight because of troubles with her love life. She told a reporter in 1948 that she was not "loathe to get married again." The only requirement was that next time she wanted a man who "amounted to something by hisself, and won't just latch onto me."

Larry Williams was a well-to-do Hollywood interior decorator originally from Michigan, whose business put him into contact with the acting community, and so he was regularly a guest at dinners and other functions sponsored by black actors and actresses. Ethel Waters told a group of her friends that Larry was actually "after her" instead of Hattie, but she would have nothing to do with him. A week or so after Hattie and Larry married, they invited some friends over, and Ethel came. She and a friend toured the house, and found that Larry had completely re-done the interior. All the linen in the bedrooms were labeled "Mr." and "Mrs.," and the bathrooms all decked out in bright pink. Ethel got into a laughing fit, and when she composed herself, said to her friend, "You see, that's why I didn't want that man in my house! I'm glad Hattie got him."[41]

And, definitely, Hattie "got him," in Yuma, Arizona, on June 11, 1949, just one day after her 54th birthday. She telephoned

Louella Parsons, to tell the columnist about her "elopement." She wanted Louella to be the first to know. "I haven't even told the producers of my show yet," Hattie exulted. "What about a honeymoon?" Louella asked. "The honeymoon will just have to wait," Hattie laughed, because of her radio work.[42]

Seven years before, when Hattie married Lloyd Crawford, she said it would "last forever." Now, upon her wedding to Larry Williams, she announced that she would be "Mrs. Hattie Williams" for the rest of her life. The marriage lasted four months.

Even before the couple got back to Los Angeles, they were arguing about money and property. Louella Parsons heard later that Williams wanted to manage Hattie, and he asked her to open a joint checking account. "I'm letting no man handle my bank account," said Hattie to Louella. "I took him right up to a lawyers' office when we got back from Yuma, and he signed a property agreement" against any claims he might have as a surviving spouse. A month into the marriage, according to reports, Hattie and Larry went to a dinner sponsored by the NAACP. At the end of the meal, Hattie asked for a "doggy bag" to take some food to Danny, her dalmatian. Larry allegedly loudly rebuked her for the act. "Here I am," he said in effect, "with a million dollar interior decorating business, and you're a big movie star; yet you want to take scraps to a dog." Hattie finally calmed him down by asserting that multimillionaires take "doggy bags" out of restaurants.[43] Hattie claimed that Williams would never go to her friends' parties, only to big premieres. "He didn't want my people," said Hattie tearfully, and as a result, her friends quit coming to her place, or inviting Hattie to their homes.[44]

Larry was a big spender, but mostly of Hattie's money. Friends reported that he bought expensive suits, shoes, and jewelry, and had the bills—which she dutifully paid—sent to Hattie. In the four months of marriage, Hattie said Williams gave her only $65.00, but always told her, "I won't ask you for money, but if you want to give me some, I won't refuse it."[45] Once Larry wanted Hattie to bankroll a trip for him to Europe. In a rage, Hattie shouted, "Europe? Europe, where? Europe, Pennsylvania? Here's fifty dollars for a Greyhound bus ticket! Take it and go!"[46]

There were rumors that the two actually physically fought and that Williams might be bisexual,[47] which Hattie heard only after she married him. Hattie hinted at this report when she told Louella Parsons that she and Larry broke up because of irreconcilable differences. "I'm only mentioning incompatibility; of course, I could say a lot more."[48]

There were also rumors that Hattie herself was bisexual, brought on apparently by Tallulah Bankhead's public proclamation that "Hattie McDaniel is my best friend!"[49] The statement caused gossips to whisper that there was an affair between Hattie and Tallulah. There is no evidence to support these beliefs, but the rumors continue to this day, the late eighties.

While Hattie was not personally bisexual, she certainly did not condemn homosexuals. In fact, she frequently liked to be in their company. Like blacks who suffered discrimination, bisexuals felt that society treated them unfairly because of sexual practices; Hattie in turn knew from personal experience that society can be prejudiced because of color. Thus victims of discrimination, from whatever source, have second class citizenship in common. This affinity created platonic comradeships. Perhaps these periodic associations with homosexuals made some people believe Hattie was one herself. She was not, but she respected people for what they were; she disdained people who tried to be something they were not.[50]

Williams apparently also tried to create dissensions among the "Beulah" cast. He told Ruby Dandridge (who played Oriole) that "it was a shame the way Hattie tries to run the show," and that Hattie blocked any new talent that might compete with her own.

Because of her marital problems, Hattie couldn't sleep, and she lost her appetite, "and you know," she said, "I'm a real hearty eater." All she could stomach, though, was "a little bit of soup" each day to keep her going. As a result, she lost about twelve pounds in a fortnight.[51]

The worst of it all, though, was that she found it difficult to concentrate on her Beulah lines. She forced her way through the program each day. The world, Monday through Friday, heard "Love dat man!" and the bright repartee of the nightly Beulah, without realizing that the voice they heard came from a person in despair. It was sheer professionalism that kept her going.

In October 1949, almost four months to the date of their marriage, Williams walked out. Hattie said it was incompatibility, "and lots of it," that caused him to do it. She still wanted to remain friends with him, and she said she was in no hurry for a divorce.

And, in fact, for the remainder of 1949, it seemed many times that a reconciliation was in the works. Ruby told everyone that Hattie's friends "were in a tizzy" over the "affaires de heart" of the actress and her husband. Larry escorted Hattie to light opera, and also to a Sigma Gamma Rho sorority formal. They continued to live separately, Hattie still on "Sugar Hill," and Larry in a plush apartment at Manhattan Place. Maybe apart, some of their acquaintances said, they could find the friendship that eluded them when they lived together.

Eventually, however, Williams simply left Hattie and Los Angeles. She was granted a divorce in early December, 1950. In tears as she walked out of the courthouse after winning the decree, trying to dodge reporters and photographers, her only comment to those gathered around was "I've been married enough; I just prefer to forget it."

"I'm not real happy," she had recently confided to a friend. "I guess I never really have been." What with failed marriages, censorship by the Armed Forces Radio Services, and little hints such as dizzy spells and tiredness, that not all was right with her health, it was a wonder that Hattie kept going as long as she did.

As television increasingly made its way into American homes in the early fifties, it was practically inevitable that producers would think of "Beulah" as a TV series. Through the press, "Beulah" fans got wind of a transition to television, and many of them simply assumed that Hattie would take the video role. Some did not like this possibility, preferring to hear Hattie on radio.

One such person was Mrs. A. N. Ferris of Inglewood, California. She told Hattie, "Please don't give up radio for TV. I like radio much better. . . . TV will never kill radio."[52]

For a time, at least, the fan got her wish. At the end of the summer of 1950, ABC Television announced that it had signed

Ethel Waters to the part. Ethel, according to reports, thought of herself as the "female Milton Berle," and believed that her role as TV 'Beulah' would make her "the first lady of television."

Ethel becoming TV 'Beulah' caused a stir among the Hollywood watchers, and it was widely reported that Hattie and Ethel were feuding over the role. Hattie frequently said that Ethel could be "evil" when she wanted to be and Ethel, to be sure, could strike right back at Hattie. Hattie went to see Ethel's Broadway performance in *Member of the Wedding*. After the show, Hattie walked backstage to visit with Ethel. When the attendant would not let Hattie in, Ethel insisted that "I've never heard of Hattie McDaniel." Hattie smiled at the incident, and told a friend, "She's heard of me all right. I'm afraid the Lord's the only one who can handle her!"[53]

Ruby Goodwin's article of August 18, 1950, started out, "There is absolutely nothing to the rumor" that Hattie and Ethel were ill-willed toward each other because of the TV 'Beulah' role. Ruby had shown Hattie a clipping about "the feud," and Hattie replied, "That's a lazy writer's way of filling a column!"[54]

Only if she had been twins, Hattie claimed, could she have added TV 'Beulah' to her repertoire. Then, in sugary-sweet language that must have set Ethel on edge, Hattie said, "My sponsors approached me several months ago about doing both shows, but I had a feeling that I couldn't do justice to both roles, so I decided to stick to radio." And then she really laid it on: "I was well aware of the intention of my sponsors, and in fairness to them I think the public should know that they gave me every consideration." It pleased Hattie mightily that a role she turned down went to Ethel Waters.[55] Hattie said that "Miss Waters is a fine actress, and I feel that Proctor and Gamble made a fine choice in selecting her for TV."[56] Hattie went on to say that this was not the first time that two people had been cast on radio and television. She cited "Life of Riley" as an example.

Ethel ran a tight show on TV "Beulah," but apparently not with the same grace and finesse accomplished by Hattie on the radio counterpart.[57] One of the new players on TV "Beulah" was Thelma "Butterfly" McQueen, who had played "Prissy" in *Gone With the Wind*, and in some subsequent movies with Hattie, such as *Affectionately Yours*. For years, as Butterfly told film historian Jack Mertes, she did not appreciate Hattie, for Hattie had no "book learning." But, then, "after I'd met Miss Ethel Waters," and worked with her on the TV "Beulah" show, Butterfly "could have worshiped the ground on which Hattie walked."[58]

The New York Times assessed the new TV "Beulah." Beulah was a "Southern jewel" who turned out cornbread and greens, and managed the Henderson household. Though it had its amusing moments, it "suffered from a trite story and was regrettably stereotyped in concept."[59]

The first TV episode concerned Mr. Harry bringing a business acquaintance home for dinner. For some reason the two quarreled, and the guest was about to leave until he smelled Beulah's "Mississippi dinner," and so there was a "happy ending." The *Times* said that the dialogue in TV "Beulah" was "hardly original." There were the calculated mistakes in grammar most commonly identified with minstrel shows," and the implication was strong that some cast members "thought of nothing else but the opposite sex."[60]

Both shows stayed high in the ratings. The Nielsens put "Beulah," audio and video, right at the very top in early 1951.

Some cynics pointed out that radio "Beulah" had always been in the top rankings, and the reason why TV "Beulah" shot up so high all of a sudden was the announcement that Ethel Waters was stepping out of the show. Her replacement? The one and only Beulah that really mattered: Hattie McDaniel.

The ABC Television network was not uninfluenced by the letters that came in concerning "Beulah." One from Sherrill Smith of Long Beach, California was fairly typical. He wrote to Hattie that "I saw 'Beulah' on television. Miss Waters is o.k., but she just isn't Beulah. I suppose your studio won't allow you on TV. Maybe later, we pray, dear. . . ."[61]

Ethel cited "pressing commitments" elsewhere upon the completion of her first fifteen week cycle of TV "Beulah." For one thing, the show was filmed at the RKO studios in Hollywood, which kept Ethel fairly well confined to the West Coast for long periods of time. She was interested in Broadway shows and doing other pictures, which necessitated more travel to New York than the "Beulah" filming allowed. Hattie was quite content living in Hollywood. It had been her home for the past twenty years, and she had no real desire to go back East for either stage or movies.[62]

Also, the NAACP had been looking into the TV "Beulah" show, as well as the TV "Amos 'n Andy." The organization feared a revival of stereotyped Negro characterization. Freeman Gosden jumped quickly to his program's defense, saying that "Amos 'n Andy" showed "the Negro in a very good light." Nevertheless, the NAACP warned that if certain changes were not forthcoming, the organization would boycott Blatz beer, the program's sponsor.[63] Hattie defended both radio and TV "Beulah." She said that Beulah was the "type of Negro woman who has worked honestly and proudly to give our nation the Marion Andersons, Roland Hayes, and Ralph Bunches."[64]

Perhaps Ethel's decision to leave TV "Beulah" was spurred by a possibility of yet another clash with the NAACP. She remembered only too well the travails of a few years before, and she did not want to repeat the experience, especially since she had "better things to do."

The decision to star Hattie as the TV "Beulah," while keeping her on the radio, was well received by the listening and viewing public. Terence O'Flaherty, writing for the *San Francisco Chronicle,* said that Hattie had become "ambidexterous." To make sure that "her right hand knows what her left hand doeth," Hattie would film her "Beulah" TV series in the summer of 1951, while radio "Beulah" was in recess until the fall. That way, perhaps, Hattie could keep scripts and characterizations from becoming confused between the two media.[65]

The *Los Angeles Radio and TV Life* hailed Hattie's transition to television. "We favor the move," the journal said. Ethel Waters was "strictly a 'than for which there is none better,'" for delivering a note of song or bringing out the blues in any role. But for the jolly Beulah, it's got to be Hattie."[66] Gertrude Gibson, writer for the Los Angeles *Sentinel,* gave her opinion that "although we have nothing against Waters, or nothing for her either, we sincerely think that Hattie is the one and only Beulah." *Variety* complimented

Hattie for never missing a single performance of radio "Beulah" and predicted similar accomplishments with television.[67]

Hattie brought Ruby Dandridge to play Oriole on TV, upsetting Butterfly McQueen, who had played that part during the Waters period. And Hattie brought her old sidekick, Ernest Whitman, to continue playing her Bill.

Hattie was exceedingly busy throughout the summer of 1951. She turned in her performances for TV "Beulah," and studied scripts submitted to her for radio "Beulah," which would resume the airwaves in the fall. In addition, she sometimes gave live performances at local theatres, where her accompanist was Selika Pettiford, a former student of Ignace Pederowski. Hattie liked to belt out George Gershwin's tunes and, even at this late date, revive "Mammy's Meditations" of *GWTW* vintage. She also enjoyed concerts and light opera, but her incredibly active schedule worked against attendance at such events.

Hattie participated in the summer of 1951 in the fifth annual 'Out Of This World Series," softball game at Gilmore Field, a benefit for the youth welfare organizations in the Los Angeles area. The two teams that paired off against each other were the "Bob Hopefuls," coached, of course, by Bob Hope; and "Cooper's Cutthroats," piloted by Gary Cooper. Included in the lineup were Gordon McRae, Robert Stack, Howard Duff, Tom Harmon, Maureen O'Hara, Celeste Holm, Marilyn Maxwell, Donna Reed, Gayle Robbins, and Lionel Hampton. The "umpires" were Bill Demarest and S. Z. "Cuddles" Sakall.

Hattie, scheduled to be one of the bat girls, thought that if she could get in the lineup and swing the bat a few times, she was confident she could hit a homerun. She'd run her own bases, she said, if she had to, but she much preferred to have Roy Rogers do it for her. He was scheduled to run the bases atop Trigger. Hattie was tentatively scheduled to bat, but she mostly performed as a bat girl, wearing blue pedal pushers and loud, red socks. There was no clear-cut winner of the "Out Of This World Series," but it did raise some $25,000 for needy children. And, of course, everyone had a good time, especially Hattie, who hustled the balls and swung the bats, dancing and singing all the while, to the vast enjoyment of her sizeable audience.[68]

Hattie had finished about six episodes of TV "Beulah" when, on August 18, two weeks before she was scheduled to start taping radio "Beulah" for the upcoming fall season, she was ordered to bed, suffering from exhaustion, and a painful boil under her left arm. She had been slated to be the mistress of ceremonies at a Sigma Gamma Rho function at the Columbia Playhouse in Hollywood. Ernest Whitman had agreed to substitute for Hattie, then he came down with the flu, and could barely talk above a whisper. Hattie's friend and secretary, Ruby Goodwin, took over for her.[69] A week later, Hattie's physician, Dr. Edward Stratton, pronounced Hattie's condition to be "not critical," but "more than serious." The physician at first diagnosed Hattie as having had a stroke; then he believed it might be diabetes. Ultimately, everyone agreed that Hattie had suffered a heart attack.[70]

It became clear that radio "Beulah" would have to be canceled altogether for the upcoming season, and that a replacement on TV "Beulah" would have to be found. (Though Hattie filmed six episodes of TV "Beulah," they were never aired.)

Hattie's replacement on TV "Beulah" was her old friend, Louise Beavers, who kept the part until 1953, turning it over to Lillian Randolph, who played the role until early 1954. Then she quit, and the "Beulah" series was discontinued, except in the memories of countless fans around the world.

Possibly Brazil had the greatest number of Beulah-Hattie fans in a foreign country. Why Brazil? The Brazilians had a racial history not unlike that of the United States. Emancipation in that South American country came only in the late 1870s, some years after slaves in the United States were freed. After liberation, there was roughly the same kind of upward struggle by Brazilian Indians and blacks just as in the United States. There was an affinity between Beulah-Hattie and the minorities in Brazil. Very frequently, the Brazilian fans addressed their letters to "Beulah McDaniel, of Hollywood." In more cases than not, the letters got through.

A reporter for the *California Eagle,* Jessie May Brown, once remarked that there was nothing "ante-bellum" about the "The

Beulah Show." In that one short statement, Miss Brown, perhaps inadvertently, summed up the influence of "Beulah." Going beyond that assessment, Beulah was a modern, non-dialect speaking black American who consistently outshone her employers all the way from economics to intellectualism. Surely, these characterisitics of a black would not have been well received by whites ten, or even five, years before. (They generally had not when Hattie played "uppity" parts in *Alice Adams* and *The Mad Miss Manton*.)

The fact that "Beulah" was "modern" and non-dialectic, was due almost entirely to Hattie McDaniel; she insisted on it. The NAACP and other black pressure groups had little to do with radio "Beulah's" non-stereotypical role. (That producers were still willing to portray stereotypes was clear in the first TV "Beulah," played by Ethel Waters.)

Since "Beulah" was the most popular show on radio, with an estimated 20 million nightly listeners, it seems reasonable to assume that the program had much to do with changing people's minds and attitudes toward blacks in the entertainment business. Hattie in radio "Beulah" did more to build respect and equality for black performers than Walter White's Hollywood Bureau. And this was ironic, in view of White's charges over the years that Hattie degraded her race by playing so many servile roles.

Though Hattie was never seen publicly in the TV "Beulah," her influence on its subsequent development was nevertheless apparent. Beavers and Randolph tended to avoid the stereotype as they played Beulah, because that is precisely what Hattie would have done. The stereotypes continued in many programs that made the transition from radio to television in the early fifties, "Amos 'n Andy" being a prime example. "Beulah," however, was the grand exception.

Once television began to move away from dependence on radio for its programming materials, a definite move occurred from depicting Negroes in false and unfair roles of dialect, shuffles, and other demeaning characterizations. The black pressure groups got most of the credit for these reforms. But those organizations would not have been nearly as successful if it had not been for the pioneering efforts of Hattie McDaniel and radio "Beulah."

The word "Beulah" was used in John Bunyan's *Pilgrim's Pro-*

gress. "Beulah" was a "land of rest," where the sun "shineth both day and night." The pilgrims stayed in "Beulah" until it was time to cross the River of Death and pass into the Celestial City. The peacefulness of the place inspired literary references to "Beulah-land," and people familiar with Bunyan frequently named their daughters "Beulah."

The name is also biblical, from the Old Testament. It is the old Hebraic word which means "married." Isaiah spoke of the land of Israel being "married" to God. Isaiah 62, says to Israel:

> *You shall be a crown of beauty in*
> *The hand of the Lord.*
> *And a royal diadem in*
> *The hand of your God.*
> *You shall no more be termed forsaken*
> *And your land shall no more be termed desolate,*
> *But you shall be called my delight is in her,*
> *And your land married*
> *For the Lord delights in you.*
> *And your land shall be married*
> *For as a young man marries a virgin,*
> *So shall your sons marry you.*
> *And as the bridegroom*
> *Rejoices over the bride*
> *So shall your God*
> *Rejoice over you.*[71]

Hattie had every right to believe that this Old Testament passage applied directly to her Beulah, and that it was a wonderful message of prophecy for her people.

CHAPTER EIGHT

"I've Played Everything But a Harp"

Great successes did little to make Hattie McDaniel happy; the older she got, the greater her disillusionments with life. Unlike many people who find a sense of serenity and accomplishment as they age, just the opposite was true for Hattie. Perhaps she had the feeling that time was her enemy, that the more it passed, the less chance she had for finding happiness.

Her depressions started essentially after her false pregnancy of 1944. Contributing also to her low moods were the incessant criticisms that she hurt her race through playing menial parts, her failed marriages, and success itself. She continued to have a Puritanical thought about success: it was a gift from God, and she always wondered how to repay the bounty. God never told her, at least to her full understanding, and the lack of an answer worried her.

Hattie's public life was jolly, easy-to-laugh, bubbling, enthusiastic, and friendly, and she was called by some reporters, "Sister Full of Love." Her close circle of friends, however, increasingly noted her intense loneliness, and her growing belief that no one really loved her for what she was, but because of what she could give them in money and charge accounts.[1] To the end of her life, Hattie remained a "soft touch"[2] to those she thought down and out, and it was not all that hard for a person to make Hattie believe that he really needed help.

Hattie frequently went on wild spending sprees herself in a sort of manic-depressive manner, as if the purchase of material objects—many of which she enjoyed just for the moment—would somehow offset her restlessness. She was an inveterate collector, and her house on Harvard was filled with mementoes, generally sent to her by fans around the world. She said of her mementoes, "I never played as a child, so now I have collections."

Around Hattie's living room walls were framed, autographed photos of all the stars with whom she had worked in movies. Many of these photos bore personal and "highly valued" messages from the stars; and she was particularly pleased with those from Clark Gable and Leslie Howard, who played Ashley Wilkes in *GWTW.* Hanging over the mantel was the largest photograph, though, of her father, Henry. On the top shelf of a large secretary stood the porcelain statues of a colonial couple, and an immense vase. The center shelf held her precious Oscar, alongside which was displayed a copy of the novel, *Gone With the Wind.* On the bottom shelf three "trumpeting elephants," stood directly in front of one hundred postal stamps commemorating the emancipation of the American black, presented to Hattie in 1940 by Eleanor Roosevelt.

Hattie's life indicated that material things and happiness do not automatically go together. Besides the low morale from failed marriages and criticisms of her roles, there was always an indefinable yearning in Hattie. Even though she received more accolades than otherwise, she seemed from the mid-forties on to doubt her ability both as a person and performer. She told friends that "I don't belong on this earth. I always feel out of place—like a visitor." Her depressions became so bad at times that she'd exclaim, "Hell can't be anything worse than what I'm living through right now."[3]

The very intensity of her life probably produced many of Hattie's problems. Even if she had had a happy marriage and children, in all likelihood her restless nature would have existed. She had an unrequited curiosity about life, which led her to many mental by-roads. Even while she was on top of the acting profession, she frequently did not know what to do with her life. Did she want to become a writer, as she often said, while working on her "memoirs," *Help Yourself,* or did she want to move away from the "wear and tear" of Hollywood, operate a ranch, and open a restaurant featuring "Mammy's Fried Chicken à la Maryland?" Her mental life was a combination of progressivism in which she wanted to move to the heights, and nostalgic repression where she asked herself, "Why should a person from my background have such high ambitions?" There was the old bugaboo that kept reminding Hattie not to forget her upbringing on the one hand, and try for great success on the other. Her mental processes were a collage of ups and downs, with her life caught right in the middle.

After Hattie's divorce from Lloyd Crawford in 1945, she began to see other men. Lt. Booker was one of them, and another was a "tall, handsome, light complexioned" young actor from New Orleans, who lived with Hattie for some time, until she caught on that he was merely using her as a meal-ticket.[4] According to neighbors, a terrible fight occurred one night between Hattie and the actor. He tore her blouse and bloodied her nose. Hattie threw him out that very night, with a neighbor's assistance.

Even so, Hattie soon missed her young actor friend. He had abused her both mentally and physically, but she apparently wanted him back. One night, some time after his departure, the doorbell rang, and Hattie told her company, "I'll bet it's that son of a bitch coming back to beg me to take him in again." When it turned out to be someone else, the look of disappointment on Hattie's face was obvious to everyone in the room.[5]

It was strange the way Hattie seemed to be attracted to men who only wanted to use her money and position for their own advantages. It was obvious that she loved these men—Lloyd Crawford, Larry Williams, and the others—but equally obvious that, perhaps with the exception of Lloyd, they did not reciprocate. Yet, in the late forties and early fifties, she kept "going for" one man after another. She was not a promiscuous woman, but she was indeed sexual. Her affinity to male "deadbeats" could have been a psychological compensation for the guilt feelings she sometimes expressed for her great successes in the world of entertainment. She seemed to have been a fairly happy person until the mid-forties; at that time, her false pregnancy, her divorces, and the charges that she hurt her race by the roles she played began to turn her into a bitter and angry person. Her outlet for these feelings of alienation were in numerous love affairs, some of which ended quite violently.

Once Hattie befriended a young white man, "who practically moved into her house." One night she came home unexpectedly from a rare location shooting, and found him in her bed, with a woman. Of course, Hattie went into a rage and threw both of them out of her house. So angered was she that she poured gasoline all around her home, and tried to set it on fire. One of her neighbors, Bessie Hicks, rushed over, restrained her and took Hattie home with her that night, where the two of them talked until dawn. Hattie was calmed down by that time, and went back to her own residence.[6]

Hattie befriended a young drama student at the University of Southern California, Michael St. John. Dan Dailey introduced Michael to Hattie, and "she and I got on immediately." Hattie suggested that Michael get a room at her friend, Bessie Hicks' place. "She's as fat as I am," Hattie laughed to Michael. "That's why we get along."

(Hattie, while keeping her old circle of friends—Bessie Hicks, Ethel Waters, Lillian Randolph, Wonderful Smith, Ernest Whitmen, *et al.*—lent a helping hand to actors and actresses just starting out. Her house was always open to these young people. She was fond of St. John, and the others, but this fondness certainly did not cause her to exclude her other friends from her life.)

During Hattie's "time of troubles" in the late forties getting movie parts, she became so despondent that she attempted suicide. After losing a role that she really wanted, Hattie telephoned St. John. "She sounded very strange," he recalled. "We only talked briefly, but afterwards I sensed there was something more to her call." St. John ran over to Hattie's house. The lights were out, and there was silence. He kept knocking on the door, and calling out to Hattie, with no response. He remembered that Hattie always left her back door open, so he jumped over the driveway gate and went into the house. He found Hattie dressed in her bathrobe, lying on her bed, and there was an empty sleeping pill bottle on the floor.[7]

"I don't know how," St. John said, "but somehow I didn't panic. I pulled Hattie up and slapped her in the face and made her move—walk—until her eyes were open. I don't know how long I did this, but I do know that I was crying. I was asking why in the hell did she try something like this. I could only see abject sadness in her eyes."[8] The press did not get hold of Hattie's effort to end her life. The event was probably as much a call for help as it was a real suicide attempt. That is why she rang up St. John before she became unconscious.[9]

Hattie apparently made no further suicide attempts, but her friends did begin to keep a closer watch on her than before. She and Michael became the best of friends; she was his teacher, his mentor. She came to rely on him as a confidante, as a person she could trust. Her favorite expression to her young acting friends was "You're full of shit!" telling them, "Just keep your mouth shut, and learn something. You don't know everything." (It was only in her later life that Hattie had learned to "swear." Her strict Baptist upbringing had dictated against drinking, swearing, and raucous behavior. Her years in socially liberal Hollywood, though, had their effects, at least to some degree.)

Some friends reported smells in Hattie's car they thought might have been marijuana. Butterfly McQueen reported that Hattie had taken to carrying a silver flask full of "refreshments, to keep her going;" it contained scotch, and was located somewhere in her cavernous purse.[10]

Hattie's parties became more numerous and larger than in the past, as though they had a compensating value for her inward turmoil. In May 1950, she threw a "party to end all parties" for Eddie "Rochester" Anderson and his wife, who were leaving with the Jack Benny Program for several weeks in Europe. Hattie always liked "Rochester," thinking of him as one of the most under-rated actors in Hollywood. She told Michael and her other young actor friends that if they really wanted to learn comedy, watch "Rochester" in action. He was a "gentle man," she believed, "who has paid his dues in every way you can think."[11] He was a true professional, with a superb sense of timing, all important to being a good comedian. In fact, some radio and TV columnists referred to Hattie as a "female Rochester."

A reporter for *The California Eagle* quipped that "It has been said that when Hattie throws a party, it's a parrrrrty!" About 250 people attended Rochester's party. It started at 4 in the afternoon, and was supposed to have ended at 11. Some guests lingered, though, until the early hours of morning. Another reporter asserted that Rochester's party "could have been a movie set all ready for the director to shoot. The glamor, the lavishness, the gaiety, the trappings were all there, as you've seen them on the screen."[12] On Hattie's well lit patio, guests listened to piano performances of a young virtuoso from Chicago, Leon Kirkpatrick. Often, the entertainment was spontaneous as Monette Moore, Ruby Barbee, and Wonderful Smith gave impromptu performances. In the "rumpus room" a jukebox blared out the hits of the day, and many guests jitterbugged the night away, between frequent visits to the well-stocked chromium bar that Hattie always maintained. Fireplaces blazed merrily in several rooms. On a table in the living room sat a replica of a large, multi-masted ship, and in front of it was an enormous three-tiered cake with the words "bon voyage" emblazoned upon it. Guests strolled throughout the rooms and gardens of Hattie's big house on Harvard. Huge bouquets of fresh flowers were situated around the grounds, with benches for the guests. As the guests kept arriving and departing, a special police force directed traffic. Many in the Los Angeles police department were quite familiar with Hattie's parties: some patrolmen even remembered the big one back in 1941 in honor of her marriage to Lloyd.[13]

All in all, Hattie's party for Rochester was *the* grand event of the year among the black community of Hollywood. Long after the event, the people who were there, spoke of it as *the party*.

Nevertheless, it was not too long after "Rochester's Party" that Hattie slipped back into the moroseness that had marked her life for some months. She decided to sell her thirty-room Harvard house in "Sugar Hill." It was too big for her, now that she was alone again after her divorce from Larry Williams, and she wanted a house all on one floor. There were too many memories attached to the Sugar Hill mansion that she would just as soon forget; if it could all have been "Rochester's Party," everything would have been fine. But life, she considered, was nowhere near "Rochester's Party." Too, she had become fond of quoting Father Divine, a well known black cleric, that "even if you do have a house with eight bedrooms in it, you can only sleep in them one at a time."

Butterfly McQueen said that Hattie wanted to re-buy the first home she owned in Los Angeles, the one on 31st Street.[14] It was not available, so she bought an eight-room "cottage" not far from Harvard, on Country Club Drive. She wanted to calm down, and possibly gain some serenity as she grew older. A small house, she felt, was proper at this stage of her life. All the while she was busy making house transactions, Hattie kept up her "Beulah" schedules, and gave numerous speeches around the area. She addressed the Home Economics Department of the California State Association of Colored Women on the subject of cooking, and was the mistress of ceremonies for several functions sponsored by Sigma Gamma Rho sorority. She also drove on a short vacation into Mexico—with an earlier short show stint in Canada, her only journeys out of the United States.

She fought off rumors in July, 1950, that she and Larry Williams were getting back together. She had been married four times, and was now resigned to staying single. She had begun to believe that no man could love her "for the right reasons,"[15] so she made no further efforts at permanent romantic attachments. She believed she'd be contented now, living in her "bungalow" on Country Club Drive, tending to her mementoes, and playing Beulah.

Those were roughly still her ambitions in August 1951, when she was stricken and had to be taken off both "Beulah" shows (as described in Chapter Seven). Her physician, Dr. Stratton, brought in a diagnostician, Jack Scheinkopf, who judged her malady to be a heart attack.

She received thousands of get well cards, and many visitors, once the doctors permitted them. She always seemed especially pleased to see her old friend, Tom McKnight, producer of "The Beulah Show." Ruby wrote to McKnight shortly after one of his visits, that "it is very important to keep Hattie interested in the things most dear to her. The gift of the plant and your references to her garden certainly achieved this." Ruby went on to tell McKnight of the great outpourings of care and concern around the country for Miss Mac "Mammy" "Beulah" McDaniel.[16]

She remained in Temple Hospital until early October when she went home to Country Club Drive, accompanied by a private nurse, to convalesce for the better part of the next year.

By then her finances had been exhausted enough to lead her to borrow. While a patient at Temple Hospital, Hattie borrowed $1,500 from the City Finance Company of Huntington Park, sending Ruby as 'my girl Friday,' . . . to collect the loan. Hattie expected to get back to work "in a few days,"[17] and she needed the money on a sixty-day note to help pay medical expenses. She also borrowed some funds from her ex-husband, Lloyd Crawford, who had written to Ruby on October 27, from Thermopolis, Wyoming of the "code of the Old West," which caused people "never to let an old friend down in sickness and trouble, in time of need." "Glad to be of some help to Hattie," he wrote to Ruby. "Let's get together and get Hattie up off the floor."[18]

And, as the fall of 1951 turned toward winter, it definitely appeared that Hattie was going to recover. She was on a regular diet and exercise program to keep her heart in proper order. Then one day in early January 1952, Wonderful Smith went to see Hattie, and found her sprawled on the bedroom floor. He at once summoned medical assistance and Hattie's doctor said that she had suffered a light stroke.[19] Again she briefly went to the hospital, but was quickly back at home on the road to recovery. She laughed and joked with all her friends, and told them that soon she would return to the "Beulah" sets. She was in the prime of life, she believed, with dozens of worthy accomplishments to perform in the years ahead. Nevertheless, she went to a Christian Science practitioner (Ruby was a Christian Scientist), Frances Dena, who charged Hattie $300 for her services, which, during this period, January–May, 1952, seemed to restore her. Though she never became a Christian Scientist, she believed that some of Mrs. Dena's practices helped her.

One of the many changes that the illnesses produced in

Hattie's routine was that for the Christmas season of 1951 she did not send out any cards. She worried about the omission, and it took a lot of persuasion from Ruby and others to convince her that her usual Yuletide recipients would much rather see her get well than to receive season's greetings.

On into the spring of 1952, Hattie's recovery was deemed "miraculous" by her admirers. She even taped the first fifteen-week cycle of radio "Beulah" for the next season, opening in the fall. Whenever inquiries were made about her health, Ruby always answered that "if Miss Mac says she's all right, then everything is all right." Everything seemed to be going well for Hattie, except for the recurrence of the boil under her left arm, which had helped to hospitalize her the previous August.

Lloyd, who had moved to Minneapolis, claimed to be much concerned about Hattie, telling Ruby in April that he had been "pondering what to do about Hattie's case for several months." He talked about her "hard sick spell," of August 1951, and believed that if she had come east for a year, as he suggested to her, she would not have had so many health problems. "But she was making big money," Lloyd asserted, "and neglecting her health."[20] "If she stays there [in Hollywood]," Lloyd prophesied, "and doesn't change climates, I look for her to die suddenly inside of a year. A change of climate, food, and water is her only salvation, and soon. I sincerely believe this from the bottom of my heart."[21]

After Hattie's initial improvement, her health once more began to decline, and the truth came out: the boil under her left arm was breast cancer. Many people believed that Hattie had guessed it all along; one reporter charged that Hattie had had the cancer for ten years, and had kept it secret, a not very likely diagnosis. Hattie herself thought her deteriorating condition was caused by physical and mental exhaustion, and primarily if she would now get enough rest and control her diet, she would regain her health.

Upon having the dreaded news confirmed to her, Hattie set about selling all her possessions. The first to go was her house on Country Club Drive, followed by some of her personal effects, the rest to be auctioned off in early 1953.[22]

Ironically, a year or so before Hattie fell ill, she went out to

Woodland Hills to help dedicate the construction of the Motion Picture Country Home and Hospital, where movie personnel could receive treatment for their maladies, and stay for long periods of convalescence. The thought was that if an entertainer were laid up for months on end, he'd probably be content among people from his own profession. Little did Hattie realize that day when she had happily dug out a shovelful of earth, that she would spend her last weeks in the building she was helping to launch. She was the first black ever to enter the Motion Picture Home and Hospital.

Newspapers reported Hattie's going into the Motion Picture Home, but with no mention of cancer, still a "hush-hush" subject. So her public never knew of her numerous radiation treatments, heavy sedations, or her doctors' lack of hope for her survival.

Though no-one talked about it openly, Hattie knew her condition when she entered the hospital. Her friends said that she became placid, calm, even serene, as though a great burden had been lifted from her. There was an air of satisfaction as she received visitors and read some of the thousands of get well cards that poured in.

Ruby, of course, visited Hattie very frequently, taking a bus for the thirty mile journey from Fullerton to Woodland Hills, often accompanied by her younger sister, Frances. As they sat by the bedside and talked with Hattie, Frances combed Hattie's hair, much to Hattie's delight.[23]

Another friend, George Schmiedel, visited Hattie in early September, and found "Miss Mac looking better." She seemed to have eliminated "most of her worries" and had taken on a visage of serenity. She did miss the "adoration and attention" of her public, but she was resigned to staying in the hospital and, hopefully, getting well enough to go home.[24] In fact, Hattie remained "very strong" right up to the end.

Her public was definitely still with her, for in September, radio "Beulah" went back on the air. A Mrs. Leo Davis wrote to Hattie: I listen every night to "Beulah" and get such a kick out of it. I can just see you going through the scenes." She prayed that "God will restore your health soon, so that you may continue the role of Beulah as only you can."[25]

In the middle of September 1952, while Hattie lay critically ill, Chessley Smith, who was the president of the Jolly-Time Popcorn Company of Sioux City, Iowa, cheered Hattie when he told her that according to the Nielsen reports, there were 43,866,120 radio homes in the United States. "And if other American families enjoy your radio show just half as much as mine does, then all 43,866,120, are tuned in to you." As a token of his appreciation for all the happy hours of "wholesome entertainment" that Hattie had given to Smith and his family, he sent her a case of Jolly-Time popcorn.[26]

On into October Hattie grew silent, sleeping much of the time, and mumbling about earlier parts of her life. Her friend George Schmiedel was "heartbroken" because to him it appeared that "Miss Mac is beyond recovery."[27]

During the week of October 20, Hattie's condition deteriorated, and doctors told her grieving friend, Ruby, that the end was near. Hattie seemed already in another world, "talking" to Henry and Susan, and her long departed brother, Otis, or perhaps was again playing "pom pom pullaway" with her childhood friend, Ruth Collamer, or picking johnny jump-ups in the springtime. Finally, on Sunday—a day Hattie had always loved—October 26, in the early morning, she sighed deeply and passed on, only fifty-seven years old.

News spread all over the world about her death. Many black newspapers used the entire front page, with huge headlines, to announce the sad news. Back in Minneapolis, Lloyd was disconsolate, and sent Ruby some money to purchase a crucifix and a big American rose for Hattie's funeral. The rose, Lloyd said, "means my heart bleeds for Hattie, my love. And I will go to church and pray for her. There will never be another Hattie."[28] He told Ruby that he had never ceased to love Hattie. "I cannot bear to bury Hattie. I can't stand it. . . . Hattie and the things I have valued the most are gone. One great lesson I have learned is that material things don't make happiness. . . ."[29] Lloyd had not visited Hattie, he said, "because I couldn't stand to see Hattie sick, and I thought she could come back east and get on her feet. . . . I didn't think death was so near for her." He closed his letter by asking Ruby to put the word "Mizpah" on Hattie's flowers, his word to her, he said, to show his love and fondness for her.[30]

Hundreds of fans wrote to Ruby immediately upon hearing of Hattie's passing, asking to have "some little personal thing" of Hattie's, a book or a handkerchief, for sentimental reasons. One woman wrote asking for "any old thing" out of Hattie's house, "that no-one else wants." (Hattie had named Ruby back in August as her power of attorney.)[31]

Typical of these fan expressions of sympathy was Elaine Mc-Deckner of Erie, Pennsylvania: "Thanks for the good times you gave to us the past six years. I'm sorry that Hattie died on Sunday. Even though I knew she was sick, it was a loss to me. I'll listen to you until you leave the air."[32] An anonymous postcard writer from Washington, D.C., was glad that the "Beulah" program had been recorded so far in advance. "I'm like most people; I think of her as Beulah, but of course, she was Hattie McDaniel."

Sadness frequently inspires poetry, and many of Hattie's fans vented their emotions through verse. Lucille Frazer of Chicago, sent this poem, " 'The Life Ahead;' In Memory of a Friend, Hattie McDaniel."

> *One thing that I regret to do*
> *Is read this poem of friendship over you.*
> *You were so very nice and kind,*
> *I will always remember you in my mind.*
> *You were a friend in time of sickness*
> *You were a friend in time of woe,*
> *All anyone had to do was just let you know.*[33]

Mickey Malone from Victorville, the "shanty Irish girl," had written numerous poems to Beulah in the past; now she wrote a final one to Hattie:

> *Dear friends, be not sad on this day*
> *Think not that our darling Hattie has gone away*
> *Nor will we ever be alone*
> *Through this life's ages*

154

For our darling Hattie
Will forever live in our heart's pages.
. . . Sweet sleep, Hattie.[34]

Ruby's brother, Charles Berkley, who had also known Hattie for a number of years, wrote this sonnet to her:

Laugh, yes laugh at life
And when it's over, it's over.
Laugh, yes laugh, and life's a bed of clover.
To take it seriously is only the role of a fool,
To live it beautifully is the way to play it cool.
To die is the only thing to do.
When it's over, it's over.
Play; yes, play in life.
Then there's never left regret
A fine thing's a part of one
The little things that brighten the sun.
Yes, play, for when it's over, it's over.
Give; yes give in life and the world
will remember you
Give; yes give and life will give to you too.
When it's over, it's over,
'Cause it's over and that's all we want
When it's through.[35]

Hattie's colleague and friend, Leigh Whipper, was the President of the Negro Actor's Guild, a benevolent association rather than a union. On October 23, he sent a check to Hattie for one month's supply of flowers. "We believe in giving flowers to the living," he told her. For the next nine months, Whipper added, Hattie would receive a check for flowers.[36]

Alas, instead of any more checks, the Guild was obliged the very next week to pass a resolution to Hattie's memory. It said in part, "we pray that God in His great understanding will keep at rest the kindly, understanding soul of Hattie McDaniel."[37] The Los Angeles city council also adapted a memorial resolution, introduced by councilman Kenneth Hahn on October 30, adjourned for the day in respect for Hattie, and sent a copy of the resolution to Sam.[38] The council was "deeply sorry" to hear of Hattie's passing, it said, recounting Hattie's wartime activities in the AWVS, and visiting army camps and naval stations to entertain America's fighting men, for which she had been cited by both President Roosevelt and Colorado Governor Ralph Carr.[39]

Inevitably, some people did not hear of Hattie's death. She received an invitation to attend a testimonial dinner in New York at the Waldorf-Astoria on November 13. The occasion was the 79th birthday of blues great W. C. Handy. If Hattie had been alive and well, she would have relished the thought of attending.

A young housewife from Roanoke, Indiana, wrote in early December, asking Hattie's financial help. Twenty-two years old, with "no-one to turn to," she decided to write to Hattie since Hattie "seemed such a sweet person on radio." The woman's husband was sick, she said, and they had a small son. "Our Christmas is not going to be white unless we can have a little bit of help," she wrote, asking Hattie for a photo and a check. Undoubt-edly, if Hattie had been alive, she would have accommodated the woman, for it was this very kind of hard luck story that had always touched her in the past.[40]

Hattie's funeral was on November 1, 1952. It was at once simple and magnificent, and it could very well have been the last scene from the movie, *Imitation of Life*. The procession was com-posed of 125 limousines, and it took two dozen large vans from the Angelus Funeral Home to bring the tons of flowers sent by Clark Gable, Claudette Colbert, Walt Disney, Eddie, "Rochester," Anderson, Ralph Edwards, and others. The rostrum and choir loft "were transformed" into a "multi-colored garden of radiant blos-soms."

The funeral started at 1 p.m. at her church for years, the People's Independent Church of God in Christ at 18th and Poloma, with the Reverend Clayton D. Russell officiating. The church's auditorium had a 1,000 seating capacity, and 5,000 people showed up for the funeral, some forming lines as early as twelve hours in advance. Uniformed policemen and motorcycle patrolmen found it difficult, and then impossible, to direct traffic in the church's vicinity. Finally, it was necessary to cut off the church completely within an area of four blocks, and detour the traffic.

Policemen also stood in the doorways inside the church and as gently as possible kept the great throngs of people from crushing in. The masses asserted that they were Hattie's friends just as much as those who had been invited, and they had a right to pay their respects. It was ironic that at her death, the love she had always wanted, and felt lacking in her life, came with such great force and intensity. It would have thrilled Hattie to see all the outpourings of affection for her.[41]

The Reverend Russell said that "it was typical of our beloved Hattie that her good works were spread upon the face of the earth." The main eulogy, entitled "Goodbye Hattie McDaniel," was delivered by veteran actor, and long-time president of the Screen Actors Guild, Edward Arnold, introduced by Louise Beavers. In his deeply resonant voice, he reviewed Hattie's life over the years, and emphasized the prominent part she took helping to entertain troops and sell bonds during World War II. Jovial good humor was Hattie's trademark, he said, for millions around the world. "All of us say," he concluded, "let your soul rest in peace. You are now resting in His arms." Sigma Gamma Rho, with Grand Besilius, Sallie Edwards in charge, provided ushering service, with the Jester Hairston Choir as a musical background to the proceedings.

Hattie's old friend—and sometimes rival for movie parts—Lillian Randolph, in rich contralto tones, gave a touching rendition of "I've Done My Work." Hattie and Lillian had always teased each other about their lives and careers. Hattie once told Lillian that she hoped to die before Lillian, because if Lillian went first and Hattie found out where she'd gone, Hattie wanted to make a detour. Lillian always answered such jibes by laughing, and telling Hattie that "I'll sing at your funeral." Now that she was actually doing it, she found it difficult; several times she had to stop and compose herself before continuing with the song. A young performer, Arthur Lee Simpkins, also sang at Hattie's funeral, "Oh Dry Those Tears." In another part of the rites, Ruby read a few lines from Hattie's favorite poet, Paul Lawrence Dunbar:

When all is done
Say not my day is o'er
And that through night
I seek a dimmer shore.
Say rather that my morn
has just begun
I greet the dawn
And not a setting sun
When all is done.

When the obsequies were finished, the pallbearers carried the green and silver casket outside, and police again had to hold back the crowds of admirers, many of whom were in tears, and wanted only to touch her casket. (The pallbearers were L. Z. Cooper, Kenneth Levy, Elmer Fain, Alton Redd, Paul Howard, and W. B. Whitman. Among the honorary pallbearers were Kenneth Hahn, Louise Beavers, Ernest Whitman, Sallie Edwards, Harold Browning, George Bryant, H. J. Paine, B. B. Irving, Lillian Randolph, Tom McKnight, Clarence Muse, Ruby Dandridge, Fay Allen, Danny Hart, and Wonderful Smith.)

The procession from the church to the cemetery was one of the largest Los Angeles had ever seen. Thousands of people lined the roadways and sidewalks to watch the hearse go by. Automobiles meeting the procession pulled off to the side of the road and stopped to show their respects. Many more now than the original 125 cars joined the journey to Hattie's final resting place.

A weeping Sam followed the casket, and at the Rosedale Cemetery, he sprinkled some fresh earth on it and said goodbye. At the interment, the Reverend H. Mansfield Collins of the Neighborhood Community Church, pointed out that Hattie was buried at the gates, "where all who pass will see her name, and where she will always be an inspiration to the young of our race, for whom she did so much."

When it became known that Hattie was to be buried in Rosedale, a number of white people in Los Angeles raised objections. They said that Rosedale was and always had been a *white* cemetery. Their objections were both overcome and ignored, and

Hattie became the first black to be buried in Rosedale Cemetery. In death as in life, Hattie McDaniel was *first*.

A few years before her death, while working on the set of *Mickey*, Hattie joked that her epitaph should be, "I've Played Everything but a Harp."[42] Her many friends on November 1, 1952, would have agreed that now indeed she was playing a harp. The quip well summed up her incredibly busy life.

When Hattie's will, dated December 10, 1951, was probated by Judge Newcomb Condee, her estate had been eroded by medical costs to less than $10,000.[43] The bulk of Hattie's modest estate was left to her brother, Sam, and his wife, Lulu, in a trust which provided them with $75.00 weekly, for as long as the money lasted. To her most immediate former husband, Larry Williams, Hattie gave $1.00. (There was no word from Williams during Hattie's illnesses.) Hattie's Oscar went to Howard University, and her papers to Ruby, who was planning to write Hattie's biography. (She never did; Ruby died in 1961.) Hattie's dalmatian, Danny, went to Sam, and various items of jewelry to her nephew, Edgar Goff, Etta's son. A niece, Marion Mumphrey, daughter of Orlena, was also listed in the immediate family. (Today, two great-nephews apparently comprise all that is left of the McDaniel clan. They are Elzi Emmanuel, grandson of Orlena, and Edgar Goff, grandson of Etta, both in the Los Angeles area.)

All through Hattie's long illness and subsequent death, the one person who was "the rock" was Ruby Berkley Goodwin, Hattie's beloved friend and guardian for almost two decades. There were even times while Hattie was ill that she could not pay Ruby. Never mind, said Ruby, some things are more important than money; the accounts of friends are settled in the heart.

A few weeks after Hattie's death, Ruby dedicated one of her "Hollywood in Bronze" articles to her.

"It may seem strange to many people who knew of my close association with Hattie McDaniel when I say that I have never shed one tear over her passing," she wrote. "There has never been any feeling of sadness at what most newspaper headlines had to say about death stilling her voice. To me, Hattie is as alive as she ever has been. True, I cannot see her, but her voice certainly isn't stilled, for every week day at 4 o'clock, I have but to turn my dial to KNX and there her voice is, jovial and booming as ever. It will be impossible to live in the shadow of such a vibrant personality. . . . and think that such a nebulous thing as the stopping of a heart beat could suddenly annihilate anything or anyone as indestructible as Hattie McDaniel."

Ruby went on to tell how she first met Hattie, on the set of *Showboat*, and spoke of her winning the Academy Award for *GWTW*. She mentioned Hattie's troubles over the type roles she played, asserting that Hattie periodically thought about early retirement because of all the criticisms. "She was the bravest woman I have ever known," said Ruby admiringly. "She never voiced bitterness that she had been struck down at the height of her career. But she was always hopeful about getting up and resuming her show ["Beulah"]."

"I believe every faith in the country prayed for her," explained Ruby. Old people at Jewish homes for the aged wrote while Hattie was ill, and said they were offering special prayers. Catholic friends told of burning candles for her, and Protestant churches remembered her in their services and broadcasts. "Miss Mac" was universally loved, and her life and career transcended political and religious boundaries. Throughout her illness, Ruby reported, Hattie never once mentioned the dread disease that caused her death. She kept assuring friends that "I'll be all right; I'll soon be up and back into harness."

"I cannot think that death has stilled her voice. For her I see death as a liberator, releasing the body and spirit of a dauntless personality. I am proud that I knew this brave woman, and I am honored that she called me 'friend.' "[44]

As time has passed, Hattie's roles, particularly as Mammy have grown in importance in the minds of the movie going public. For example, in 1967, the Rivoli Theatre in New York sponsored a week's screening of *Gone With the Wind*. The Harlem Citizens for Community Action, headed by the Reverend A. Kendall Smith, forced the manager to put Hattie's name on the marquee, along with Clark Gable, Vivien Leigh, Leslie Howard, and Olivia de Havilland. Perhaps the duress on this occasion caused spectators to show increased attention to Hattie's artistry, for in subsequent showings all over the country, Hattie was afforded star billing.[45] As the fiftieth anniversary of the movie approaches (1989), Hattie's stature will no doubt be increasingly vitalized.

Beyond being a wonderful movie star, Hattie was also a grand person. In her best form she could thrill and delight, not for her own self-aggrandizement, but to make people around her feel important. Making others realize their own value and significance is no small accomplishment. Perhaps that trait was the most important legacy Hattie McDaniel left to the world.

Epilogue

After winning her Oscar in 1940, one of Hattie McDaniel's acquaintances said to her, "Hattie, you're getting too prominent to continue mingling with the common people. You'd better begin eliminating them." Hattie looked him squarely in the face, and answered, "That's a good idea. I'll start right now by eliminating you." Then she walked away from him. The story illustrates an important point about Hattie. She met everyone, high and low, black and white, on a basis of equality. This was simply her natural way; she was automatically a friend to everyone she met. This trait had been ingrained into her from earliest childhood.

It was this naturalness that helped her to contribute greatly in her day, and beyond, to racial pride and equality. She was not a "deliberate" reformer; most of the time she did not even realize that her work, especially as radio Beulah, was so important in reform. She was a gradualist, "inadvertent," reformer, and she accomplished more in this capacity than many of those who had set out specifically to change the system.

Walter White and the NAACP were the insistent advocates of this point of view, and it sometimes appeared that White's credo became "If you are not for me, you are against me." That stance was unacceptable to Hattie and her friends, who felt that gentle, good-willed pressures and a willingness to compromise went further than direct confrontation. Opening doors for young black entertainers, and by extension, young blacks from all walks of life, was as significant in Hattie's opinion as boycotting an "unacceptable" movie. Her way was not as quick or dramatic as others, but she believed it would have a lasting impact.

Hattie was the product of her age as her career overlapped the technological achievements of radio and the movies. The airwaves made her reputation.

When she began her radio-movie career, there was no such thing as a civil rights movement. When her radio-movie career ended, the civil rights revolution was just around the corner. Hattie's fight against restrictive covenants, and her straight playing of radio Beulah influenced that revolution more than she or anyone around her realized. She influenced the civil rights movement by proving to listeners that a black person could have a comedy role without degradation. She showed the "new role" of which the Negro had always been capable. She was able to instill a mood of rising expectations in young blacks on their way up in the entertainment and business worlds. It is usually when people *see* the possibilities of upward mobility that they begin to remove the obstacles in their way. Hattie showed that it could be done, and her example certainly was not ignored by the generations that followed.

Hattie's life and career reflected her dream of progress within a nationalistic setting. Her dreams came together with the oft-repeated, but only spasmodically fulfilled ideal that in America a person, regardless of race, color, or national origin, is free to go as far as his talent will take him. She gave hope, comfort, and inspiration to her people, especially those with singing and acting abilities, and made them think that "If Hattie can do it, so can I."

It is a well known "law" of reform that a change in one area of society is likely to produce changes elsewhere. If non-stereotypical roles, which Hattie helped to procure, became standard fare for black players in television and movies in the early fifties, could one reasonably expect that their process would stop right there? No. The process had great influence on the thinking that led to events like *Brown v The Topeka Board of Education,* and to the sit-ins of the sixties that ultimately broke one racial barrier after another. Far then from degrading her race, as Walter White and others frequently charged, Hattie cracked open a few doors that had been tightly shut before.

The real dream, though, is that there are probably some more "Hattie McDaniels" in this world even today, smiling, singing, dancing, acting, and just waiting for someone to pay serious attention to them. To all those talents, Hattie would add one word: sincerity. And that now they will be judged on their talent, not the color of their skin. If so, Hattie McDaniel had a great deal to do with it. Her legacy lives on.

Chronology

June 10, 1895: Born, Wichita, Kansas; 13th child of Henry and Susan (Holbert) McDaniel.

1900–1901: Moved with her family to Colorado; first to Ft. Collins and then to Denver. Was a student at Franklin School in Ft. Collins and at 24th Street and East High in Denver.

1910: At age fifteen, won a gold medal from Women's Christian Temperance Union, for reciting "Convict Joe." Decides on an entertainment career.

1911: Left high school for the theatre.

1911–1916: On the road, with father Henry and brother Otis. Played entire Colorado circuit.

1916–1920: Traveled with various performing groups to West Coast, and short stints into Canada.

1922: Married George Langford and was widowed shortly thereafter.

1920–1925: Associated with Professor George Morrison's "Melody Hounds." Sang on Denver radio station, KOA.

1924–1929: Played on Orpheum, Pantages, TOBA, Shriner, Elks circuits. In road production of *Showboat* when depression struck.

1929–1931: In Milwaukee, at Sam Pick's Club Madrid, first as ladies' room attendant; then as featured vocalist.

1931: Moved to Hollywood, California. Took bit parts in movies; "Hi-Hat Hattie" on KNX radio program, "Optimistic Do-Nuts." (See pp. 20–21.)

1932: Acted in first major picture, *The Golden West*.

1932–1938: Played in several movies, usually as a household maid or cook.

1938: Married and divorced Howard Hickman.

1939: Played in movie, *Gone With the Wind*.

1940: Became the first black person ever to win an Academy Award. She won Oscar for being the Best Supporting Actress in *Gone With the Wind*.

1941: Married James Lloyd Crawford.

1941–1945: Continued to play maid-cooks, also sang in movies, including *The Great Lie* and *Since You Went Away*.

1945: Along with about fifty other blacks on Sugar Hill, a racially changing neighborhood in Los Angeles, won a restrictive covenant case. Divorced from Lloyd Crawford.

1946: Played Aunt Tempey in *Song of the South*.

1946–1948: Involved in numerous controversies with Walter White and the NAACP.

1947: Began the comedy series "Beulah," on CBS radio.

1948: Made a comeback in the movies with *Family Honeymoon*.

1949: Married Larry Williams.

1950: Divorced Larry Williams.

1950: Television "Beulah," ABC Network.

1951: Became ill; canceled both radio and TV "Beulah" shows.

October 26, 1952: Died at Motion Picture Country Home and Hospital, Woodland Hills, California. Buried at Rosedale Cemetery.

Filmography

Altogether, Hattie played in some 300 movies. Most of these were very short, unattributed performances. It was not until after her Academy Award performance that she automatically got screen credit for pictures in which she played. The following is a partial listing. The studio and the director are listed with the films.

1932

The Golden West, Fox; David Howard.

The Blonde Venus, Paramount Publix; Josef von Sternberg.

Hypnotized, Winter Garden; Mack Sennett.

Washington Masquerade, MGM; Charles Brahin.

1933

The Story of Temple Drake, Paramount; Stephen Roberts.

I'm No Angel, Paramount; Wesley Ruggles.

1934

Judge Priest, Fox; John Ford.

Operator Thirteen, MGM; Richard Boleslavsky.

Lost in the Stratosphere, Monogram; Melville Brown.

Babbitt, RKO; William Keighley.

Little Men, Mascot Production; Phil Rosen.

Appeared in some Charley Chase film shorts.

1935

Music is Magic, Fox; George Marshall.

Another Face, RKO; Christy Cabanne.

Alice Adams, RKO; George Stevens.

China Seas, MGM; Tay Garnett.

Traveling Saleslady, First National; Ray Enright.

The Little Colonel, Fox; David Butler.

Our Gang Shorts.

1936

Showboat, Universal; James Whale.

The First Baby, Fox; Lewis Seiler.

Hearts Divided, Warner; Frank Borzage.

High Tension, Fox; Allan Dwan.

Star for a Night, Fox; Lewis Seiler.

Postal Inspector, Universal; Otto Brower.

The Bride Walks Out, RKO; Leigh Jason.

Valiant is the Word for Carrie, Paramount; Wesley Ruggles.

Can This Be Dixie?, Fox; George Marshall.

Gentle Julia, Fox; John Blystone.

Next Time We Love, Universal; Edward H. Griffith.

Libeled Lady, MGM; Jack Conway.

The Singing Kid, Warner; William Keighley.

Reunion, Fox; Norman Taurog.

1937

Racing Lady, RKO; Wallace Fox.

Don't Tell the Wife, RKO; Christy Cabanne.

The Crime Nobody Saw, Paramount; Charles Barton.

True Confession, Paramount; Wesley Ruggles.

Over the Goal, Warner; Noel Smith.

45 Fathers, Fox; James Tinling.

Nothing Sacred, United Artists; William Wellman.

Saratoga, MGM; Jack Conway.

The Wildcatter, Universal; Lewis D. Collins.

1938

Battle of Broadway, Fox; George Marshall.

The Shining Hour, MGM; Frank Borzage.

The Mad Miss Manton, RKO; Leigh Jason.

Carefree, RKO; Mark Sandrich.

The Shopworn Angel, MGM; H. C. Potter.

Everybody's Baby, Fox; Malcolm St. Clair.

1939

Zenobia, Hal Roach; Gordon Douglas.

Gone With the Wind, MGM; Victor Fleming.

1940

Maryland, Fox; Henry King.

1941

Affectionately Yours, Warner; Lloyd Bacon.

The Great Lie, Warner; Edmund Goulding.

They Died With Their Boots On, Warner; Raoul Walsh.

1942

The Male Animal, Warner; Elliott Nugent.
In This Our Life, Warner; John Huston.
George Washington Slept Here, Warner; William Keighley.

1943

Thank Your Lucky Stars, Warner; David Butler.
Johnny Come Lately, United Artists; William K. Howard.

1944

Since You Went Away, United Artists; John Cromwell.
Three is a Family, United Artists; Edward Ludwig.
Janie, Warner; Michael Curtiz.
Hi Beautiful, Universal; Leslie Goodwin.

1946

Margie, Fox; Henry King.
Never Say Goodbye, Warner; James V. Kern.
Janie Gets Married, Warner; Vincent Sherman.
Song of the South, Walt Disney.

1947

The Flame, Republic; John H. Auer.

1948

Mickey, Eagle-Lion; Ralph Murphey.
Family Honeymoon, Universal-International; Claude Binyon.

Radio Appearances

1931: "Optimistic Do-Nuts," KNX, Los Angeles.

1932–33: "NBC Musical Series," NBC Network.

1940: "Wings Over Jordan," WGAR; Cleveland, Ohio.

1941: "Rudy Vallee Show," Eddie Cantor's *Time to Smile*, NBC Network.

1943: "Blueberry Hill," CBS Network.

1944: "Billie Burke Show," CBS Network.

1945: "Amos 'n Andy Show," NBC Network.

1947: "The Beulah Show," CBS Network.

1948: "Bing Crosby's Philco Radio Time," WJZ, New York; ABC Network.

Favorite Recipes

Due to the fact that Hattie McDaniel played so many cooks in motion pictures, radio, and television, she received many requests for her recipes through the years. Several of her favorites follow.

Roast Turkey

In preparing roast turkey, Hattie rubbed butter all over it before cooking. This action, she said, gave it a "wonderful flavor." She placed her turkey on slices of salt pork, laid in the bottom of the dripping pan. She then rubbed the turkey with salt, sprinkled with pepper, and dredged with flour. She recommended three and a half hours of cooking at 450 degrees for a ten pound turkey. Anything faster than that would make it too dry.

Of course, all good turkeys need dressing, and here was Hattie's, a fairly conventional method:

Remove the crust from two small baker's loaves. Slice and pack with dripping bits. Season with two and a half teaspoons of salt, one half teaspoon of powdered sage, and one medium sized onion, chopped fine. Mix well, using two forks, and two cups of cornbread.

Melt two thirds of a cup of butter in three fourths of a cup of boiling water, and add to the first mixture. Toss lightly with two forks. Add two eggs, slightly beaten, mix well, and fill the body and breast of the turkey. If crumbly stuffing is desired, omit eggs.

Hattie noted that "I make my cornbread for my dressing like I make for the table, only not as rich."

Dumplings

Ingredients include two cups of flour, four teaspoons of baking powder, one half teaspoon of salt, one teaspoon of favorite shortening, and three fourths of a cup of water. Sift the flour twice. Mix flour, baking powder and salt. Rub in shortening with finger. Add water gradually, mixing with knife. Put in drippings from the cooking turkey or chicken. Cook until done.

Mammy's Icebox Cake

Hattie said, while writing this recipe, "Nowadays, with the new frigidaires, when you want to feel a little bit extravagant, here is a recipe for icebox cake."

Ingredients include one half pound of butter, one pound of powdered sugar, six eggs, one teaspoon of vanilla, one pound of graham crackers, one half pint of whipping cream, one cup of pecans.

Cream butter and add powdered sugar a little at a time. Separate yolks of eggs from the whites, and add yolks one at a time. Mix thoroughly after each egg yolk is added. Fold in beaten whites. Add vanilla. Whip the cream and add. Mix in the pecans. Crumb the graham crackers. Roll fine with a rolling pin. Take a loaf cake pan. Take wax paper and fit in pan neatly allowing enough to hang over on each side so that cake can be lifted out with paper when ready. Put a layer of crumbs and a layer of filling. Layer crumbs and filling alternately. Let the last layer of crumbs be on top. Put in frigidaire until cold and it is ready to serve. When ready, remove from pan by lifting from the ends of the waxed paper, lay on a board, slice, and serve.

Hattie went on with other delectable recipes. She told her fans about the joys of homemade French dressing, creamed onions, candied yams, sweet corn, Southern baked ham, and greens in ham liquor. Her pride and joy, though was "Mammy's Fried Chicken, à la Maryland." (She was working at this time on the movie *Maryland*. One of the reviews said that in the movie Hattie spent a lot of time "dishing up biscuits," but the fried chicken was her *tour de force*. Though most of her chicken recipe was conventional, she added enough personal methods to make it at least somewhat her "own.")

Mammy's Fried Chicken à la Maryland

Ingredients include one four pound fryer, one tablespoon of salt and pepper, one cup of flour, two cups of shortening or bacon fat. Cut the chicken into sizeable serving pieces. Wash well and dry with absorbent paper. Mix flour, salt, and pepper, and put in a heavy brown paper bag and shake pieces of chicken until well floured. Put into hot fat. Fry until golden brown. Turn, cover, and reduce temperature. Cook at moderate temperature until done. Place chicken in roasting pan, cover, and cook at 325 degrees until tender. Remove to hot platter and garnish with sprigs of parsley and spiced apricots or peaches.

Dances

The cakewalk was historically an observance of the harvest season by plantation blacks. Sometimes called the "chalk-line walk," the dance was actually a contest which featured fancy steps and difficult turns. Generally, the music stopped abruptly, and everyone froze into place. Those who could do it best won the cake.

In plantation days the cakewalk was so popular that the competition became quite keen. One "acid test" in the cakewalk was for the participants to dance with a glass of water balanced atop their heads. The winner was the person who had the fanciest steps and the least spilled water. Frequently, some of the plantation slaves were so good at the cakewalk that their masters took them "on tour," entering them in cakewalk contests throughout the South. Some slaves earned large sums of money just by being good at the cakewalk.

There was some social content to the cakewalk. It was a dance that lent itself to improvisation. Thus, it was not unusual for cakewalkers to "put a strut" into a minuet, a mimic of the fancy dances favored by their white owners. Generally, the black satirist had little fear of reprimand; if a white did notice that he was being made fun of, he did not want to broadcast it to his associates.

The juba dance has been described as a merger of European jigs and reels with African rhythms. Variously spelled Giouba and Djouba, the dance came to Caribbean areas like Cuba and Haiti before being exported to the plantations of Georgia and the Carolinas. Two dancers were ringed by a circle of other performers. The ones in the center began the dance, and called out different variations (somewhat in the manner of square dances) for the group to follow. An author, William Smith, described the juba as each performer "jigging it away in the merriest possible gaiety of heart, having the most ludicrous twists, wry jokes, and flexible contortions of the body and limbs, that human imagination could devise."

One "instruction" to the dancers, always accompanied by banjo playing, was:

> *Juba circle, raise de latch*
> *Juba dance dat Long Dog Scratch*
> *Juba! Juba!*

This intonation caused the dancers to switch to a step called "dog scratch," which, as one might imagine, involved the arms and legs in twisting movements resembling the scratching motions of a dog.

> *Another variation, (among hundreds) was:*
> *Juba jump and Juba sing*
> *Juba cut dat Pigeon's wing.* . . . .

causing the dancers to flutter their hands in a way to resemble a stricken bird.

One variation that was mostly self explanatory went this way:

> *Juba up and Juba down*
> *Juba runnin' all around.*

One early performer in the United States was a free black man named William Henry Lane. He became so enamored of the dance that he changed his name to Master Juba, and made concert appearances all over the country and in England. He is sometimes credited with establishing tap dancing as a form of theatrical art. Thus, juba was extremely popular with both blacks and whites throughout the antebellum period.

Later, in post slavery times, the juba inspired another dance called The Hambone. It, too, emphasized circles of dancers, step changes, and clapping hands (or patting) to the time of the banjo players. By the time Hattie and her friends were doing the dance, it was intermittently referred to as both juba and hambone.

Source Notes

CHAPTER ONE

1. Alexander G. Murdoch, "Convict Joe," in *The Speaker's Garland*. Philadelphia: Penn Publishing, 1888, p. 70.

2. *Ibid.* p. 73.

3. Hedda Hopper, "Hattie Hates Nobody," *Chicago Sunday Tribune,* December 14, 1947, p. 10. Louella Parsons, "Mammy's Gold Oscar Most Popular Award," *International News Service,* March 9, 1940. Tamara Andreeva, "Hattie is Hep," *Rocky Mountain Empire Magazine,* April 11, 1948.

4. While it is likely that they married somewhere in Tennessee, it seems clear that they did not wed in Nashville. The marriage records for Davidson County do not show such a union.

5. Nancy Sparks, "Miss McDaniel Native of City," Wichita (Kansas) *Beacon,* October 31, 1967.

6. *Ibid.*

7. Interview, Edgar Goff (Hattie McDaniel's nephew), May 15, 1985.

8. Some studio publicity biographies listed Hattie's year of birth as 1898. This does not seem likely. Susan was twenty-six when she married Henry. If Hattie had been born in 1898, that would have made Susan forty-nine, and still bearing children. Of course, such is possible, but not likely. It seems fairly accurate, then, to put Hattie's birth year as 1895. In her later life, she was coy with anyone who wanted to know how old she was. She'd wink and say, "a woman who'd tell her age would tell anything." Tamara Andreeva, "Hattie is Hep," *Rocky Mountain Empire Magazine,* April 11, 1948.

9. Denver, Colorado, Telephone Directory, 1901–1922.

10. Taped notes, Ruth Collamer Dermody, Ft. Collins, Colorado, to the author, undated, 1985.

11. *Ibid.*

12. *Ibid.*

13. Denver Telephone Directory, 1901–1922.

14. 1910 Census U.S. Colorado, Denver; Precinct 4; Supervisor's District No. 1 Enumeration District No. 66. Ward of City 4, Sheet No. 5A, April 18, 1910.

15. Cary Stiff, "The Rise of Colorado's Klan," *Empire Magazine* (Denver, Colorado) September 21, 1969. Also Stiff, "When the Klan Ruled Colorado," *Empire Magazine,* (Denver, Colorado), September 28, 1969.

16. Louise Poirson, undated letter to Hattie McDaniel. Ruby Berkley Goodwin Collection, North Hollywood, California. Also the Hattie McDaniel Collection at the Margaret Herrick Library of the Academy of Motion Picture Arts and Sciences, Beverly Hills, California.

17. Hattie to Ruby B. Goodwin, undated note, Goodwin Collection.

18. Interview of Marian Morrison Robinson (daughter of George Morrison), by Joan Reese in Denver, Colorado, January 15, 1985. In the sixth grade, Hattie's teacher was Mrs. H. D. Abbott. Hattie performed well in all her subjects, but she did have some problems with spelling. She spelled 'stratagem' as 'stratagam,' 'firmament' as 'firmement,' 'separate' as 'seperate,' and 'sovereign' as 'soveriengn.' Despite these errors, she sailed through 'ornithologist,' 'judicious,' 'percolated,' 'particularly,' and 'vacillation.' McDaniel Collection, Herrick Library; Beverly Hills, California.

19. *Ibid.*

20. Three instructive books on dance in America, particularly as it pertained to the black experience are: Lynne Fauley Emery, *Black Dance in the United States from 1619 to 1970.* Palo Alto, California; National Press Books, 1972; Ellen Jacob, *Dancing: A Guide For the Dancer You Can Be.* Reading, Massachusetts: Addison-Wesley, 1981; and C. V. Robert Toll, *Blacking Up: The Minstrel in Nineteenth Century America.* New York: Oxford University Press, 1974.

21. Advertisement in *Colorado Statesman,* November 28, 1908.

22. Advertisement in *Colorado Statesman,* March 6, 1909.

23. *Colorado Statesman,* March 13, 1908.

24. Otis' obituary appeared in the *Colorado Statesman,* December 18, 1916.

25. These reviews were summarized in the *Colorado Statesman,* February 14, 1925.

26. Henry's obituary appeared in the *Colorado Statesman,* December 9, 1922.

27. *Colorado Statesman,* December 5, 1925.

28. Gunther Schuller, *Early Jazz: Its Roots and Musical Development,* New York: Oxford University Press, 1968, pp. 370–371.

29. *Ibid.*

30. This song was registered with the copyright office on May 27, 1927.

31. This song was registered with the copyright office on May 27, 1927.

32. One performer who got his start at Club Madrid was a young pianist named Waldo Liberace.

33. In doing the research on this biography of Hattie McDaniel, the author sent letters to newspaper editors in the Milwaukee area soliciting memories of Hattie at Club Madrid. About two dozen people responded, some giving quite lengthy descriptions and explanations of Hattie's start at the place.

34. Mark Steger, letter to the author, October 18, 1984.

35. *Ibid.*

36. This figure varies from article to article. Some authors have the sum as high as $150.00 and others as low as $30.00. The safest estimate is that she had more than the usual tipping to which she was accustomed. James H. Briggs, "Pluck Marks Work of Hattie McDaniel," *Los Angeles Times,* August 25, 1942, puts the figure at $90.00.

CHAPTER TWO

1. Hedda Hopper, "Hattie Hates Nobody," *Chicago Sunday Tribune,* December 14, 1947.

2. Harry Levette, "I Knew Hattie McDaniel," American Negro Press, November 5, 1952.

3. *Ibid.* Also, Hopper, "Hattie Hates Nobody;" Parsons, "Mammy's Gold Oscar Most Popular Award;" Andreeva, "Hattie Is Hep." Also, Lisa Mitchell, "Hattie McDaniel; More than a Mammy," *Hollywood Studio,* April, 1979; James H. Briggs, "Pluck Marks Work of Hattie McDaniel," Los Angeles *Times,* April 6, 1941; and E. B. Rea, "Natural Talent Made Her a Star," *Washington [D.C.] Afro-American,* November 18, 1952.

4. E. B. Rea, "Natural Talent Made Her A Star. . . ."

5. *Ibid.* Also Jane Holmes, "Lightning Strikes Twice," unpublished essay, Goodwin Collection, North Hollywood, California.

6. Holmes, "Lightning Strikes Twice. . . ." In the months and years ahead, even while playing in the movies, Hattie continued her radio career with programs like Captain Henry's *Showboat, Wings Over Jordan,* a national black radio show, *What's On Your Mind, Good News, Billie Burke,* Eddie Cantor's *Time To Smile, Gulf Screen Guild Theatre, The Rudy Vallee Show, No Time For Comedy,* and, of course, *Beulah.*

7. Jane Holmes, "Lightning Strikes Twice," unpublished essay, Goodwin Collection, North Hollywood, California.

8. Hedda Hopper, "Hattie Hates Nobody," *Chicago Sunday Tribune,* December 14, 1947.

9. *Ibid.*

10. *The Golden West* is rarely seen these days (1980s). It is on file at the Film Center at the University of Wisconsin at Madison.

11. Holmes, "Lighting Strikes Twice."

12. *Ibid.*

13. *Ibid.*

14. According to reports, she paid approximately $10,000 for this home.

15. Interview, Wonderful Smith, in Los Angeles, May 15, 1985. Wonderful is his real name, given to him by a doting grandmother in Arkansas.

16. *Ibid.*

17. Ruby Berkley Goodwin, "Hollywood in Bronze," undated essay, 1952. Goodwin Collection, North Hollywood, California.

18. *Ibid.*

19. *The New York Times,* May 15, 1936.

20. Extensive searches by the author failed to turn up any information on Howard Hickman and the second marriage. No one in the present day Goodwin family has any recollection of this marriage. Apparently, the only extant reference to the marriage and subsequent divorce is in this letter from Ruby to Hattie in November, 1938. The letter is in the Goodwin Collection, North Hollywood, California.

21. Interview, Carlton Moss in Los Angeles, May 14, 1985.

22. Edward D. C. Campbell, Jr. *The Celluloid South: Hollywood and the Southern Myth.* Knoxville: The University of Tennessee Press, 1981, pp. 76–77.

23. Film in the Film Resources Center, University of Wisconsin, Madison. See also Ronny Zeigler, "Hattie McDaniel: '(I'd) . . . rather play a maid,' " *Amsterdam News,* April 28, 1979.

24. Film in the Film Resources Center, University of Wisconsin, Madison.

25. Film in the Film Resources Center, University of Wisconsin, Madison.

26. Dialogue is from the movie, *Star for a Night.* Film in the Film Resources Center, University of Wisconsin, Madison. Used by permission of Twentieth Century Fox.

27. These expressions are from the movie, *Racing Lady.* Film in the Film Resources Center, University of Wisconsin, Madison.

28. Dialogue is from the movie, *Can This Be Dixie?* Film in the Film Resources Center, University of Wisconsin, Madison. Used by permission of Twentieth Century Fox.

29. Ronny Zeigler, "Hattie McDaniel: '(I'd) . . . rather play a maid,' " *N.Y. Amsterdam News,* April 28, 1979. This quote is also frequently attributed to Butterfly McQueen, Ethel Waters, Louise Beavers, and numerous other black actresses.

30. McDaniel to Goodwin, undated note, 1950, Goodwin Collection, North Hollywood, California.

31. Jane Holmes, "Lightning Strikes Twice," unpublished essay, Goodwin Collection, North Hollywood, California.

CHAPTER THREE

1. David O. Selznick Memo, October 5, 1938. Selznick Papers, University of Texas, Austin, Texas.
2. *Ibid.* December 5, 1938.
3. Sol Lindser to George Cukor, November 10, 1936. Selznick Papers.
4. *Ibid.*
5. Eleanor Roosevelt to Katharine Brown, April 22, 1937. Selznick Papers.
6. Bessie Mack to David O. Selznick, February 16, 1939. Selznick Papers.
7. David O. Selznick Memo, December 5, 1937. Selznick Papers.
8. Bing Crosby to David O. Selznick, January 15, 1937. Selznick Papers.
9. David O. Selznick to Bing Crosby, January 19, 1937. Selznick Papers.
10. Audition for "Mammy" is usually shown on television every April when the academy award presentations are being made.
11. *Time,* December 25, 1939. Also, Bob Thomas, *The Story of Gone With the Wind.* Hollywood: Metro-Goldwyn-Mayer, 1967.
12. David O. Selznick Memo, December 8, 1938. Selznick Papers.
13. Susan Myrick to Margaret Mitchell, January 15, 1939. Mitchell Papers, University of Georgia, Athens, Georgia.
14. A copy of this contract is on file in the Selznick Papers at the University of Texas in Austin.
15. David O. Selznick Memo to Henry Ginsberg, March 29, 1939. Selznick Papers.
16. This contract, signed December 30, 1939, is on file in the Selznick Papers at the University of Texas in Austin. Hattie listed her address as that of her new-found agent, MCA Artists, at 9370 Burton Way, Beverly Hills, California.
17. Carl Strange to David O. Selznick, October 10, 1936. Selznick Papers.
18. *Ibid.*
19. Selznick to Strange, October 13, 1936. Selznick Papers.
20. David O. Selznick Memo to Hal Kern, May 11, 1939. Selznick Papers.
21. The newspaper wrote to Selznick with the idea on July 19, 1938. Selznick Papers.
22. E. Dolly Blount Lamar to David O. Selznick, June 29, 1938. Selznick Papers.
23. Lamar to Clark Gable, June 29, 1938. Selznick Papers.
24. Susan Myrick Memo, undated, 1939. Selznick Papers.
25. David Platt, *The Daily Worker,* October 29, 1936.
26. Dona Popel, *Journal of Negro Life,* April, 1937.
27. L. D. Reddick, *The Journal of Negro History,* July 19, 1937.
28. Rabbi Barnett Brickner to David O. Selznick, May 17, 1939.
29. Lewis Gannett to Walter White, June 9, 1938. NAACP Collection, Library of Congress, Washington, D.C.

30. Earl Morris, "Sailing With the Breeze," *Pittsburgh Courier,* February 4, 1939; February 18, 1939 and March 11, 1939.

31. Morris observed much of the filming of *Gone With the Wind* in February and March, 1939.

32. Walter White to David O. Selznick, June 28, 1938. NAACP Collection.

33. Marcella Rabwin to John Hay Whitney, February 11, 1939. Selznick Papers.

34. Marcella Rabwin to Katharine Brown, January 29, 1939. Selznick Papers.

35. David O. Selznick to John Hay Whitney, February 10, 1939. Selznick Papers.

36. Susan Myrick, *White Columns in Hollywood: Reports from the GWTW Sets.* Edited, with an introduction by Richard Harwell. Macon, Georgia: Mercer University Press, 1982, p. 214. In terms of roles, the Selznick people believed that Aunt Pittypat in the movie was more of a stereotype than all the black players put together. Susan Myrick echoed this sentiment and stated that "in the finer Southern homes, the servants are not expected to be clowns. They reflect the dignity of the people they work for. Many people without a Southern background do not know that this distinction exists. Many times, the Negroes, though in the capacity of servants, actually ran the estates, attended to much of the business, and treated their bosses as though they were children." Myrick, *White Columns. . . .* p. 214; Also David O. Selznick to Walter White, February 10, 1939. Selznick Papers.

37. See Gavin Lambert, *GWTW: The Making of Gone With the Wind.* Boston: Little-Brown, 1982. pp. 203–4. Also Val Lewton to David O. Selznick, June 7, 1939. Selznick Papers.

38. Val Lewton to David O. Selznick, June 7, 1939. Selznick Papers.

39. Marcella Rabwin to Katharine Brown, January 29, 1939. Selznick Papers.

40. David O. Selznick to John Hay Whitney, February 10, 1939. Selznick Papers.

41. *Ibid.*

42. Hattie told this story several times in her skit, "Mammy's Meditations," that she gave to audiences, primarily throughout the 1940s. A full copy of "Mammy's Meditations" is in the Selznick Papers at the University of Texas, Austin.

43. *Ibid.*

44. *Ibid.*

45. *Ibid.*

46. Myrick, *White Columns in Hollywood . . . ,* p. 268.

47. *Ibid.,* p. 229.

48. *Ibid.,* p. 293.

49. From *Gone With the Wind.* Quoted with the permission of the Mitchell Estate and Turner Entertainment.

50. "Gone With the Wind," *Photoplay,* August, 1961.

51. *Variety,* June 12, 1940.

52. Report on Hays Office, April 28, 1939. Selznick Papers.

53. David O. Selznick to Hattie McDaniel, October 23, 1939. Selznick Papers.

54. David O. Selznick to Howard Dietz (MGM), November 30, 1939. Selznick Papers.

55. *Ibid.* November 29, 1939. Selznick Papers. Additional information on the question of bringing *GWTW*'s black performers to Atlanta can be found in Howard Dietz to Katharine Brown, December, 1939; David O. Selznick to Katharine Brown, November 30, 1939; David O. Selznick to Robert Willis November 30, 1939; Katharine Brown to David O. Selznick, December 8, 1939. Selznick Papers.

56. *Ibid.* Also, Anne Edwards, *Road to Tara: The Life of Margaret Mitchell.* New Haven and New York: Ticknor & Fields, 1983, p. 297.

57. Hattie McDaniel to David O. Selznick, December 11, 1939. Selznick Papers.

58. Hedda Hopper, "Hattie Hates Nobody," *Chicago Tribune*, December 14, 1947.

59. *Ibid.*

60. *The New York Times*, December 22, 24, 1939.

61. *Ibid.*

62. *The Daily Worker*, January 9, 1940.

63. David O. Selznick to John F. Wharton, January 19, 1940. Selznick Papers.

64. *Ibid.* January 12, 1940. Selznick Papers.

65. John F. Wharton to David O. Selznick, January 16, 1940. Selznick Papers.

66. Resolution of the American Labor Party, January 18, 1940. Selznick Papers.

67. A. E. Harding to David O. Selznick, January 27, 1940. Selznick Papers.

68. Sons of Union Veterans of the Civil War, Undated resolution, 1940. Selznick Papers. Mrs. Maude D. Warren, national secretary of the SUVCW sent this resolution to Selznick.

69. Bertha Black and Beulah Palmer to David O. Selznick, undated letter, 1940. Selznick Papers.

70. David O. Selznick to Bertha Black and Beulah Palmer, February 3, 1940. Selznick Papers.

71. Louella Parsons, "Mammy's Gold Oscar Most Popular Award," *International News Service*, March 9, 1940.

72. Although no newspapers printed Hattie McDaniel's Oscar speech, copies of it are fairly numerous. Selznick Papers.

73. "Gone With the Wind," *Photoplay*, August, 1961. Miss de Havilland said about the event: "As the end of the evening drew near, though my British upper lip did remain stiff, from across the table Irene Selznick perceived, trembling on

the lower lid of my left eye, a single tear; understanding the feelings of disappointment that I was hiding, she came round the table, said 'Come with me,' and led me out to the kitchen at the Ambassador Hotel, where, aged 23, I did indeed, cry." She was surprised, since she was one of the four stars in the film, when Selznick entered her in the awards competition as a supporting, rather than best, actress. Olivia de Havilland to the author; February 5, 1989.

74. Olivia de Havilland to the author, June 12, 1985.

75. Parsons, "Mammy's Gold Oscar . . ." March 9, 1940.

76. *The Atlanta Constitution*, March 8, 9, 1940.

77. *New York Amsterdam News*, March 9, 1940.

78. *Ibid.*

CHAPTER FOUR

1. Susan Myrick, *White Columns in Hollywood*: On the inside cover of this book are the signatures and best wishes of all the GWTW stars to Miss Myrick.

2. David O. Selznick to Katharine Brown, October 4, 1940. Selznick Papers.

3. *Ibid.*

4. Hattie Owen Edge to Selznick International Pictures, September 17, 1954. Selznick Papers.

5. Her cooking abilities are discussed in "Found: A Cook on the Screen Who Can Cook," *New York Herald Tribune*, July 21, 1940.

6. Hedda Hopper, "Hattie Hates Nobody," *Chicago Tribune*, December 14, 1947.

7. *Modern Screen*, February, 1942.

8. *Ibid.*

9. William John to Daniel O'Shea, March 13, 1940. Selznick Papers.

10. *Ibid.*

11. Roy Bradt to C. E. Carrier, April 4, 1940. Selznick Papers.

12. C. E. Carrier to Daniel O'Shea, April 16, 1940. Selznick Papers.

13. C. E. Carrier to Roy Bradt, March 21, 1940. Selznick Papers.

14. Daniel O'Shea to C. E. Carrier, March 20, 1940. Selznick Papers.

15. Roy Bradt to C. E. Carrier, April 4, 1940. Selznick Papers.

16. David O. Selznick to Daniel O'Shea, November 29, 1939. Selznick Papers.

17. David O. Selznick to William Paley, January 3, 1940. Selznick Papers.

18. David O. Selznick to Daniel O'Shea, October 10, 1940. Selznick Papers.

19. William Paley to David O. Selznick, January 19, 1940. Selznick Papers.

20. Memo to David O. Selznick, March 27, 1940. Selznick Papers.

21. Will Price to David O. Selznick, September 9, 1940. Selznick Papers.

22. *Ibid.*

23. Daniel O'Shea to David O. Selznick, January 8, 1940. Selznick Papers.

24. Russell Bergwell to Daniel O'Shea, January 11, 1940. Selznick Papers.

25. The first "Good News" skit was performed on January 11, 1940.

26. *Ibid.*

27. M. Janov (Selznick International Paymaster) to A. M. Davis, January 29, 1940. Selznick Papers.

28. Daniel O'Shea to A. M. Gilbert, January 23, 1940. Selznick Papers.

29. *Ibid.*

30. A. M. Davis to Daniel O'Shea, January 27, 1940. Selznick Papers.

31. George Glass to David O. Selznick, May 1, 1940. Selznick Papers.

32. *Time*, June 10, 1940.

33. Copy in the Selznick Papers, University of Texas, Austin.

34. Daniel O'Shea to David O. Selznick, December 8, 1939. Selznick Papers.

35. Contract between Selznick International and Twentieth Century Fox, December 13, 1940. On file in the Selznick Papers.

36. David O. Selznick, undated memo, December 1940. Selznick Papers.

37. This dialogue is from the movie *Maryland*.

38. David O. Selznick to Daniel O'Shea, February 15, 1940. Selznick Papers.

39. Hattie McDaniel to Ruth Collamer Dermody, March 29, 1940. Dermody Collection, Ft. Collins, Colorado.

40. *Ibid.*

41. *Ibid.*

42. David O. Selznick to L. V. Calvert, March 20, 1940. Selznick Papers. Also, C. E. Carrier to Daniel O'Shea, April 16, 1940.

43. Selznick to Calvert, March 20, 1940.

44. *Ibid.*

45. *Ibid.*

46. *Ibid.*

47. Ray Klune to Daniel O'Shea, April 12, 1940. Also Ray Klune to David O. Selznick, April 18, 1940. Selznick Papers.

48. Daniel O'Shea to Hattie McDaniel, April 25, 1940. Selznick Papers.

49. "Mammy's Meditations." Selznick Papers.

50. Daniel O'Shea to Phil Bloom, May 4, 1940. Selznick Papers.

51. Daniel O'Shea wrote to a man named Scanlon, July 2, 1940, within Selznick International that Twentieth Century Fox should be billed "for the services of Hattie McDaniel on retakes from the date she left her engagement until the date she started again in Baltimore at the rate of $1,500 per week, plus her round trip transportation and $75.00 a week for her maid during the time Hattie was gone." Selznick Papers.

52. E. G. Smith to David O. Selznick, undated, 1940. Selznick Papers. Selznick wrote back to Smith on May 28, 1940, thanking him for his kind sentiments.

53. Claude Barnett to David O. Selznick, June 18, 1940. Selznick Papers.

54. *Ibid.*

55. *Ibid.*

56. Claude Barnett to Daniel O'Shea, July 1, 1940. Selznick Papers.
57. David O. Selznick to Daniel O'Shea, June 24, 1940. Selznick Papers.
58. John G. Turner to David O. Selznick, June 26, 1941. Selznick Papers.
59. *Ibid.*
60. Hattie McDaniel to Daniel O'Shea, July 17, 1940. Selznick Papers.
61. Daniel O'Shea to David O. Selznick, October 16, 1940. Selznick Papers.
62. Katharine Brown to Daniel O'Shea, October 18, 1940. Selznick Papers. She said further that "we have had a tremendous disturbance in New York," and that there was a "definite political situation about Hattie McDaniel."
63. E. J. Haley to Phil Bloom, May 30, 1940. Selznick Papers.
64. Phil Bloom to E. J. Haley, June 3, 1940. Selznick Papers.
65. Daniel O'Shea to Phil Bloom, June 4, 1940. Selznick Papers.
66. Etta Moten to Hattie McDaniel, April 20, 1940. Claude Barnett Papers, Chicago Historical Society.

CHAPTER FIVE

1. David O. Selznick to Daniel O'Shea, October 22, 1940. Selznick Papers.
2. *Ibid.*
3. *Ibid.*
4. *Hollywood Reporter*, April 4, 1941.
5. Warner Brothers Collection, Pressbook, University of Southern California, Los Angeles, California.
6. *Ibid.*
7. *The New York World-Telegram*, April 12, 1941.
8. *California Eagle*, April 2, 1941.
9. Though there are many references to Hattie's autobiography, there are apparently no extant copies, at least in the various collections of materials about her. One report stated that she was "correcting the galleys" on *Help Yourself.* There is no indication that her autobiography was ever published.
10. Financial Statement, undated, January 1942; Warner Brothers Collection, University of Southern California, Los Angeles, California.
11. Ruby Berkley Goodwin, handwritten notes, undated; Goodwin Collection, North Hollywood, California.
12. *Ibid.*
13. *Ibid.*
14. Hattie McDaniel to Ruby Berkley Goodwin, March 31, 1941. Goodwin Collection.
15. *Ibid.* April 6, 1941.
16. *Rocky Mountain News*, April 14, 1941.
17. *Denver Star*, April 12, 1941.
18. *Ibid.*
19. *Ibid.* Also, *The Colorado Statesman*, April, 1941; and *Crisis* Magazine, November, 1943.

20. Ruby Goodwin notes, Goodwin Collection.

21. *Ibid.*

22. Hattie McDaniel to Ruth Collamer Dermody, July 15, 1941. Dermody Collection, Ft. Collins, Colorado.

23. Hattie McDaniel to Ruby Berkley Goodwin, December 14, 1941. Goodwin Collection.

24. *Ibid.* December 2, 1941.

25. *Ibid.* January 8, 1942.

26. Jack Warner to Hal Wallis, October 25, 1941. Warner Collection, USC.

27. Telephone interview, Ernest Anderson, May 16, 1985, in Los Angeles.

28. Dialogue is from *In This Our Life*. Film Resources Center, University of Wisconsin, Madison.

29. John S. Holley to Jack Warner, August 9, 1942. Warner Collection, USC.

30. Lola Kobner to Walter White, November 28, 1942. NAACP Collection, Library of Congress.

31. S. Charles Einfeld to Walter White, undated, 1942. NAACP Collection.

32. Herbert King to John Huston, July 31, 1942. NAACP Collection.

33. Inez Richardson Wilson to Warner Brothers, May 26, 1942. NAACP Collection.

34. Darius Johnson to Warner Brothers, June, 1942. NAACP Collection.

35. Edith Peacock McDougal to Warner Brothers, August 10, 1942. NAACP Collection.

36. John Holley to Jack Warner, August 9, 1942. Warner Collection, USC.

37. Walter White to Olivia de Havilland, May 25, 1942. NAACP Collection.

38. Olivia de Havilland to Walter White, November 21, 1942. NAACP Collection.

39. Olivia de Havilland to the author, April 28, 1985.

40. Details of these meetings are filed in the Goodwin Papers, North Hollywood, California.

41. Descriptions of Camp Haan are in the Goodwin Papers.

42. Hattie McDaniel to Ruth Dermody, July 10, 1942. Dermody Papers, Ft. Collins, Colorado.

43. Hattie McDaniel speech, August 30, 1942, in Indianapolis, Indiana. Goodwin Papers.

44. *Ibid.*

45. *Ibid.*

46. Story related in the Warner Brothers Press Book for *In This Our Life*, October, 1941. Warner Brothers Collection, USC.

47. Mitchell Rawson to David O. Selznick and Daniel O'Shea, January 19, 1944. Selznick Papers.

48. "Hattie Steals Movie Scenes," *American Negro Press*, October 29, 1943.

49. Barbara Keon to Mr. Sidleman, September 13, 1943. Selznick Papers.

50. Herman Hill, "Hill's Side," *Pittsburgh Courier*, November 18, 1944.

Though she took voice lessons from time to time, Hattie never did take any formal training for acting—a fact that only increases one's admiration for her phenomenal career. A few years later, in 1945, *Since You Went Away* was dubbed into Spanish. Hattie's voice was that of a Cuban Negro actress. Selznick was upset by her performance, saying that she had no resemblance to Hattie's personality or quality.

Another film for Hattie in 1944 was *Janie*, which had been a successful stage play in New York. One minor fad that this movie started around the country was "Op" language, a language that Janie and her friends used when they didn't want the grown-ups to understand. Warner publicity was kept fairly busy answering letters from curious people about "Op." Agnes Johnson of Warner's explained to Marilyn Latham of Burlington, Iowa, that you just put an "Op" before every vowel. Thus, Hattie McDaniel would be "Hopattopiope McDopanopiopel." Warner Brothers would come out as "Woparnoper Bropothopers," and so on. The studio insisted that once you got the hang of it, "Op" wasn't so bad. Though "Op" was one of the frills of the late forties, it did not exactly start a national craze. Agnes Johnson to Marilyn Latham, December 5, 1944. Warner Brothers Collection, USC. Hattie told her friend Ruth in a letter, April 18, 1944, how much she enjoyed working on the "cute" story of *Janie*. Dermody Collection, Ft. Collins, Colorado.

51. Hattie McDaniel to Ruth Dermody, September 15, 1945. Dermody Collection, Ft. Collins, Colorado.

52. *Los Angeles Examiner*, May 25, 1944.

53. Hattie McDaniel to Ruth Dermody, September 18, 1944. Dermody Collection, Fort Collins, Colorado.

54. Alexander Keeland to Ruby B. Goodwin, April 6, 20, 1944. Goodwin Collection.

55. *Ibid.* June 1, 1944.

56. Hattie McDaniel to Ruth Dermody, September 18, 1944. Dermody Collection.

57. *Ibid.*

58. Ruth Dermody, Telephone interview with the author, June, 1985.

59. Anonymous interview, Michael St. John, May 20, 1985, in Berkeley, California.

60. Butterfly McQueen to the author, May 8, 1984.

61. Interview, Joel Fluellen, May 14, 1985, in Los Angeles.

62. Interview, Frances Williams, May 15, 1985, in Los Angeles.

63. *Ibid.* Also Fluellen and Moss interviews, May 14, 1985.

64. *Los Angeles Examiner*, December 20, 1945; also *Los Angeles Tribune*, December 6, 1945.

65. *Ibid.*

66. Hattie McDaniel to Ruth Dermody, September 15, 1945. Dermody Collection.

67. Interviews, Carlton Moss and Joel Fluellen, May 14, 15, 1985, in Los Angeles.

68. "Hattie McDaniel Wins Divorce," *American Negro Press*, December 26, 1945.

69. Clore Warren to Claude Barnett, January 4, 1946. Barnett Papers, Chicago Historical Society.

70. *Ibid.*

71. Claude Barnett to Clore Warren, January 6, 1946. Barnett Papers, Chicago Historical Society.

CHAPTER SIX

1. Jane Holmes, "Lightning Strikes Twice," unpublished essay in the Goodwin Collection, North Hollywood, California. A "Mammy," said writer Jamaica Kincaid, "is different from your mother because while your mother is expected to love you, Mammies love you for no reason at all." Mammies are "fair, loving, loyal, nurturing, supportive, protective, generous, and devoted." A Mammy is the kind of person to whom you can say, "I just raped 14 children and I killed eight of them, and she'll say, 'isn't that terrible, I love you anyway.' " Jamaica Kincaid, "If Mammies Ruled the World," *The Village Voice*, May 5, 1975.

2. Walter White to Edwin Embree, October 30, 1942. NAACP Collection, Library of Congress, Washington, D.C.

3. *Ibid.*

4. White described this interview in a letter to Melvyn Douglas, March 12, 1942. NAACP Collection.

5. Walter White to Arch Reeve, August 5, 1942. NAACP Collection.

6. Negro Motion Picture Players Association; Resolution, 1942, to NAACP. Library of Congress.

7. Samuel Bischoff to John Holley, December 8, 1941. NAACP Collection. One report, "Motion Pictures and the Social Attitudes of Children," told of some tests given to children in Crystal Lake, Illinois, where the population was 5,700 whites and not one Negro. The first test was to 434 children, all of whom showed a "marked liberality," toward Negroes. Then they were shown the movie *The Birth of a Nation*, and retested. "There was almost a one hundred percent shift in their opinions. Prejudice was definitely inculcated by *The Birth of a Nation*." Ruth Peterson and J. L. Thurston researched and wrote this article, which apparently went unpublished. A copy of this report is on file in the NAACP Collection, Library of Congress.

8. Walter White note, NAACP Collection.

9. Roy Wilkins to Walter White, February 10, 1942. NAACP Collection. Lillian Murray echoed Wilkins when she wrote NAACP executive, Madison Jones, that "I go to the movies . . . but I seldom see anything good that a colored person do. I know they do lots of things that are just as good as any white person can do, but you never read or see it in the papers other than our own. Why don't something be done about it?" Lillian Murray to Madison Jones, October 24, 1946. NAACP Collection.

10. *Variety*, June 17, 1942.

11. *Ibid.*

12. George S. Schuyler, *Pittsburgh Courier*, September 5, 1942.

13. Archer Winsten to Walter White, February 3, 1942. NAACP Collection.

14. Undated report, NAACP Collection.

15. *The People's Voice*, September 12, 1942.

16. Hedda Hopper, "Hattie Hates Nobody," *Chicago Tribune*, December 14, 1947.

17. *Ibid.*

18. The minutes of this meeting are filed in the Goodwin Papers, North Hollywood, California.

19. *Ibid.*

20. He wrote this article in early 1942, and it was distributed by a few black newspapers around the country after it was published several months later. It was printed "exclusively" in the *Pittsburgh Courier*, September 12, 1942. A copy of this article is in the NAACP Collection, Library of Congress.

21. *Ibid.*

22. *Ibid.*

23. *Ibid.*

24. *Ibid.*

25. Almena Davis to Walter White, May 11, 1942. NAACP Collection.

26. Alice D. Webb to Irving Mills, March 11, 1943. NAACP Collection.

27. William Grant Still to Walter White, June 2, 1943. NAACP Collection.

28. Walter White to Norman Houston, September 10, 1943. NAACP Collection.

29. Norman Houston to Walter White, September 16, 1943. NAACP Collection.

30. Interview, Carlton Moss, May 15, 1985, in Los Angeles.

31. Lena Horne, with Richard Schickel, *Lena*. New York: Doubleday & Co., 1965, pp. 136–137.

32. Terry Francois to Walter White, March, 1945. NAACP Collection.

33. James Jackson to Walter White, April 6, 1945. NAACP Collection.

34. *Ibid.*

35. *Ibid.*

36. *Ibid.*

37. Paul W. Byers to Walter White, February 20, 1946. NAACP Collection.

38. Robert Brown to Walter White, December 6, 1948. NAACP Collection.

39. Hattie McDaniel to George V. Byrnes, March 29, 1945. Goodwin Collection.

40. *Ibid.*

41. *Ibid.*

42. *Ibid.*

43. White's memo suggesting the formation of the Hollywood Bureau is in the NAACP Collection, Library of Congress.

44. Lawrence F. Lamar, "Hollywood Performers Rap Walter White Plan," *New York Amsterdam News,* February 2, 1946.

45. Walter White to Roy Wilkins, January 28, 1946. NAACP Collection.

46. *Ibid.*

47. *Ibid.* Also, Franklin Williams to White, August 5, 1947. NAACP Collection.

48. Walter White to Roy Wilkins, January 28, 1946. NAACP Collection.

49. *Ibid.*

50. *Ibid.*

51. *Ibid.*

52. Walter White to *Chicago Defender,* February 21, 1946. NAACP Collection.

53. White's Hollywood Bureau memo, NAACP Collection.

54. *The Chicago Defender,* editorial, February 23, 1946.

55. *The People's Choice,* February 9, 1946.

56. Lilly Rowe, "Notebook," *Pittsburgh Courier,* February 9, 1946.

57. Interview, Joel Fluellen, May 15, 1985, in Los Angeles.

58. *Ibid.*

59. John Dales, Jr., to Walter White, April 10, 1946. NAACP Collection.

60. Franklin Williams to Walter White, August 5, 1947. NAACP Collection.

61. Interview, Carlton Moss, May 14, 1985, in Los Angeles.

62. Walt Disney to Walter White, July 25, 1944. NAACP Collection.

63. Walter White to Walt Disney, August 1, 1944. NAACP Collection.

64. Richard Condon to Walter White, August 13, 1946. NAACP Collection.

65. June Blythe to Walter White, September 5, 1946. NAACP Collection.

66. Gloster B. Current to Walter White, November 22, 1946. NAACP Collection.

67. Hope Spingarn to Walter White, November 23, 1946. NAACP Collection.

68. Carl Phillips to Walter White, November 22, 1946. NAACP Collection.

69. White sent this telegram to all the wire services on November 27, 1946. White chafed, too, when the programs for *Song of the South,* to be sold at cinemas whenever the movie played, had the word "Negro" spelled with a lower-case 'n.' This had been the practice of Joel Chandler Harris, who wrote the "Uncle Remus" stories, but, after all, said White, that was in the nineteenth century. Disney, here in the middle of the twentieth, should know better. White memo, NAACP Collection.

70. *Time,* November 18, 1946.

71. *The New York Times,* December 8, 1946. In 1987, *Song of the South* was nationally re-released, and there was no controversy about it. Whether the lack of controversy meant that blacks no longer object to the movie or that the civil rights movements have come full circle is a debatable question.

72. Walter White to *Parent's Magazine,* January 9, 1947. NAACP Collection.

73. Katherine C. Edwards to Walter White, January 14, 1947. NAACP Collection.

74. Walter White to Hope Spingarn, *et al,* January 18, 1947. NAACP Collection.

75. Los Angeles *Tribune,* August 23, 1947.

76. Stanley Bates to Walter White, August 19, 1947. NAACP Collection.

77. *Ibid.*

78. Omaha *World-Herald,* January 29, 1948.

79. Walter White to J. Parnell Thomas, October 16, 1947. NAACP Collection.

80. Hedda Hopper, "Hattie Hates Nobody," *Chicago Tribune,* December 14, 1947.

81. Lisa Mitchell, "Hattie McDaniel, More Than a Mammy," *Hollywood Studio Magazine,* April, 1979.

82. Carl Cain, *California Eagle,* January 1, 1948.

83. Interview, Wonderful Smith, May 15, 1985, in Los Angeles.

84. Universal Studios Press Release, June 4, 1948. Universal Collection, USC. Though much of *Family Honeymoon* was filmed at the Grand Canyon (where the greatest crisis that occurred was the escape of two dozen trained bed bugs, requiring a frantic casting official to order more of the little creatures from Hollywood), all of Hattie's shots were done in the studio. She got $1,000 a week for her services, with a two week guarantee of work.

85. Hedda Hopper, "Hattie Hates Nobody," *Chicago Tribune,* December 14, 1947.

86. Pola Grinsfaun to Universal Studios. Universal Collection.

87. Henry Lee Moon to Leonard Lyons, September 30, 1949. NAACP Collection.

88. Darryl F. Zanuck to Walter White, September 21, 1948. NAACP Collections.

CHAPTER SEVEN

1. Thomas Reddy, "Hattie Makes Hit on Stage," *Los Angeles Examiner,* September 25, 1947.

2. *Pittsburgh Courier,* November 18, 1950. Ruby Goodwin later incorrectly put the starting date of the show as December 9, 1947.

3. *Pittsburgh Courier,* November 18, 1950.

4. John Crosby, "Radio in Review," *New York Herald Tribune,* December 30, 1947.

5. Michael St. John, Notes on Hattie McDaniel, May 2, 1985.

6. John Crosby, "Radio in Review," *New York Herald Tribune,* March 14, 1947.

7. *Pittsburgh Courier,* November 18, 1950.

8. A copy of this contract is filed in the Goodwin Papers, North Hollywood, California.

9. *Fortnight,* January 16, 1948.

10. Hattie McDaniel to William Tarrance, February, 1951. Goodwin Papers, North Hollywood, California.

11. John Crosby, "Radio Wins With Lady Rochester," *New York Herald Tribune,* December 30, 1947.

12. Many "Beulah" scripts are on file in the Goodwin Papers, North Hollywood, California.

13. *Time,* December 1, 1947.

14. Gertrude Gibson, Undated note, Goodwin Papers.

15. Maxine Hampton to "Beulah McDaniel," May 8, 1951. Goodwin Papers.

16. These letters are on file in the Goodwin Papers, North Hollywood, California.

17. Louella Parsons, *New York Journal-American,* March 10, 1950.

18. Gaynell Tipton to "Beulah," May 21, 1951. Goodwin Papers.

19. Dora Bart to "Beulah McDaniel," undated, Goodwin Papers.

20. Azille McAllister to Hattie McDaniel, undated, Goodwin Papers.

21. Elmira Mayfield to "Beulah," May 13, 1951. Goodwin Papers.

22. Beulah Bass to Hattie McDaniel, August 27, 1952. Goodwin Papers.

23. Clara Frison to Hattie McDaniel, undated, Goodwin Papers.

24. This letter is on file in the Goodwin Papers.

25. This letter, from Pass Christian, Mississippi, is on file in the Goodwin Papers.

26. This letter from "D.R." is on file in the Goodwin Papers.

27. This letter from "R.H.," June 28, 1951, is on file in the Goodwin Papers.

28. Mickey Malone to Hattie McDaniel, April 25, 1950. Goodwin Papers.

29. A copy of "Beulah's Boogie" is on file in the Goodwin Papers. An extensive search by the author has failed to find Mr. Johnson's whereabouts. Also, a report from the Library of Congress indicates that a copyright was never taken out for "Beulah's Boogie."

30. There are several copies of this article on file in the Goodwin Papers.

31. Larry Walters, "Radio Gag Bag," *Chicago Tribune,* January 18, 1948.

32. Many of these descriptions of Hattie's lifestyle were given in Gene Handsaker, Prescott (Arizona) *Courier,* January 22, 1948.

33. These descriptions of "The Beulah Show" are in the Goodwin Papers, North Hollywood, California.

34. Major William Tarrance to Hattie McDaniel, May 24, 1951. Goodwin Papers.

35. *Ibid.*

36. S. W. Garlington, "Amusement Row," *New York Amsterdam News,* February 17, March 3, 1951.

37. This letter was written sometime in February, 1951. Apparently it was

never published by the wire services. A copy of this letter is in the Goodwin Papers. Hattie said at the Interracial Unity Committee's award presentation that "I am proud of my standing as a woman interested in her race." More than once Hattie used her influence at Warner Brothers to obtain the studio's large California ranch for entertaining delegations meeting in Los Angeles. Two such occasions were the regional gatherings of the NAACP and the Negro Doctors and Pharmacists. She was one of few people who could come and go at will at the Warner studio gates. Her distinguished guests included Adam Clayton Powell, Sr. and Jr.; Mrs. Portis Washington Pittman, daughter of Booker T. Washington, and General Benjamin O. Davis.

38. William Tarrance to Hattie McDaniel, March 20, 1951. Goodwin Papers. If the "primary mission" was "troop education," one wonders how all the baseball and football games were broadcast, along with programs like the "Grand Ol' Opry." Thousands of GIs would have chuckled, or worse, at the Major's suggestion.

39. Tarrance to McDaniel, March 20, 1951. Goodwin Papers.

40. Dorothy O'Leary, "Regarding Miss Hattie McDaniel," *New York Times,* March 7, 1948.

41. Interview, Joel Fluellen, May 14, 1985, in Los Angeles.

42. Louella Parsons, " 'Beulah' McDaniel to Wed Today," *Los Angeles Examiner,* June 11, 1949.

43. Parsons, " 'Beulah,' Mate Incompatible," *Los Angeles Examiner,* October 26, 1949.

44. *Los Angeles Herald-Express,* December 6, 1950.

45. *Ibid.* Also Los Angeles *Times,* December 6, 1950.

46. Anonymous interview, Michael St. John, May 20, 1985, in Berkeley, California.

47. This question was discussed in the Goff interview, May 15, 1985; Moss and Fluellen interviews, May 14, 1985; and an anonymous interview, May 20, 1985.

48. *New York Journal-American,* October 26, 1949.

49. Interview, Carlton Moss, May 14, 1985.

50. These thoughts about Hattie were collectively expressed in interviews and discussions with various people who knew her. Michael St. John was her next door neighbor for some time, and knew her well. Joel Fluellen played on some of the Beulah episodes with her, and Carlton Moss knew her for many years. Her nephew Edgar Goff also has many memories about Hattie McDaniel.

51. *Los Angeles Herald-Express,* December 6, 1950.

52. Mrs. A. N. Ferris to Hattie McDaniel, April 28, 1950. Goodwin Papers.

53. Michael St. John Notes On Hattie McDaniel; May 2, 1985.

54. Ruby Berkley Goodwin, "The Call," Calvin News Service, August 18, 1950. Many copies of this article are in the Goodwin Papers.

55. *Ibid.*

56. *Ibid.*

57. Jacqueline Trescott, "Butterfly McQueen: In Prissy's Shadow," *The Washington Post,* November 7, 1976.

58. Butterfly McQueen to Jack Mertes, undated; Jack Mertes Collection, Peoria, Illinois.

59. *The New York Times,* October 4, 1950.

60. *Ibid.*

61. Sherrill Smith to Hattie McDaniel, April 24, 1951. Goodwin Collection.

62. For stories about Miss Waters' departure from the TV "Beulah" show, see Terence O'Flaherty, San Francisco *Chronicle,* June 26, 1951 and *Los Angeles Radio and Television Life,* June 29, 1951.

63. *Newsweek,* July 23, 1951.

64. *Ibid.*

65. O'Flaherty, June 26, 1951.

66. *L.A. Radio and TV Life,* June 29, 1951.

67. *Variety,* June 13, 1951.

68. The "Out of this World" Series was described by the *Los Angeles Tribune,* July 7, 1951. Also Gene Hansaker, *Santa Ana Register,* August 7, 1951.

69. *Los Angeles Tribune,* August 25, 1951.

70. Los Angeles *News,* August 28, 1951.

71. *Old Testament,* Isaiah 62:3, 4.

CHAPTER EIGHT

1. Michael St. John, Notes, May 2, 1985.

2. Telephone interview, Wonderful Smith, May 16, 1985.

3. St. John Notes, May 2, 1985.

4. *Ibid.*

5. *Ibid.*

6. *Ibid.*

7. *Ibid.*

8. *Ibid.*

9. *Ibid.*

10. Butterfly McQueen to the author, May 8, 1984.

11. St. John Notes, May 2, 1985.

12. *The California Eagle,* May 11, 1950.

13. *Ibid.*

14. Butterfly McQueen to the author, May 8, 1984.

15. St. John Notes, May 2, 1985.

16. Ruby Goodwin to Tom McKnight, September 15, 1951. Goodwin Papers.

17. Hattie McDaniel to City Finance Company, September 6, 1951. Goodwin Papers.

18. James L. Crawford to Ruby Goodwin, October 27, 1951. Goodwin Papers.

19. Lisa Mitchell, "Hattie McDaniel, More than a Mammy," *Hollywood Studio Magazine*, April, 1977.

20. James L. Crawford to Ruby Goodwin, April 27, 1952. Goodwin Papers.

21. *Ibid.*

22. Interview, Joel Fluellen, May 14, 1985, in Los Angeles.

23. Interview, Frances Melton, May 21, 1985, in Oakland, California.

24. George Schmiedel to Ruby Goodwin, September 6, 1952. Goodwin Papers.

25. Mrs. Leo Davis to Hattie McDaniel, September 24, 1952. Goodwin Papers.

26. Chessley Smith to Hattie McDaniel, September 12, 1952. Goodwin Papers.

27. George Schmiedel to Ruby Goodwin, October 24, 1952. Goodwin Papers.

28. James L. Crawford to Ruby Goodwin, October 27, 1952. Goodwin Collection.

29. *Ibid.*

30. *Ibid.*

31. The power of attorney was dated August 6, 1952. It is on file in the Goodwin Papers.

32. Elaine McDeckner to "The Beulah Show," October 28, 1952.

33. A copy of this poem is in the Goodwin Papers.

34. Mickey Malone to Ruby Goodwin, October 27, 1952. Goodwin Papers.

35. A copy of this sonnet is in the Goodwin Papers.

36. Leigh Whipper to Hattie McDaniel, October 23, 1952. Goodwin Papers.

37. Negro Actor's Guild, Resolution on the Death of Miss Hattie McDaniel. Herrick Library, Beverly Hills, California.

38. F. Walter Patterson to Sam McDaniel, October 30, 1952. Goodwin Papers.

39. A copy of this resolution is on file at the Herrick Library.

40. "J.T." to Hattie McDaniel, December 10, 1952. Goodwin Papers.

41. Of course, newspapers around the world covered Hattie's funeral. One was the *Los Angeles Examiner,* November 2, 1952.

42. *World Telegram,* April 26, 1948.

43. A copy of this will is in the Goodwin Papers.

44. Many copies of this article by Ruby, distributed to the wire services in December, 1952, are on file in the Goodwin Papers, North Hollywood, California.

45. *The New York Times,* October 14, 1967.

Bibliography

Original Sources

1. MSS

Claude Barnett Papers, Chicago Historical Society.

Ruth Collamer Dermody Papers and Notes to the Author, Ft. Collins, Colorado.

Ruby Berkley Goodwin Papers, North Hollywood, California.

Hattie McDaniel Papers, Margaret Herrick Library; Academy of Motion Picture Arts and Sciences, Beverly Hills, California.

Margaret Mitchell Collection, University of Georgia, Athens, Georgia.

MGM, Fox, Universal, Paramount, Warner Collections, University of Southern California, Los Angeles.

Jack Mertes Collection; Peoria, Illinois.

National Association for the Advancement of Colored People Collection, Library of Congress, Washington, D.C.

David O. Selznick Collection, University of Texas, Austin, Texas.

Michael St. John Notes, Berkeley, California.

2. LETTERS TO THE AUTHOR, FROM:

Olivia de Havilland, April 28, June 12, 1985; February 5, 1989.

Butterfly McQueen, May 8, 1984.

From Milwaukee: Allen W. Bathke, October 9, 1984; Ken Bernaski, October 9, 1984; Stephanie Ehlers, October 10, 1984; Barbara Mohr, October 11, 1984; Ken Ohst, November 1, 1984; Geraldine Race, October 9, 1984; Eila Rasmussen, October 11, 1984; Geneva Roethal, October 11, 1984; Dolores Schiefen, November 13, 1984; Dorothy Schmutzler, October 11, 1984; Gerri Solomon, October 16, 1984; Kurt Sommerich, October 11, 1984; Mark Steger, October 18, 1984; Mabel Weber, November 1, 1984; Helen Williams, October 8, 1984.

3. INTERVIEWS BY THE AUTHOR

Ernest Anderson (by telephone), May 16, 1985; Leon Bennett, May 16, 1985; Joel Fluellen, May 14, 1985; Edgar Goff, May 15, 1985; Carlton Moss, May 14, 1985; Wonderful Smith (by telephone), May 16, 1985; Frances Williams, May 14, 1985.

4. OTHER INTERVIEWS

Joan Reese: Interview of Marian Morrison Robinson (daughter of George Morrison), January 15, 1985.

Secondary Sources

1. BOOKS

Bogle, Donald. *Toms, Coons, Mulattoes, Mammies and Bucks: An Interpretive History of Blacks in American Films*. New York: Viking Press, 1973.

Campbell, Edward D. C. *The Celluloid South: Hollywood and the Southern Myth*. Knoxville: University of Tennessee Press, 1983.

Cripps, Thomas. *Slow Fade To Black: The Negro in American Film, 1900–1942*. New York: Oxford University Press, 1977.

Edwards, Anne. *Vivien Leigh, A Biography*. New York: Simon and Schuster, 1977.

Emery, Lynne Fauley. *Black Dance in the United States From 1619 to 1970*. Palo Alto California: National Press Books, 1972.

Horne, Lena, with Richard Schickel. *Lena.* New York: Doubleday, 1965.

Jacob, Ellen. *Dancing: A Guide For The Dancer You Can Be.* Reading, Massachusetts: Addison-Wesley, 1981.

Murdoch, Alexander G. "Convict Joe," in *The Speaker's Garland.* Philadelphia: Penn Publishing Co., 1888.

Myrick, Susan. *White Columns in Hollywood. Reports from the GWTW Sets.* (Richard Harwell, editor). Macon, Georgia: Mercer University Press, 1982.

Rust, Brian. *Jazz Records, 1897–1942.* 2 vols. (4th revised & enlarged edition), New Rochelle, New York: Arlington House Publishers, 1978.

Schuller, Gunther. *Early Jazz: Its Roots And Musical Development.* New York: Oxford University Press, 1968.

Thomas, Bob. *The Story of GWTW.* Hollywood, California: MGM, 1967.

Toll, C. V. Robert. *Blacking Up: The Minstrel in Nineteenth Century America.* New York: Oxford University Press, 1974.

2. ARTICLES AND PERIODICALS

Adams, Julius J. "Did Walter White Set Negroes Back in Radio?" New York *Amsterdam News;* November 19, 1949.

Andreeva, Tamara. "Hattie Is Hep," *Denver Post;* April 11, 1948.

Crosby, John. "Radio in Review: Beulah," New York *Herald-Tribune;* March 14, 1947.

Crowther, Bosley. Review of *Song of the South, New York Times;* December 8, 1946.

Dale, Edgar. "The Movies and Race Relations," *The Crisis;* Vol. 44; No. 10, October, 1937, 296.

"Good News About Hattie McDaniel," *Modern Screen;* February, 1942.

Hamilton, Sara. "Round Up Of Pace Setters," *Photoplay,* Vol. 54; June, 1940, 70–80.

Hopper, Hedda. "Hattie Hates Nobody," *Chicago Sunday Tribune;* December 14, 1947, 10.

Kinkaid, Jamaica. "If Mammies Ruled the World," *Village Voice;* May 5, 1975.

Levette, Harry. "I Knew Hattie McDaniel," *American Negro Press;* November 5, 1952.

Mitchell, Lisa. "Hattie McDaniel, More Than A Mammy," *Hollywood Studio Magazine;* April, 1977, 19–20.

Mitchell, Lisa. " 'Mammy' McDaniel As The Definitive Matriarch," *Los Angeles Times;* November 7, 1976.

Myrick, Susan. "40 Years of Such Interesting People," *Atlanta Journal and Constitution Magazine;* September 8, 1974, 8–10.

Myrick, Susan. "Pardon My Un-Southern Accent," *Collier's;* December, 1939, 20–21; 32.

Nugent, Frank. "Gone With, Etc., Or The Making Of A Movie," *New York Times Magazine;* December 10, 1939, 6; 17–18.

O'Leary, Dorothy. "Regarding Miss Hattie McDaniel," *New York Times;* March 7, 1948.

Parsons, Louella. "Mammy's Gold Oscar: Most Popular Award," Syndicated column, *International News Service,* March 9, 1940.

Photoplay, August, 1961, 30; 85–88.

Rea, E. B. "Natural Talent Made Her A Star," Washington *Afro-American;* November 18, 1952.

Sparks, Nancy. "Viewpoint," Wichita *Beacon;* October 31, 1967.

Stevens, John D. "The Black Reaction to Gone With the Wind," *Journal of Popular Film,* Vol. 11, No. 4, Fall, 1973, 366–371.

Time, Review of *Song of the South,* November 18, 1946. Also *Time,* December 25, 1939, 32; June 10, 1940, 69; December 1, 1947, 102; and May 5, 1961, 16.

Trescott, Jacqueline. "Butterfly McQueen; In Prissy's Shadow," *The Washington Post;* November 7, 1976, El; E5–E6.

Variety, June 12, 1940, 14; Also *Variety,* June 17, 1942, 5.

Weaver, William R. Review of *Gone With the Wind. Motion Picture Herald,* December 16, 1939.

Zeigler, Ronny. "Hattie McDaniel (I'd) . . . Rather Play a Maid." *Amsterdam News;* April 28, 1979, 37.

3. NEWSPAPERS

Amsterdam News, January 21, 1939; March 9, 16, 23, 1940.

Atlanta Constitution, March 8, 9, 1940; March 4, 1983.

California Eagle, April 2, 1941; January 1, 1948; May 11, 1950.

Chicago Sunday Tribune; December 14, 1947; January 18, 1948; January 13, 1950.

Colorado Statesman, March 12, 20, 1908; November 28, 1908; March 6, 1909; December 18, 1916; December 9, 1922; January 20, 1923; February 14, May 9, December 5, 1925; April, 1941.

Daily Worker, January 9, 1940.

Dallas *Times-Herald,* November 4, 1952.

Detroit News, October 27, 1952.

Denver *Post,* September 21, 1969.

Los Angeles Examiner, March 21, 1941; May 25, 1944; December 20, 1945.

Los Angeles *Herald-Express,* December 6, 1950.

Los Angeles *Mirror,* December 18, 1948; October 27, 1952.

Los Angeles *News,* August 31, 1951.

Los Angeles *Sentinel,* March 4, 1948; July 13, 1950.

Los Angeles *Sunday News,* August 29, 1948.

Los Angeles *Times,* December 6, 1950; October 27, November 2, 1952.

Los Angeles *Tribune,* July 7, 1951; August 18, 1951.

New York *Journal-American,* October 26, 1949; March 10, 1950.

New York *Post,* December 17, 1941.

New York *Radio Daily,* February 27, 1950.

New York *Sun,* February 19, 1940.

New York *World Telegram,* April 12, 1941.

Omaha World-Herald, January 29, 1948.

Pittsburgh Courier, November 1, 1952.

Prescott (Arizona) *Courier,* January 22, 1948.

Punch, May 8, 1940.

San Francisco *Examiner,* September 4, 1951.

The Daily Telegraph, August 17, 1940.

The Denver Star, November 1, 1952.

The Hollywood Reporter, December 13, 1939.

The *New York Times,* February 5, 1939; February 12, 1940; April 22, 1941; June 4, 1952; October 14, 27, 1952; November 2, 1952.

Bibliography

The Observer, April 21, 1940.
The Oregon Journal, January 15, 1950.
The Washington Eagle, January 19, 1948.
Washington Afro-American, November 28, 1952.
Wichita Beacon, October 31, 1967.

Index

Mad Miss Manton, 28, 141
Maid Of Salem, The, 35, 62
Male Animal, The, 83
Malone, Mickey, 126, 154, 155
"Mammy's Meditations," 65–72;
  139
Marquette University, 17
Maritime Federation, 50
Marky, Gene, 84
Maryland, 63, 67, 76, 99, 179
Maxwell House Coffee, 59
Mayan Theatre, 24
Maytag News, The, 57
Maytag West Coast Company, 57
Member Of The Wedding, 136
MGM, 57
Mickey, 118, 159
Miller, Loren, 90
Miller, Marvin, 121
Mills Brothers, 22
*Mr. Blandings Builds His Dream
  House,* 34
Mitchell, Lisa, 116
Mitchell, Margaret, 33, 34, 35,
  37, 38, 40, 42, 46, 55, 56
Moore, Monette, 148
Morgan, Frank, 75
Moreland, Mantan, 99, 100, 105
Morris, Earl, 41
Morrison, George, 12–14; 77
Moss, Carlton, 26, 49, 109
Moten, Robert, 62
Motion Picture Country Home
  and Hospital, 152
Moton, Etta, 72
Motion Picture Producers and
  Distributors of America, 46
Mumphrey, Marion, 159
Murdoch, Alexander G., 2

Muse, Clarence, 30, 95, 97, 99,
  100, 101–103; 105, 109,
  114, 158
Myrick, Susan, 36, 37, 40, 44,
  45, 55

National Association for the
  Advancement of Colored
  People, xi, xii, 8, 41, 80, 96–
  120; 122, 128, 133, 138,
  141, 163
National Parent-Teacher Associa-
  tion, 123, 128
Negro Actors' Guild, 155
Negro Motion Picture Players
  Association, 97
New York Post, The, 99
New York Times, The, 25, 114,
  137
New York World's Fair, 1940, 70
Nicholas, Fayard, 83
Nielsen ratings, 137, 153
Noel, Hattie, 35
Nugent, Frank, 25
Nye, Carrol, 45

Oberon, Merle, 75
O'Flaherty, Terence, 138
O'Hara, Maureen, 87, 139
Old Testament, 142
Olivier, Laurence, 61
"One Man's Family," 130
"Op," fn. 195
Operator 13, 22
Oregon Daily Journal, 12
Oregonian, The, 12
Orpheum Theatre Circuit, 13,
  14, 16
O'Shea, Daniel, 57, 58, 59, 61,
  66, 69, 71

Carlton Jackson is a Professor of History at Western Kentucky University, specializing in the social history of the United States. A native of Alabama, Professor Jackson has held three Fulbright senior lecture awards, and has lectured extensively on U.S. history in Asia, Europe, and South America.